David Armstrong

Philosophy Now

Series Editor: John Shand

This is a fresh and vital series of new introductions to today's most read, discussed and important philosophers. Combining rigorous analysis with authoritative exposition, each book gives a clear, comprehensive and enthralling access to the ideas of those philosophers who have made a truly fundamental and original contribution to the subject. Together the volumes comprise a remarkable gallery of the thinkers who have been at the forefront of philosophical ideas.

Published

David Armstrong
Stephen Mumford

Donald Davidson
Marc Joseph

Nelson Goodman
Daniel Cohnitz & Marcus Rossberg

Saul Kripke
G. W. Fitch

David Lewis
Daniel Nolan

John McDowell
Tim Thornton

Hilary Putnam
Maximilian de Gaynesford

John Rawls
Catherine Audard

Wilfrid Sellars
Willem A. deVries

Peter Strawson
Clifford Brown

Bernard Williams
Mark P. Jenkins

Forthcoming

Robert Brandom
Jeremy Wanderer

Thomas Nagel
Alan Thomas

David Armstrong

Stephen Mumford

McGill-Queen's University Press
Montreal & Kingston • Ithaca

© Stephen Mumford 2007

ISBN 978-0-7735-3330-1 (bound)
ISBN 978-0-7735-3331-8 (paper)

Legal deposit second quarter 2007
Bibliothèque nationale du Québec

Published simultaneously in the United Kingdom by Acumen
Publishing Limited and in North America by McGill-Queen's
University Press

Library and Archives Canada Cataloguing in Publication

Mumford, Stephen
   David Armstrong / Stephen Mumford.
(Philosophy now)

Includes bibliographical references and index.
ISBN 978-0-7735-3330-1 (bound)
ISBN 978-0-7735-3331-8 (pbk.)

   1. Armstrong, D. M. (David Malet), 1926–.   I. Title.   II. Series.

B5704.A754M84 2007   199'.94   C2007-902076-3

Typeset by Graphicraft Limited, Hong Kong.
Printed and bound by Cromwell Press, Trowbridge.

Contents

Preface

David Malet Armstrong has a claim to being the greatest philosopher produced by the young and vast country of Australia. It is primarily through his work that Australian philosophy, and Australian metaphysics in particular, enjoys such a high reputation in the rest of the world. Students of an older generation will know of Armstrong chiefly as a philosopher of mind. He was one of the big three Australian materialists, who argued that our mental lives are nothing more that a series of states in our brains or central nervous systems. Not content with overturning centuries of thinking about the mind, however, Armstrong went on to have a second career as a philosopher. In providing his theory of mind, he came to see that we needed accounts of states, properties, dispositions, the nature of identity, causation and laws of nature. He saw that metaphysics was an area where serious work was yet to be done. Perhaps with the intention of being a better philosopher of mind, he became a metaphysician in the mid-1970s. He only seldom returned to his former discipline, however, perhaps seeing that metaphysics was where all the real action was.

This book aims to offer an introduction to the full range of Armstrong's thought for readers already familiar with the nature and methods of twentieth-century analytic philosophy. I have deliberately not, however, offered a purely chronological account of his work. I would maintain that Armstrong's chief philosophical achievement is the development of a core metaphysical programme, embracing the topics of universals, laws, modality and facts. It is a naturalistic metaphysics, consistent with a scientific view of the natural world. The philosophy of mind is important, particularly to those of us who want to understand our minds. But minds, and even human beings, are just one small part of the natural world. I have presented Armstrong's thought, therefore, with the core programme first and his accounts of mind, sensation and knowledge afterwards, as special topics of this naturalistic metaphysics.

There are still issues about the order of presentation, however. "Metaphysics is a serpent that has itself by the tail", Armstrong once said (WSA: 28). A theory of metaphysics is often integrated and interconnected. But this makes order of exposition a problem. One part of the theory cannot be understood without the other parts. How, then, is one to explain that theory in a sequential order? My approach has been to start with what I think are the key commitments. I begin with Armstrong's naturalism, his most general commitment, and then move on to his realism about universals. Once they are in place, theories of laws, modality and dispositions follow quickly. We can then move on to see these all in terms of facts or states of affairs. By that point we will have all the basics of his core theory. We will then move through perception, mind and belief before a further metaphysical flourish in the last two chapters, looking at truth and the new view of instantiation. I have attempted to present a dispassionate, fair and unbiased account of Armstrong's thought. His is a body of work that I regard highly and think of as significant, but I have drawn the reader's attention to areas of weakness and issues about which there is room for further debate. My own views on these matters are often at odds with Armstrong's but I have been careful not to use this book as a forum to air my alternatives. This book definitely is about Armstrong's work, not about mine.

I have used a system of referencing in which Armstrong's books have abbreviated titles. See the list of abbreviations that follows. Papers by him are referred to with just a date. For works by other authors, I have used a standard system of referencing.

A significant portion of this book has been written "on the road" so I must thank various people and institutions for their invitations and financial assistance that allowed this research time away. Chapter 4 was written in Buenos Aires, where I was the guest of GAF (Grupo de acción filosósfica) at the invitation of Eduardo Barrio. Chapter 6 was written at the 2006 APA in Chicago, for which I am grateful to the British Academy for their travel grant and the University of Nottingham's Overseas Conference Fund. Chapter 7 was written in Tromsø, in the Arctic Circle. I was the guest of the University of Tromsø for their Alternative Conception of Nature conference, at the invitation of Svein Anders Noer Lie. I was able to work through the whole draft of the book while at Niagara Falls, Canada, at the IAPS conference (with a view of the Falls from my room, no less), again funded by the University of Nottingham. Other parts of the book were written on visits to the Universities of Lund and Halle-Wittenberg, and the final, revised draft was completed at the University of Stellenbosch, South Africa, at the Philosophical Society of Southern Africa 2007 conference. Finally, the end period of research on this book was assisted by the AHRC-funded *Metaphysics of Science* project.

I am grateful to Rani Lill Anjum and Sonya Barcant, who read the whole manuscript and offered many comments, making it a better and more readable book. As an undergraduate, Sonya Barcant worked through the consequences of Armstrong's new theory of instantiation before the same points were published as objections by Peter Simons (2005). Chapter 11 in particular benefits from her input. I am grateful to the two anonymous readers for Acumen who gave constructive feedback on the manuscript. I must also express my gratitude to Lindsay Hutchinson, who made 2005–07 very smooth years for philosophy at Nottingham. Without her highly efficient running of the department, this book would not have been completed so soon. Maggie, William, Oliver and Charlie are to be thanked for their support and tolerance of frequent work-related absences. I thank also E. J. Lowe and D. H. Mellor for their continued support, and David Armstrong himself for his encouragement of my own work in recent years. I did discuss with Armstrong the possibility that he should see the manuscript of this book before publication. He had, after all, commented on a draft of my previous book. He was keen, however, that in this case he should not comment on the draft. Perhaps there was a principle behind this thinking: the subjects of books in this series ought not to be inputting into nor influencing their own volumes. These books should be another's view, distanced and critical, of the thinker in question.

A special issue of the *Australasian Journal of Philosophy*, volume 84 (2006), number 2, on the work of David Armstrong appeared just too late to be of use during the writing of this book. But readers looking for some more detailed critiques of special topics in Armstrong's work may wish to turn there next.

Abbreviations

Chapter 1
Naturalism

A philosopher who gives a systematic account of the whole world will usually have some fundamental commitment that drives and unites its various elements. David Armstrong is one who does offer a grand vision of the world. His work shows how that vision accounts systematically for philosophically difficult phenomena such as properties, laws, truth, the mind and knowledge. These are some of the key problems that philosophy should aim to solve.

Three general commitments drive Armstrong's philosophy. He is a naturalist, a physicalist, and he thinks that the world is a world of states of affairs. This last view should be called factualism. These commitments form the background against which his sizeable body of work can be set. In various places, he offers philosophical accounts of perception, universals, laws of nature and causation, modality and truthmaking. These can all be understood as naturalistic theories where some problematic area of philosophy is explained in terms of states of affairs, all of which are physical states of affairs. Our first aim is to understand these three commitments better.

In one place he gives explicit endorsement of three theses (N&R: 126):

1. The world contains nothing but particulars having properties and being related to each other
2. The world is nothing but a single spatiotemporal system
3. The world is completely described in terms of a (completed) physics.

The first thesis is a commitment to an ontology of states of affairs. Some call these *Tractarian facts*. Such *factualism* will not be a primary concern in this chapter, though something can be said about the place of this commitment among his others. I will do this, briefly, in the next section before moving on to the main topics of this chapter: Armstrong's naturalism (thesis 2) and his physicalism (thesis 3).

First philosophy

A state of affairs is a particular bearing, a property, for example: an apple being red; an electron having negative unit charge, a person believing Sydney to be the capital of Australia (falsely). Armstrong thinks that the whole world consists of nothing more than such states of affairs. Some people prefer to call these things *facts*, although they are not facts in the sense of being true propositions. They are certainly intended to be things in the world, in non-propositional reality, like Wittgenstein's (1921) facts in the *Tractatus*. According to a factualist, the whole of reality can be thought of in such terms: one gigantic collection of states of affairs or facts. States of affairs will be the smallest units of existence. They seem to have components – particulars and universals – but these are not themselves capable of independent existence outside those facts. The simplest, smallest thing that exists in the world will be a simple state of affairs. A simple state of affairs consists in a simple particular instantiating a simple property. Many complicated issues are involved in this ontology. We will need to understand what is a universal, what is a particular, and what is instantiation. We will need to know what it is that makes any of these simple. But I will not say more here about states of affairs because the subject will get a chapter all of its own (Chapter 6) and we will need to build up to that difficult topic gradually. Besides, our concern here is with the generalities of Armstrong's philosophy so that we can understand what drives all the detailed argument that awaits us.

Armstrong sees the commitment to states of affairs as his commitment of "first philosophy". Naturalism and physicalism are his most fundamental doctrines but *first philosophy*, to use Aristotle's phrase, is concerned with *ontology* or the most general categories of all (NoM: 160–61). First philosophy is about what sorts of thing there are in general: whether there are particulars, universals, causes, laws, numbers, substances and so on. In committing to an ontology of states of affairs, Armstrong is saying that all the things that need to be accounted for can be accounted for in terms of such states of affairs. Armstrong accepts that there are causes, for instance, but he has an account in terms of states of affairs that shows what causes are. Similarly he can account for universals, particulars, laws and numbers in terms of states of affairs. A large portion of Armstrong's work is the development of this programme.

The rest of this chapter is about the other fundamental commitments, of which naturalism is the most fundamental. It is what guides the rest of the philosophy. The exact nature of naturalism is hard to pin down, however. While it seems to be Armstrong's most basic commitment, and the one that determines his choice of philosophical topics, and his solutions to them, it is a subject he only occasionally discusses directly. It is always there, and allusion to naturalism is made in various places, but the discussion is invariably brief. Like all of our most fundamental assumptions, arguments in its favour cannot be deep or lengthy. There is nothing more basic that could be employed in its justification. Often, therefore, we can only state our fundamental commitments, making them transparent and clear, and perhaps give some rough indication of why they are sensible.

Forebears

From where did Armstrong get these basic commitments? What is his background? He is, of course, an Australian philosopher and, it can be argued, a *distinctly* Australian philosopher. A major figure who probably more than any other shaped twentieth-century Australian philosophy is John Anderson, not so much for his personal output as for the powerful influence he had over his students, many of whom went on to fill other Australian academic posts. The influence that Anderson had over Armstrong is not so easy to specify, though. Anderson was for a long time a radical while Armstrong was not. By the time Armstrong was being taught, however, Anderson had jettisoned a significant portion of his radicalism. And while Armstrong was influenced by his ideas, he reacted strongly against Anderson's methods, which he saw had the effect of recruiting followers. Armstrong saw no role for this in philosophy. But there was nevertheless a real and lasting philosophical influence of Anderson on Armstrong, which is evident most obviously in their shared commitment to naturalism.

3

There were other important influences on Armstrong during his career. After Anderson, the next figure to mention would be C. B. (Charlie) Martin. Armstrong and Martin were briefly colleagues at Melbourne and later again at Sydney. From Martin, Armstrong took the truthmaker principle, which would stay with him throughout his philosophical life, often being deployed in many of his arguments. He also gained from Martin an interest in dispositions, seeing that they played an important role in explaining many problematic phenomena. He would dissent from Martin's treatment, however, largely developing an alternative to Martin's ontology of real causal powers. This dissent seems, in no small part, down to Armstrong's discovery of the *categorical*: a notion to which he was introduced by H. H. Price when undertaking graduate studies in Oxford. While Armstrong remained a thoroughly straight-talking Australian philosopher, this idea gained in England became a key part of his position in mind and metaphysics.

Let us now return to the main idea of naturalism. In attempting to pin down this doctrine, Anderson offers us little help. He was not a vastly productive philosopher by current standards, and his main work, which was to be a book on logic, remained uncompleted (Franklin 2003: 19). He was also not given to simple statements of his view. Some of the best summaries come, therefore, from his former students. Mackie summed up Anderson's philosophy thus:

> His central doctrine is that there is only one way of being, that of ordinary things in space and time, and that every question is a simple issue of truth or falsity, that there are no different degrees or kinds of truth. His propositional view of reality implies that things are irreducibly complex, and we can never arrive at simple elements in any field. Anderson rejects systematically the notion of entities that are constituted, wholly or partly, by their relations: there can be no ideas or sensa whose nature it is to be known or perceived, no consciousness whose nature it is to know, no values whose nature it is to be ends or to direct action. Knowledge is a matter of finding what is objectively the case; all knowledge depends on observation and is fallible; . . .
> (Mackie 1962: 265)

Most of the Andersonian doctrines outlined in this passage appear in Armstrong's work at some point. Being is univocal and it is what the world of spacetime, and only the world of spacetime, has. Neither being nor truth comes in degrees. The propositional structure of reality shows itself in Armstrong's ontology of states of affairs, which he explicitly credits to the influence of Anderson (WSA: 3). Anderson's subject–predicate logic corresponds to the basic entities of the world, being irreducible complexes of particulars and universals. Nothing can be constituted in whole or in part by its relations, for all real relations are external (WSA: 1); that is, they exist extra to their relata. Additionally, Armstrong gained his direct realism about perception from Anderson (1984: 15).

Perhaps most importantly, Armstrong's brand of realism about universals came from Anderson. He gave the following account of his teacher's view:

> Anderson held that the world was the spatio-temporal world, and that nothing else existed except this world. Not only was there no God, or non-spatial minds, but there were no "abstract" entities in the Quinean/North American sense of that term: entities over and above the spatio-temporal world. So among the other things which Anderson excluded, there were no Platonic forms or realm of universals descried by the eye of reason. Realism about universals for Anderson meant that different things in the spatio-temporal world could have the *same* quality or property, or be of the *same* kind or sort. It was a thoroughly down to earth (down to space-time) form of realism.
>
> (1984: 41–2)

As well as adopting and developing such an Andersonian vision, Armstrong also took from him a view of what topics were important in philosophy. Armstrong's life work in philosophy developed naturalistic accounts of mind, metaphysics, truth and knowledge. In contrast, he largely avoided areas of philosophy such as ethics and aesthetics, except where he might try to justify leaving them alone (for example, Armstrong 1982). Ethical and aesthetic values seem to have no place in the objective world of spacetime, where one fact is as significant or insignificant as another. If one is to study nature, therefore, rather than just the narrow concerns of man, values will not be a high priority. Anderson did have something to say of morals but argued that they cannot intrinsically be action guiding (Franklin 2003: 39–41), as that would be for them to have a relational nature. The naturalist philosopher will prefer, therefore, to stick to what we can know and what is a part of the natural world.

The statement of naturalism

What exactly is the position of naturalism? It would be helpful if we could find a simple and clear statement of the naturalistic thesis that Armstrong supports. We certainly find statements of this kind – a number of them – spread over the range of his work. They suffice in their rough and ready form to give us an idea of the background to his work. One very simple statement of the position is as follows:

> Naturalism I define as the doctrine that reality consists of nothing but a single all-embracing spatio-temporal system.
>
> (NoM: 149)

He presents similar statements in a variety of other places, for example:

> It is the contention that the world, the totality of entities, is nothing more than the spacetime system. (WSA: 5)

However, while such statements are simple and to the point, they may seem rather brief and leave us little the wiser. They are bare and abstract presentations of the view. What, we may wonder, is the nature of this spacetime? What can be contained within it and what is excluded from it? What is time and what is space? What are the entities of which the spacetime system is the totality? Armstrong did not try to answer these questions. He has a principled reason for remaining silent. The nature of spacetime is a problem that Armstrong thinks is best left to science, which is the proper empirical investigation of the natural world. The nature of spacetime is an *a posteriori* matter, not to be decided by the *a priori* methods of philosophy, which employs reason alone. What exists is a matter for science to decide. Philosophers can decide the categories of things that exist, when they do first philosophy; but what, if any, things exist within those categories can only be decided by the empirical evidence. Armstrong will therefore think it right to state naturalism in a very abstract way. The world can be seen as a totality of, in some way occupied, spacetime points. Armstrong takes these to be a structure of states of affairs. They are the basic or fundamental particulars bearing simple properties, which is to say that they are the simple states of affairs.

The doctrine of naturalism has a positive and negative aspect. The positive aspect is that there is a world of spacetime. The negative aspect is that there is nothing more than a world of spacetime.

Idealists will deny the positive aspect; that is, they deny the reality of the spacetime world. Those who deny the negative aspect of the doctrine are a diverse bunch. Only once one sees what Armstrong opposes to the doctrine of naturalism does one start to get a more concrete idea of what he thinks the doctrine is about.

Some may attempt to deny the doctrine for religious reasons, if they think there exists a God, spirits or heaven. This is usually understood as a claim that there is a supernatural realm in addition to the natural one. God and heaven are outside space and time although they, in some sense to be outlined by the theist, sit above it (the *super* in supernatural). Non-theists have, however, also tried to deny the doctrine of naturalism. An early philosophical denial is found in Plato with the theory of the Forms. Things such as squareness or justice could not be found in the world of spacetime, although their shadows or imperfect copies could be. The universal, the Form, existed in a transcendent world, now usually called the Platonic realm. Some have thought that other abstract objects might inhabit such a realm. Numbers might be there, as they seem to have a transcendent existence, beyond space and time, and perhaps propositions might be there. But Armstrong would deny all this so he is obliged to offer naturalistic accounts of universals, numbers and propositions. Another denial of naturalism, or a kind of naturalism, would be David Lewis's modal realism. Lewis proposes a plurality of worlds, many of them more or less like ours (Lewis 1986). If we are to account for modality, or the truth of counterfactual and causal claims, Lewis thinks we have to grant that our world is just one of countless many and that these different worlds are spatiotemporally discontinuous. This is against the spirit of Armstrong's naturalism, which admits just the one world of spacetime. A Lewisian might protest that each of these worlds could be a separate naturalistic world of spacetime. That the worlds are spatiotemporally distinct, nevertheless, does not seem to be a spatiotemporal fact itself. So for there to be a plurality of worlds there would have to be further, non-natural facts about their separateness. What are the gaps between these "island universes"? What keeps worlds apart? Armstrong's commitment to naturalism is strong enough for him to look for other accounts of modality, counterfactuals and causes, where the truth-makers for all such claims can be found in this world. Armstrong's naturalism is an immanentist thesis. All that there is is around us and accessible to us. There are no further hidden, supernatural, disconnected or transcendent realms.

David Armstrong

An argument for naturalism?

But how safe is the thesis of naturalism? Is there an argument for it or is it mere assumption? As I have already indicated, there is little that you can do to justify your most fundamental assumptions. Often they are accepted simply on the basis of how productive they are or how much sense they allow one to make of things. But these factors are of a pragmatic nature: they are about how useful one's assumptions are rather than a guarantee of their truth. As a realist, Armstrong is not likely to be satisfied with purely pragmatic considerations. It will be good, therefore, if we can say at least something further to justify our main commitments.

Armstrong does offer some more justification. He sets out first to defend the positive part of the position: the claim that there is a spatiotemporal system. This positive component of the doctrine Armstrong declares "fairly secure" and "uncontroversial" (WSA: 7). The world certainly does appear to us, both superficially and scientifically, to be a spatiotemporal system. Only philosophers and theists have ever denied that the reality and the appearance are the same. We can name Leibniz, Parmenides, Hegel, Bradley and some Eastern religions as all having denied that reality matches the spatiotemporal appearance. The denials will usually be forms of idealism: that the world is in whole or in part the creation of minds. The arguments of such philosophers, however, are all *a priori*. Armstrong sees himself as an empiricist, which he thinks prohibits the *a priori* as a method of discovering what there is or is not. Is this a justification of naturalism, though, or merely another assertion of it? This seems to be Armstrong's only argument for the first part of the doctrine: the world looks spatiotemporal and we cannot trust any argument that claims otherwise. The argument has a Moorean quality to it (Moore 1925): the world seems self-evidently spatiotemporal and our belief in this has more conviction than we can have in any argument to a contrary conclusion.

The negative part of the doctrine is that this spatiotemporal system constitutes the whole of reality. This is an additional view that requires a distinct justification. The negative part of the doctrine has been denied by a variety of people who need not necessarily deny also the positive part of the thesis. An idealist denies both the negative and positive claims but a theist or a dualist, for instance, might accept that there is a world of spacetime but think that there is more besides.

Many entities outside spacetime have been proposed. Naturalism rules out such things as concrete possible worlds and transcendent realms inhabited by universals. It would also rule out the existence of heaven or the existence of God (ToU: 156) as a being outside of space and time. Naturalism is, admittedly, a very austere ontology, but Armstrong sees such economy as a virtue:

> A bewildering variety of additional entities have been deemed necessary by some philosophers. There have been postulations of transcendent universals, a realm of numbers, transcendent standards of value, timeless propositions, non-existent objects such as the golden mountain, *possibilia* and/or possible worlds, "abstract" classes which are something more than the aggregate of their members, including unit-classes and the null-class.
>
> (N&R: 128)

For these additional entities, Armstrong offers a challenge: can they act upon the spatiotemporal system? Can they act in nature? Suppose one claimed that they can, as many claim of God and Descartes claimed of mental substances. There are many difficulties associated with such an interactionist view. How could something that is not located in spacetime have causal power over something that is so located? The effect occurs in a place at a time. Does not the cause have to be at an adjacent place and time? That is usually a prerequisite for us to grant that one thing caused another. In the present case, the cause is supposed to be in no place and no time, however. Can it really interact with the natural world? But is there in any case any room for such causation from outside the system? As natural science sees the spatiotemporal system, it is causally self-enclosed (NoM: 153). There is no room for causation from outside the system unless we allowed that natural history could be overdetermined, that is, having two distinct but also sufficient causes. Suppose instead, then, that such entities do not and cannot act on nature. That may be plausible for such alleged entities as Platonic Forms, numbers and propositions. Epiphenomenalists say the same about the mind: it can be caused by physical things but can itself have no effects. But if these things can never act on or in nature, then we have no reason to postulate them (NoM: 154). Here, Armstrong invokes the Eleatic principle from Plato's *Sophist* (247d–e). The principle suggests that "if a thing lacks any power, if it has no possible effects, then, although it may exist, we can never have any *good reason* to believe that it exists" (NoM: 156). Better, thinks Armstrong, to allow only a single, causally closed world.

The particulars-having-properties, the states of affairs, will suffice as the causal relata.

This may still look a bit too pragmatic for some. Armstrong's conclusion is not quite that there is nothing other than the world of spacetime but, rather, that we have no good reason to believe in anything other than spacetime. It may allow room for uncertainty about the existence of such things rather than motivate their outright rejection. Armstrong acknowledges this weakness of the Eleatic principle (WSA: 42). But in philosophy it is always very difficult to prove that something does not exist. Concluding that we have no good reason to believe in such a thing is often as close as we can get.

Physicalism

There is a further basic commitment of Armstrong's philosophy which, although allied to naturalism, needs to be separated from it. It is the doctrine that all in this natural world is physical. As he says, "the only particulars that the spacetime system contains are physical entities governed by nothing more than the laws of physics" (WSA: 6).

One could be a naturalist without thinking that the entities of spacetime are all physical. Materialism, which we can take to mean the same as physicalism, is thus depicted as a sub-species of naturalism. Following Smart (1963), Armstrong describes it as the view that "the world contains nothing but the entities recognized by physics" (NoM: 156). Furthermore, the materialist is a realist about the theoretical entities of physics, such as the fundamental particles. The materialist is thus rejecting the various anti-realist interpretations of physics, such as instrumentalism and operationalism, which at their worst descend into forms of idealism. We have already seen that there are basic Andersonian commitments that warn against forms of idealism: things cannot be constituted by their relations to other things, such as minds.

If one claims, however, that the entire natural world is physical, then one is obliged to explain away the apparent irreducibly non-physical appearances of such things as the intentionality of the mental and the irreducible simplicity of the secondary qualities. Armstrong does attempt such explanations in physical terms, as we shall see. These are cases where philosophical argument *can* be used to overthrow the appearances. But there are good reasons why we think we should do so. The same sort of argument used against the anti-naturalists can be invoked. Do intentional states and secondary qualities, as irreducibly non-physical things, bestow any causal power? Armstrong thinks they do not and so he sees no reason to postulate them. If there is no reason to postulate them as irreducibly non-physical, then physicalism is saved.

We can again notice the very abstract nature of Armstrong's commitment. The entities that make up the world are simply those recognized by physics or governed by the laws of nature. Furthermore, it is clear from the third of Armstrong's theses, with which we began, that the real entities in the world will not be those recognized by an ancient, false or incomplete physics. The real entities will be those invoked by a completed physics: a full and true account of the physical world. It is a safe assumption that our current physics is far from complete. So we are not yet sure what the commitment of physicalism is. To say that everything is physical, where this simply means that everything is as a final theory of physics tells us it is, may seem to tell us little. We may have a folk theory of matter, and thus an idea of what it is for something to be material, but in some degree this is very likely to be overthrown, if it has not been already, by a more sophisticated theory. The completed theory may deal only in point-like entities, if they can be called entities at all, or perhaps only in fields and their various features. The commitment of physicalism could turn out to look quite different from what we expect.

Why, though, should we defer to science on the nature of the physical at all, and thus on the nature of the physicalist commitment? Does Armstrong concede too much to science? To understand his attitude to science, we need to consider his view of empiricism.

Empiricism

Empiricism is distinct from naturalism. The latter is a metaphysical thesis while the former is an epistemological one. And yet Armstrong concedes that what there is should be determined by *a posteriori* investigation rather than *a priori* reasoning. Armstrong's theory of universals is, for example, an *a posteriori* realism, which he sometimes calls scientific realism. In looking for a theory of higher-order universals – properties of properties, for instance – Armstrong notes that previous such theories have been rationalist ones, where the existence of higher-order universals has been decided *a priori*.

Armstrong tries to develop an empiricist theory of higher-order universals (ToU: 134). Philosophy can tell us what something must be like if it is a real universal, but it is only through an empirical investigation that we find what universals there actually are in the world.

The naturalist is urged therefore to adopt a general epistemological stance. Certainly Armstrong thinks knowledge is possible but in most cases the naturalist has to leave it to science to discover such knowledge. Science is, after all, the most systematic and rigorous study of the natural world. It is also the only field in which substantial agreement has been reached on what is the case (NoM: 2). Hence "An epistemological stance comes rather naturally with Naturalism thus defined. It is the contention that, except for the primitive verities of ordinary experience, it is natural science that gives us whatever detailed knowledge we have of the world" (WSA: 5). We shall see in Chapter 9 why we should allow the verities of ordinary experience to count as knowledge, namely that it is the kind of non-inferential and reliable knowledge that we need in order to avoid a regress of justification.

There is, thus, a naturalist view of what natural science is about, as Armstrong outlines:

> Natural science traditionally concerns itself with at least three tasks. The first is to discover the geography and history of the universe, taking "geography" to cover all space and "history" to cover all time, including future time. . . . A second task is to discover what sorts of thing and what sorts of property there are in the universe and how they are constituted, with particular emphasis upon the sorts of thing and the sorts of property in terms of which other things are explained . . . The third task is to state the laws which things in space and time obey. Or, putting it in the terms used in describing the second task, the third task is to state the laws which link sort of thing with sort of thing, and property with property. (WLN: 3)

Although naturalism is a philosophical commitment to the validity of science, in one place science seems to be part of the justification for naturalism. He says his commitment to naturalism is "held all the more strongly because the ground for it is to be found more in the natural sciences rather than philosophy" (DaD: 91). It is clear also that the naturalist must understand science realistically and accept its capacity to discover the way the world really is.

Armstrong seems happy to call this empiricism but, as it stands, this commitment is not quite the same empiricism as that of Locke, Berkeley and Hume. That was a theory of concept acquisition: that all the contents of the mind derive from experience. But Armstrong says that his commitment to empiricism is to the "method of observation and experiment, the method of the natural sciences, as opposed to the attempt to gain knowledge by a priori reasoning" (NoM: 161). One may gain a hypothesis from anywhere and it does not need to be founded on experience, but any claim about what there is must be derived from experience. This generates his *a posteriori* realism in metaphysics, which might be a less misleading name for his view than empiricism.

Metaphysics and philosophy

Science is important, but what role is there for philosophy, and metaphysics in particular, in this naturalistic view of the world? Physics can tell us what particular things exist while metaphysics purports to tell us the types of thing that there are. But how does it do so? Philosophy's method is non-empirical. How then do we find truth in metaphysics?

In his introductory book on universals, Armstrong permits himself some general reflections on the nature of metaphysics. He says:

> We have to accept, I think, that straight refutation (or proof) of a view in philosophy is rarely possible. What has to be done is to build a case against, or to build a case for, a position. One does this, usually, by examining many different arguments and considerations against and for a position and comparing them with what can be said against and for alternative views. What one should hope to arrive at, and what I try to achieve in this book, is something like an intellectual cost–benefit analysis of the view considered. . . . One important way in which different philosophical and scientific theories about the same topic may be compared is in respect of intellectual economy. In general, the theory that explains the phenomena by means of the least number of entities and principles (in particular, by the least number of sorts of entities and principles) is to be preferred. (U: 19–20)

Moreover:

> Metaphysicians should not expect any certainties in their inquiries. One day, perhaps, the subject will be transformed, but for the present the philosopher can do no more than survey the field as conscientiously as he or she can, taking note of the opinions and arguments of predecessors and contemporaries, and then make a fallible judgement arrived at and backed up as rationally as he or she knows how.   (U: 135)

One of Armstrong's great achievements was to show how a scientific naturalism could be combined with a metaphysical realism. This is not always the case. He notes, for instance, how naturalists would often be nominalists (U: 76) as they could not accept a realm of universals in addition to particulars. To save naturalists from nominalism, Armstrong shows how universals can exist in particulars, immanently, instead of in a transcendent realm (see Chapter 2, below, and Armstrong 1988).

Elsewhere, Armstrong considers philosophy in general and addresses G. E. Moore's so-called paradox of analysis. When philosophers investigate some phenomenon X, and ask "what is X?", they are caught between two unpalatable situations. Either they already know what X is, in which case it is pointless for them to ask what X is. Or they do not know what X is, in which case they cannot even begin to investigate what X is. This is perhaps not a serious problem, and not literally a paradox. If it were, it would be a problem for any investigation, not just philosophy. But Armstrong answers it in an interesting and elegant way. "We do not go from black night to daylight, but from twilight to daylight" (WLN: 5):

> we do not start with blank ignorance of what an X is. Instead, we start with an unreflective, unselfconscious or merely practical grasp of the thing. The philosophical object is to pass from this to an articulate, explicit and reasoned grasp of what an X is.
>
> *(Ibid.)*

The emphasis is always on such kinds of argument, reason and compromise. While Armstrong took his general realism from Anderson, and his non-Platonic realism about universals in particular, he was neither a *follower* of Anderson, nor does he want philosophical disciples of his own. Philosophy is about reasoned argument, not an appeal to authority. Anderson was specifically criticized on this issue:

> His [Anderson's] real intellectual weakness lies in his desire to make disciples, his encouragement of the growth of an

Andersonian orthodoxy, his unwillingness to take criticism seriously. By a tragic paradox, his work in arousing in so many students some real feeling for the Western intellectual tradition, and his considerable achievement in the field of pure philosophy, have been largely stultified by his encouragement of an Andersonian provincialism in place of those other provincialisms he so vigorously attacked in the name of culture.

(Armstrong 1958: 152, quoted in Franklin 2003: 47)

Elsewhere, Armstrong expressed his personal unwillingness to become an Andersonian: "I am not a natural disciple, and, although I was immensely influenced, I never became one of the loyal circle. This caused Anderson to regard me with suspicion" (1984: 8). Armstrong of course wishes to persuade others through his argument. But it is not persuasion for the sake of persuasion and it is specifically not for the purpose of gaining followers. Rather, the arguments should stand up for themselves and we all should follow the good arguments where they lead. If we follow the same chain of reasoning as Armstrong, and end at the same destination, then that is perfectly all right. But if we end at the same destination merely because we wish to follow Armstrong, bowing to his authority, then that is wrong. In contrast to Anderson, Armstrong was proud of the fact that, although there were some persuaded by immanent realism or by combinatorialism, there were no Armstrongians. Instead, one should follow Armstrong by being an independently minded philosopher, engaging in metaphysics, mind and epistemology, and being prepared to overthrow Armstrong himself, if that is what the argument justifies.

This is not, of course, a new idea. It is philosophy in a pure form where there is no appeal to authority to settle any particular point of dispute. But Armstrong can make a good claim to have followed this ideal through. Furthermore, he has exhibited an increasingly conciliatory attitude to truth in philosophy. Nothing is ever so clear cut as to vindicate dogmatism in the slightest. Philosophy is about weight of argument and sometimes one position may have the better over a rival only very slightly or there may be almost nothing to choose between two theories. The philosopher should, therefore, always maintain an open mind. As he says:

This makes it important, I think, that philosophers should be prepared to explore, and bring into their discussions, positions for which they have sympathy but which differ from the views they actually take. "Fall-back" positions are particularly important to

> specify, that is, positions which one would adopt if forced out of
> one's actual position. (WSA: xii)

The philosophical enterprise should also involve discussion with
those with whom you disagree. Armstrong was an indefatigable
talker and traveller, even entering his ninth decade. A philosophical
discussion with an opponent, as long as they agree on a general basis
on which to progress, is likely to be more profitable than discussion
with a disciple. Hence Armstrong, far more so than Anderson, toler-
ated criticism and alternative views as long as they were informed
and argued. One particularly fruitful philosophical relationship
was the one between Armstrong and David Lewis. Both constructed
systematic metaphysical positions and they differed enormously. But
each of these positions benefited from the input and criticisms of the
other. Both gained by developing the arguments of their opponents
until they saw them in their strongest light.

A methodological approach that developed out of extended argument with others was Armstrong's capacity to "multiply arguments
beyond apparent necessity" (1984: 16). Suppose one has three
arguments for a position. They might fail and one might come to
reject them. So Armstrong tends to overdetermine his position.
If you have a fourth, fifth, sixth or seventh argument for a view,
you should present it. It is worth giving seventeen arguments for
the same conclusion, if you have that many, just in case sixteen
of them fail.

Metaphysics is currently in good shape. It has had to fight a
rearguard action for much of the twentieth century, faced with
the dual attacks of logical positivism and then ordinary-language
philosophy. Arguably, Armstrong was the first of the new, contemporary metaphysicians. Some might claim this instead for Lewis,
much of whose work in metaphysics pre-dates that of Armstrong.
But Armstrong was the first to engage in serious this-worldly ontology; to try to give fundamental accounts about our world, rather
than displace ontological questions with talk about other worlds. The
current flourishing of metaphysics has occurred in part because
others followed Armstrong's lead. Here, his Sydney influences
overcame his Oxford learning. While taking the BPhil at Oxford,
he had attended J. L. Austin's lectures, to which he "listened with
some incredulity that such matter could be of philosophical interest"
(1984: 10). Conceptual analysis could be important, but he could
never accept that it was the whole of philosophy (*ibid.*: 11).

This chapter is designed to set the context for Armstrong's work. The theories he offers us, of the various troublesome problems of philosophy, are all designed to be naturalistic theories, or at least to be compatible with or restrained by naturalism. Given that this is a commitment to a single world of spacetime, it imposes limitations on the materials available to Armstrong. He cannot invoke any other-worldly entities. Thus, of the theory of possibility, he says

> Every systematic philosophy must give some account of the nature of possibility. The main constraint I wish to place on such an account is that it be compatible with *Naturalism*. The term "Naturalism" is often used rather vaguely, but I shall understand by it the doctrine that nothing at all exists except the single world of space and time. So my objective is to give an account of possibility which is in no way other-worldly.
>
> (CTP: 3)

If Armstrong is able to find this-worldly, naturalistic theories of the mind, perception, modality, truth, universals and so on, it will be a considerable achievement and a great advance for the cause of scientific realism as a philosophical stance.

Chapter 2
Universals

What sorts of thing are there in the world? Perhaps we might answer with a list: there are people, tables and chairs, cats and dogs, plants, mountains, planets, nuts, bolts, television sets and motor cars. The list is practically endless. It is notable, however, that the things mentioned in this list are all particulars or at least kinds of particulars. A table is a physical object that has a location in space (in my dining room) and a location in time (20 September 2006). For a naturalist like Armstrong, who says that all there is is a single world of space and time, particulars are relatively unproblematic, and few would deny that they exist even though there may be other interesting things to say about them. But some philosophers have suggested that there is another kind of thing that exists. My table is square and the wheels on my car are round. Might it be that squareness itself and roundness itself are also things that exist? Things of this latter kind are known as universals, perhaps because they can be located at any place and any time. Thus, while the table being in my room at a certain time prevents it from being in other places at the same time, squareness being in my room in no way prevents it from appearing elsewhere simultaneously. I may, of course, chop my table in half so that while half of it is in my room, the other half is at the same time in your room. In the case of universals, however, they seem capable of being *fully present* at different spatiotemporal locations simultaneously, whereas my butchered table is only half present in two different places. There is, therefore, at least a *prima facie* distinction between universals and particulars.

How is a naturalist to account for the apparent existence of universals? The problem of universals is one of the oldest in philosophy, being a main concern of Plato in various dialogues such as the *Republic*. As Rodriguez-Pereyra (2002: 1) notes, however, it is slightly misleading to call this the problem of universals because the claim that there exist universals such as squareness and roundness is actually a putative solution to the problem. Plato's problem was the One over Many: how there could be a seeming identity in diversity. A wheel on my car is round but so is a compact disc. It seems to be the very same roundness that can be found in millions of distinct objects. How is it that they can all be round? How can roundness, seemingly a single thing, be fully present in many different places? Plato suggests in the dialogues that there is a heavenly object called *the Form of roundness*, to which all the particular round things relate. For the Platonist, roundness really is a thing. A naturalist such as Armstrong will not accept that there is a Platonic heaven, which stands outside the ordinary world of space and time. Plato's solution will be rejected, therefore, so the problem remains. How can one thing – roundness – be distributed over many objects?

Before Armstrong's theory of universals gained the influence it currently holds, naturalists tended to opt for some version of nominalism. This is a position that maintains that all that exists is only a particular. The alleged Platonic Forms, if they exist, are particulars (squareness becomes a single thing) but they are also universals, capable of multiple instantiation. Nothing that exists is a universal, according to the nominalist. This leaves the nominalist with a task of accounting for obvious truths such as that objects *a* and *b* are both round or both red. It looks in these cases as if we are saying that there is a single feature, quality or property that is had by two distinct things. Can we avoid invoking roundness and redness as universals? Many philosophers have defended forms of nominalism but Armstrong was not satisfied with any defence. As far as he was concerned, there were very serious problems for any metaphysic that denied the existence of universals.

Here was Armstrong's problem, which he hoped to solve in his two-volume work collectively titled *Universals and Scientific Realism*. He was trying to walk a middle line and hold a position that was realist about universals but without committing to any transcendent realm in which they existed. If universals are real, thought Armstrong, they must exist in the natural world, immanently, here and now. One of his achievements was to formulate a credible theory of immanent realism about universals. It is not a theory that everyone holds – there is probably no such theory in all of philosophy – but it is a theory that many people think is among the viable contenders. The concern of this chapter is with this theory. Before looking at the details, however, it will be best to consider further the perceived failings of the two other main options, nominalism and transcendent realism. Armstrong outlines his objections to them in the first volume of the work, entitled *Nominalism and Realism*.

Nominalism

The defenders of nominalism try to offer a reductive analysis. According to Armstrong it is plain obvious that we appeal to identity across distinct individuals. We can say that two different objects are both blue, meaning that they are the same colour. Two plants may be said to be of the same kind. The case of relations looks even more clearly to be a case of identity across distinct individuals. I bear a relation of *being a father of* to a certain child, but of course this exact fatherhood relation exists between many other pairs of individuals. James Mill was the father of John Stuart Mill and clearly this is exactly the same relation that I bear to my children even though the respective relata of the relation, the things related, differ.

The nominalist analysis is an attempt to show that we can explain away the apparent appeals to universals that seem to be made. The analyses are claims that only the particulars are required. Armstrong is not convinced that the nominalist analysis can work, however, because at some stage the nominalist will be forced to admit at least one universal. But if one universal is admitted, then the nominalist is defeated and they might as well admit all the other universals as well.

As an example, let us consider the claims of predicate nominalism. Armstrong identifies this variety of nominalism as consisting in the claim that there is nothing more to something having the property F than that thing falling under the predicate "F" (N&R: 13). While there is a predicate "red", therefore, the predicate nominalist will say that there is no corresponding property of redness. Particulars a and b are both red simply because they both fall under the predicate "red". The nominalist thinks that they have admitted nothing more than particulars and predicates, so they have an ontology free of universals.

But now, Armstrong objects (N&R: 19), the predicate nominalist says it is true of a and b that they both fall under the predicate "red".

It certainly appears that they are invoking a relation of *falling under* that holds between *a* and "red" and also between *b* and "red". It is exactly the same *falling under* relation that holds in both instances. This looks to be invoking a real universal, therefore, in which case the nominalist analysis has failed. The predicate nominalist may try to deploy the same strategy in accounting for what it is for *a* to fall under a predicate "F". They may say that *falling under* is not a universal but that there is only a two-place predicate "falls under". But it is quite clear that exactly the same problem applies. What is it for things to fall under the "falls under" predicate? The charge is that unless at some stage the predicate nominalist is prepared to allow a real universal, such as a *falling under* relation, their account produces an infinite regress.

This kind of regress problem affects the other forms of nominalism. Resemblance nominalism, for instance, tells us that *a*, *b* and *c* are all red if they resemble each other. This requires that there be a resemblance between *a* and *b*, a resemblance between *a* and *c*, and a resemblance between *b* and *c*. But is resemblance itself a universal? To say so is to abandon nominalism. Can I invoke the resemblance nominalist theory to account for it? To do so, I would have to say that the resemblance between *a* and *b* is one resemblance (R_1), the resemblance between *a* and *c* is another resemblance (R_2) and that between *b* and *c* is a third (R_3). R_1, R_2 and R_3 are all resemblances not, allegedly, because they are instances of the same resemblance-universal but, presumably, because they resemble each other. There would have to be, therefore, a second-order resemblance between R_1 and R_2, another between R_1 and R_3, and a third between R_2 and R_3. The same problem clearly arises and the analysis can extend infinitely, which is to say that the analysis is incomplete. This argument is known as Russell's regress (from Russell 1912: 150–51) and Armstrong endorses it as sound (N&R: 55), although we shall see in the section on resemblance nominalism (p. 38) that he later abandons it. We shall also see shortly that the power of such regress arguments against nominalism have been challenged.

A second kind of problem that Armstrong finds with predicate nominalism is the plausibility of the idea that there exist properties for which there are no corresponding predicates. Certainly we cannot offer any current examples of this but the idea is plausible enough because we know of cases from history. We now say that some things are electrically charged. But such a predication was not available for our use prior to Faraday's discoveries. In the past, therefore, there have been many properties for which there was no predicate and it would be foolhardy to now claim that we have created predicates for every property there is. The number of properties may be infinite but the class of predicates, though large, is finite.

To say that the number of properties that exist is infinite may seem to be question begging against nominalism, but Armstrong has another argument that makes this more plausible. Nominalism has the order of analysis the wrong way round, he insists. There is a strong intuitive attraction to the idea that the predicate "red" is true of a and b because a and b are red. Predicate nominalism tells us it is the other way round: a and b are both red because, and solely because, the predicate "red" applies to them. But suppose a particular undergoes change and different predicates become true of it: "The change in the object could have occurred even if the predicates had never existed" (Armstrong 1992: 161). Similarly, resemblance nominalism tells us that a and b are red because they *resemble* each other and all other red things. They do not, the position tells us, resemble because they have the same property, as we might think intuitive: they have the same property because they resemble, where resemblance has to be taken as a primitive and unanalysed fact.

Armstrong sees some strength in Price's version of resemblance nominalism (Price 1953: ch. 1), where "having the same property" consists in resembling some class of exemplars. We can call this "aristocratic" resemblance nominalism. But any resemblance nominalism faces a particular difficulty, not shared, for instance, by predicate nominalism. What if there is something that is one of a kind? What, for example, if there is only one white thing, only one thing that is 113,826.317 miles long, or only one thing that exemplifies a certain spacetime worm (N&R: 51)? Here there are no exemplars for such a thing to resemble. How then can we make sense of being white, of being that length, or exemplifying that spacetime worm, in terms of resembling something else? There seems nothing to rule out properties that have but a single instance, so, even if we permitted resemblance as a primitive, it is not available to account for the possession of these properties.

A further variant on nominalism is class nominalism, where to be F means nothing more than belonging to a certain class of particulars. We could call this the F-class. Only particulars exist, however, although we may want to add to this the thesis that such particulars fall into primitive natural classes (see Quinton 1957). Special problems hit this form of nominalism, however. We might note that two classes sometimes share the same members, which means, on standard set theory, that they are the same. Hence, if the class of things with kidneys coincides with the class of things with hearts, then being renate and being cordate turn out to be the same property, as do being triangular and being trilateral (U: 25–6). Further, change in the membership of a class produces a new class, given the identity conditions for classes (U: 27). If one thing ceases to be blue, then the blue-class changes and blueness becomes a different property, which is counterintuitive. Finally, does not it seem more plausible that sameness of property determines membership of a class rather than, as the class nominalist requires, class membership determines sameness of property (U: 27–8)? Class nominalism, like all forms of nominalism, seems to get the analysis the wrong way round.

A final form of nominalism that ought to be mentioned is what Armstrong calls "ostrich" nominalism (N&R: 16), so called because it is basically a denial that there is any problem of universals. Such nominalists deny that there are universals but then claim that there is nothing they have left unaccounted for so they do not have to go on to give some analysis of property ascriptions in terms of classes or resemblances. Quine (1948) and Devitt (1980) are labelled with this position. As Armstrong (1980) argues, this view has no answer to the problem of the One over Many: the way that the one thing, such as redness, can be distributed over many different particulars. Ostrich nominalists are denying that there is any such problem. There are two ways they can go. They could say that the existence of a alone accounts for the truth that a is red, so, according to such a view, we do not need to posit redness in addition. But this is not a plausible view, as some nominalists now concede (Rodriguez-Pereyra 2002: 45). While a may be F, it could also be the case that a is G and a is H as well. So it seems to be some specific feature of a in virtue of which it is F, and this differs from the feature in virtue of which it is G. To speak of the different *features* of a, in virtue of which it is F, G and H, seems to be to say that a has different properties. Lewis has a different kind of ostrich approach (1983: 21). The One over Many needs no reply. The fact that there is sameness of type can simply be taken as primitive. After all, perhaps no analysis of sameness of type is possible. The onus is on Armstrong to prove that it is.

Transcendent realism

At this point, Armstrong is satisfied that nominalism, in any of its forms, cannot give a credible account of properties and relations. What is the alternative? Plato offers us realism about universals, where such universals are understood to be transcendent. We will see that Armstrong offered a third option: an Aristotelian account that was realist about universals but without being committed to transcendent objects. Let us begin, however, by looking at the case for realism, pure and simple, and we will come after that to the distinction between its transcendent and immanent varieties.

In the first place, there are certain statements that seem to be about universals rather than particulars, for example (N&R: 58):

(1) Red resembles orange more than it resembles blue
(2) Red is a colour.

If one tried to say that there were no universals, one would have to say that (1) and (2) could be analysed as statements about particulars alone. But what would they be? It is not clearly true that if x is a red particular, y an orange particular, and z a blue particular, that x resembles y more than z. x and z might both be cars, of the same make and model, while z is an orange sock. The red car almost certainly resembles the blue car more than it does the orange sock. One might say, more plausibly, that x at least colour-resembles y more than it colour-resembles z. But one is then appealing again to colour, a universal.

For (2), to avoid reference to universals one would have to say instead of "red is a colour", something like:

(2′) For any x, if x is red, then x is coloured.

But Frank Jackson (1977) showed that (2′) does not entail (2), so cannot replace it. (2) may entail (2′) but it also entails the further necessary truth:

(3′) For any x, if x is red, then x is extended

and it is plain to see that (3′) does not entail:

(3) Red is an extension.

The first argument for universals is, then, that they are ineliminable, though Armstrong concedes that certain forms of nominalism may be able to side-step this argument. There is further debate about these examples in Devitt (1980), to which Armstrong (1980) replies.

The second, and more general consideration, is that particulars and universals are metaphysically irreducible to each other. Both nominalism and the bundle theory of substance are potentially one-category ontologies. The former is the view that one can give a reductive account of properties in terms of particulars, while the latter is the view that one can give a reductive account of particulars in terms of properties. Each view is metaphysically untenable, however, as one assumes that there can be propertyless particulars while the other assumes that there can be properties that are instantiated by no particular. Armstrong rejects both. The "thin" particular, which is supposed to be the particular alone, stripped of all properties, is a mere philosopher's abstraction. But properties without particulars are equally an abstraction: abstracting the qualitative out of the particulars in which it is found. We need, therefore, to concede the reality of both.

We come now to the nature of such universals. In the *Republic*, Plato describes the world of transcendent Forms, apprehended only by the philosopher. They are not empirically accessible but Plato nevertheless provides a variety of arguments for their existence, which Armstrong summarises (N&R: 64–6). There are some properties that are uninstantiated, such as Hume's missing shade of blue or *travelling faster than light*. If these do not exist in our world – if they do not exist immanently – where do they exist? They could only exist transcendentally. Related to this, there are ideal, limiting cases. Nothing in this world is perfectly circular or perfectly good. If true circularity or goodness exists anywhere, it exists only in the Platonic heaven. Last, there are logical or mathematical objects, such as the number four or, some might think, propositions. Although such things have instances in our world, the number or the proposition itself cannot be any one of them. Their existence must be, therefore, transcendent.

The problem with any transcendent form of realism, as has long been acknowledged, is to explain how the instances relate to the universal. Whiteness or triangularity are supposed to be particulars residing in the Platonic heaven. So in what way is this particular shirt in my wardrobe white or this shape in a painting a triangle? Transcendent realism is a relational theory and it thus owes us an account of the relation involved. In Plato, the relation between a Form and the instances is sometimes called *imitation* and at other times *participation*. It is not adequately described what these relations consist in, however, and there seem to be difficulties for any such account. By participation, do we mean that the instances are literally a *part* of the Form? That would be a problem because while the parts of whiteness may themselves be white, the parts of a circle need not be circular and the proper parts of a metre length will not themselves be a metre long.

The Platonic version of realism is, as Armstrong states, a "transcendent version of Resemblance Nominalism", which treats "transcendent universals as celestial paradigms" (N&R: 69–70). It is, thus, subject to many of the same criticisms as resemblance nominalism. Would not something still be white even if there were no Form of whiteness? And would not there be various regresses waiting to scupper the account? Whatever the relation is between a Form and its instances (imitation, participation), it is still a relation and has many instances. There has to be, therefore, a Form of participation, which somehow must relate to its instances, so a regress is already under way.

To top it off, transcendent realism offends against naturalism. It requires that there be more than a single world of spacetime: a transcendent realm of heavenly objects is added. If naturalism is an overarching commitment, then transcendent realism is immediately repugnant. But Armstrong has shown that nominalism, so often favoured by naturalists, is also untenable. Where is the naturalist then to turn?

Tropes

Before moving on to Armstrong's own preferred form of realism about universals, we should first inspect his take on the other great rival view: that properties and relations are tropes. A trope is a particular but, as some say, an abstract particular (Campbell 1990). D. C. Williams (1953) is most famously associated with the metaphysics of tropes, although there are a number of other followers (see Maurin 2002). Just as there are particular tables and chairs, there are also particular rednesses and squarenesses. A sock is blue, for instance, and its matching companion is also blue. These are distinct blues even if there is an exact similarity between them. Blues can, thus, be taken to be particulars but they are *qualitative* particulars: individual portions of blueness. Qualities are admitted, but as particulars instead of universals.

It is conceded that there is some attraction in this view and, over time, Armstrong has become more accepting of trope theory as a viable option. He has said, for instance: "I underestimated the strength of a tropes + resemblance (+ substance-attribute) view. In my present estimation . . . it is a close second to the first choice, which is a Realism about universals" (U: 120. See also 1992: 168). Initially, when building the case for immanent realism, Armstrong was keener to talk down the plausibility of tropes. Its attraction can just as easily be explained by his own states-of-affairs ontology, he thought, about which we shall learn more in Chapter 6. Particulars always instantiate properties and properties are always instantiated by particulars. A sock's blueness appears to be a kind of particular, but this need not entail that the blue of the sock literally is itself a particular. Rather, it is this-sock-being-blue that is a particular: the state of affairs of this particular sock instantiating the property of blueness. States of affairs are indeed particulars. They are composite objects, of sorts, comprising a particular (such as this sock) and a universal (such as blue). But where we have a particular plus universal connected together in this way, we have a further particular: a state of affairs. Armstrong refers to this as the *victory of particularity*: a particular + a universal = a particular (N&R: 115).

We are not, therefore, obliged to accept a trope ontology in order to explain the apparent particularity of a property's instances. But Armstrong also offers a number of arguments against the trope view (N&R: 82–7). Distinct tropes resemble each other. How is this so? The realist would say that they are distinct instances of the same property, but the trope theorist must say something else. Because properties are particulars, they are not a One running through Many. Is the resemblance that holds between distinct tropes itself a universal? Are there resemblance tropes? If so, there is clearly the possibility of a Russellian regress. Where *a* and *b* resemble each other, such resemblance must either be admitted as a universal or taken as a trope: a resemblance trope. But then all the different resemblance tropes would have to resemble each other, so exactly the same difficulty recurs.

Immanent realism

The reality of both particulars and universals is to be admitted, therefore. But how are they related? Where it is the case that the apple is red, what holds the apple and the redness together? Any relational tie between particular and universal looks problematic. In the Lockean substratum theory, for example, "thin" particulars are said to *support* their properties. But how can they do so? That *a* supports F would have to be understood as a universal, *supporting*, borne by *a* to F. So the same question arises of how *a* supports this universal: how *a* supports *supporting*. Once again an infinite regress is initiated (N&R: 106). Clearly, this problem is likely to arise for any relational tie that is supposed to connect particulars and universals. This kind of problem is known as Bradley's regress and Armstrong's reconsideration of it led later to a major change of mind on his part, though we shall not look at that until Chapter 11.

Bradley's regress means that the particularity and universality in a thing cannot be regarded as two components standing in some relation to each other. The alternative is to understand the distinction between particulars and universals to be a formal distinction, which is how Aristotle and Duns Scotus understood the distinction and, more significantly for Armstrong, as John Anderson did (1962: ch. 11). Armstrong explains this formal distinction so:

> One model that does seem helpful is the way that the size of a thing stands to its shape. Size and shape are inseparable in particulars, yet they are not related. At the same time they are distinguishable, and particular size and shape vary independently.
>
> (N&R: 110)

The chief commitments of this view are that "Universals are nothing without particulars. Particulars are nothing without universals" (N&R: 113). These two claims can be articulated as the basic principles of immanent realism:

> *Principle of Instantiation*: For each universal, U, there exist at least N particulars such that they are U.
> *Rejection of Bare Particulars*: For each particular, *x*, there exists at least one universal, U, such that *x* is U.

(Armstrong also provides a strong version of this latter principle where U must be a non-relational universal. It is this version of the principle that Armstrong eventually defends in ToU: ch. 19, III.)

Armstrong's view can be represented in a grid (Figure 2.1). The vertical axis lists all the particulars, in lower case, and the horizontal axis lists all the properties, in upper case. The ticks indicate the states of affairs, for example particular *b* bearing property F. The states of affairs are the things that exist, while the particulars and

	A	B	C	D	E	F	G	...
a	✓		✓		✓	✓		
b		✓				✓		
c	✓						✓	
d				✓	✓			
e		✓		✓		✓	✓	
f	✓						✓	
g			✓	✓		✓		
...								

Figure 2.1   Grid for instantiation of properties

universals are, respectively, that about that state of affairs that is particular and that about the state of affairs that is universal. The two principles outlined above place formal restrictions on our grid. Each particular instantiates at least one property, so each row of our grid must contain at least one tick. But there cannot be uninstantiated universals. Each universal must be instantiated by at least one particular, so there must be at least one tick in every column. A particular such as *a*, abstracted away from all its properties, is not an existent in its own right. Such "thin" particulars would be propertyless substrata, which Armstrong rejects. They are mere abstractions. All particulars that exist are thick, as stated by the *Rejection of Bare Particulars*.

If "thin" particulars and universals are formally distinguished from among the states of affairs, what is the basis for the distinction? What distinguishes the "thin" particularity of a state of affairs from its universality?

Particularity is distinguished by total spatiotemporal position: the spacetime "worm" of a thick particular, considered in four dimensions. Four-dimensionalism, the view that all times and places are equally real, is a theme to which Armstrong returns repeatedly. It is a thesis attractive to naturalism because it is scientifically plausible. In Armstrong's case, there is little cost in accommodating such an "omnitemporal" view of the world; indeed on more than one occasion such four-dimensionalism benefits his theory. Here is the first such case. Distinct particulars may occupy the same places at different times but if we consider four-dimensional location – total position in place and time – then *where we have particulars with different total positions we can say that we have different particulars* (N&R: 122). It is at least logically possible that distinct particulars occupy the same total position, a "visual" cube and a "tactual" cube is Armstrong's example, and it is possible that there be two particulars with all the same properties, as is commonly objected to the bundle theory of substance. But if we call the totality of a thing's properties its nature, then we can hold that *particulars are identical if and only if they have the same total positions and the same natures* (N&R: 123). Such a thing is an unrepeatable, or "substance" (ToU: 4).

What, then, of universals? A universal is for Armstrong, as we have seen, a One that runs through Many. It is "genuinely identical in different particulars" (ToU: 19). Squareness, for example, is that which is identical in all square particulars. It is identical in that it is the very same thing in all these instances. Hence a universal is repeatable, unlike a substance; it can appear in any number of different places at the same or different times, as was suggested at the beginning of this chapter.

A *posteriori* realism

Armstrong's immanent realism is also an *a posteriori* realism, in the sense described in Chapter 1 (p. 13). This is also called *scientific* realism. We cannot know *a priori* which universals there are. Indeed, an apparent *a priori* proof for the existence of some universal is a good reason to think that there is no such universal. Armstrong calls this his *Irish principle*: "if it can be proved a priori that a thing falls under a certain universal, then there is no such universal" (ToU: 11). Hence there is no universal of *being identical with itself*, as we would know *a priori* that every particular had this universal. This invalidates, among other things, the argument from meaning, which would be simply to argue from the existence of a predicate to

the existence of a corresponding universal. Rather, for each predicate, there may be no, one, or many corresponding universals
(ToU: 9). How then do we discover, *a posteriori*, the real universals?
One guide that Armstrong suggests is to exploit the connection
between universals and laws of nature. Laws are connections
between the universals that particulars instantiate (more in
Chapter 3). If we discover all the laws of nature, we would thereby
have found a list of all the universals, namely all the universals
mentioned in those laws (ToU: 8, 9). Another pointer exploits the
connection between the properties of a thing and its causal powers
(see also Chapter 5). A genuine universal would make some
causal difference to the things that instantiated it (ToU: 11). This
is based on the Eleatic principle from Plato's *Sophist* (247d–e),
which we have already encountered in the argument for naturalism.
Armstrong takes from it four claims about the nature of properties
(ToU: 43–4):

(a) The active and passive powers of particulars are determined by
    their properties
(b) Every property bestows some active and/or passive power upon
    the particulars of which it is a property
(c) A property bestows the very same power upon any particular
    of which it is a property
(d) Each different property bestows a different power upon the
    particulars of which it is a property.

The status of these claims is controversial, though. In the first
instance, we might wonder what justifies their truth. While (a)
seems to stem from Armstrong's metaphysical commitments, he
can justify (b)–(d) on epistemological or pragmatic grounds only.
Also controversial, however, is the relation between properties and
powers if (a)–(d) are true. Some, such as Shoemaker (1980), take
powers to be exhaustive of properties, but Armstrong does not go
that far. (a)–(d) provide only identity conditions for properties but
not a reductive analysis. We need to get an initial grip on at least
some properties before we can identify the others in terms of them.
We do this when properties exercise their powers on our own senses
in ways that naturally resemble (ToU: 48), which is not to suggest
that our initial classifications cannot be subsequently revised as
science progresses. We may have begun with a very naive account of
the world's properties, starting from the "epistemic state of nature"

(1992: 166), but that account is painstakingly improved as science progresses.

Disjunctive and negative predications are among the cases where there is no corresponding universal. One might say of something that it is F or G, where it is not both F and G. But *F or G* should not be regarded as a genuine universal. Armstrong produces a number of reasons why not (ToU: ch. 14, I). Two particulars, *a* and *b*, might both be F or G although they have nothing in common. *a* might be F and not-G, while *b* is G and not-F, so while one could truly predicate "F or G" of *a* and *b*, there is no corresponding universal because there is no genuine identity running through the Many. For the same reason, there is no genuine universal of being *not*-F (ToU: ch. 14, II). Different things of which it is true that "not-F" might have nothing in common. Particular *a* might be not-blue because it is all green, while *b* may be not-blue because it is all red, and so on. Again there is no One distributed over the Many.

These arguments, however, have an appearance of begging the question. Only if *being F or G* is not a genuine universal can one say that particulars of which it is true that "F or G" can have nothing in common. Similarly for negative properties. Armstrong was to concede this and preferred afterwards to talk of more or less *natural* properties. The issue of naturalness dominates his later book on universals (*Universals*), for instance. These were not the only arguments against disjunctive and negative properties, but the others might similarly be thought question-begging. There are no extra causal powers brought by being F or G or being not-F, Armstrong says, so the link is broken between properties and powers. But this is to overlook the possibility of disjunctive and negative causal powers, which we have not yet ruled out. There is certainly something odd about disjunctive and negative properties, but we have no such feeling about conjunctive universals, which Armstrong is happy to concede (ToU: ch. 15). Where *a* is both F and G, we can allow that it has the conjunctive universal *F and G*, as long as we accept that *being F and G* is not an additional universal over and above *being F* and *being G*. While we may dislike conjunctive universals because of the mere suggestion that they are additions to being, we ought to allow them because, as far as we know, apparently simple universals may turn out, upon a completed physics, really to be conjunctive or complex. The world's universals might be infinitely complex, and philosophers should not judge against such a possibility *a priori* (ToU: 67).

David Armstrong

Relations

What of relations? Thus far, everything true of properties (monadic universals) can be extended to relations (polyadic universals), but we ought to be able to say something about the difference between monadic and polyadic universals. And need we admit relations at all as something over and above particulars and their properties? Armstrong concedes the logical possibility that all relations might be reducible to non-relational properties of particulars, but this is not, as a matter of fact, the case (ToU: 84). It is contingent what relations exist, just as it is contingent which properties exist, as all need to satisfy the instantiation requirement. Of those relations that are instantiated, some are irreducibly relational. These are the *external* relations, where the non-relational properties of the related particulars alone do not necessitate the holding of a relation (ToU: 85). Internal relations are reducible, as they are logically necessitated by the non-relational properties of their relata. *Resemblance* would be an internal relation necessitated, for example, by both the related particulars having the non-relational property of *being white*. Although Armstrong is not as clear as he could be (ToU: 88–91), he allows that we can take *spatiotemporal relations* to be external. Hence *a* and *b* may stand in a relation of being one metre apart, but that they stand in such a relation is not reducible to the non-relational properties of *a* and *b*.

I have spoken of non-relational properties, which is to suggest that there is such a thing as relational properties. Armstrong admits such things. For example, the earth has the relational property of *revolving around a star* (ToU: 78) and I once had the relational property of *being over Walvisbaai*. But relational properties, though real enough, are a reducible category. They are reducible to properties and relations so need not be posited as a fundamental ontological category. All we need for the reduction of such a relational property are the property *being a star* and the relation *revolving around*.

Finally on relations, Armstrong conspicuously denies reflexive relations, where a particular bears some relation to itself (ToU: 91–4). Putative examples are *being identical with itself* or *being the same colour as itself*. Many of the usual arguments apply against these being genuine universals. For a start, we would be able to know *a priori* that every particular had these features so, by the Irish principle, there are none such. But they would also make no difference to the causal powers of things. All genuine relations are therefore polyadic, having always more than one relatum.

Resemblance, determinables and determinates

One further difficulty that Armstrong considers is the notion of resemblance. Two particulars resemble each other through having the same property or having resembling properties. But how do properties resemble each other? Clearly there are such resemblances among universals. Indeed, there can also be degrees of resemblance. Hence, as we have already seen, redness resembles orangeness more than it resembles blueness. After finding faults with all previous accounts (ToU: ch. 21), Armstrong constructs a new one.

If we take as examples the class of colours and the class of shapes, what Armstrong wishes to explain are the following *prima facie* truths (ToU: 116):

(i) The members of the two classes all have something in common (they are all shapes, they are all colours)

(ii) But while they have something in common, they differ in that very respect (they all differ as shapes, they all differ as colours)

(iii) They exhibit a resemblance-order based upon their intrinsic natures (triangularity is more like quadrilaterality than circularity, redness is more like orangeness than blueness)

(iv) They form a set of incompatibles (the same particular cannot simultaneously be both triangular and circular, all red and all blue).

First, Armstrong denies that determinables are genuine universals (ToU: 117). A determinable would be a universal that came in more specific varieties or determinates. There is no genuine (scientific) property of being coloured, nor even of being red. Many distinct determinate shades of red exist, and being the same property means having identity through all instances. We cannot have properties that agree but differ in the same respect, redness for instance. All universals must be, therefore, determinates.

What unifies certain (determinate) properties as a class? Armstrong's suggestion is a series of partial identities holding between members of the class (ToU: 121). Lengths, for instance, contain lesser lengths as parts. *One metre* is partially identical with a *half metre*. This explains what is common to a class of properties: for any two different lengths, there will be a part–whole relation between them: one will be a part of the other. Furthermore, degrees of resemblance can be explained for lengths because there is a distinct order among the partial identities. Partial identities can be more or less close. One foot is a larger part of a yard than it is of a mile; hence it resembles a yard more than a mile. Incompatibilities are also explained because the proper parts of a certain length cannot be identical with that length. Nothing could, that is, instantiate a length and a proper part of that length at the same time in the same dimension.

Armstrong proceeds to suggest that this same account might be extended to other classes of property, such as shapes and colours. Shapes can also have part–whole relations, with ordering principles for overlap. Colours are a difficult case because the phenomenological appearance is of complete simplicity. Only where we have complexity can we talk of overlapping part–whole relations. But this is a case, Armstrong thinks (ToU: 126), where we need to banish the fallacy of the infallibility of perception. A physicalist reduction of phenomenologically simple colour to physically complex light wavelength, and other physical factors, seems plausible – at least for the naturalist – so the case of colour may not be so different from the case of length after all. We can be aware of the resemblance between colours without being aware of the true nature of colour properties from which such resemblances flow, just as we can be aware that two faces resemble without being able to see or articulate the exact respect in which they resemble (ToU: 127). Although this escapes one immediate difficulty, it does lead to another uncomfortable result for Armstrong's theory of universals. All properties are absolutely determinate and are likely to be far more differentiated than our powers of discrimination (ToU: 131). We have to face the possibility, therefore, that we may experience only determinables, which is the same as to say that we may never experience a genuine property. A theory of universals that declares them unknown may be thought counterintuitive.

There is one final concern about this account. *Part–whole* seems to be a relation, so we seem to have invoked a further universal in order to explain resemblance, and we may wonder whether the various part–whole relations resemble. But Armstrong does not accept this as a relation, certainly not an external, hence irreducible, one, even if there is a two-place predicate "— is a part of —" (ToU: 127). Some universals are parts of others simply in virtue of what they are.

Armstrong concludes his two-volume study of universals with a look at higher-order universals. These are putative properties of properties or, in one special and interesting case, relations holding between properties. As this generates Armstrong's theory of laws, I will leave this topic until Chapter 3.

Resemblance nominalism exhumed?

For some time after its appearance, Armstrong's theory of universals held sway. It was in essence a modern revival of Aristotelian realism, so was not new in that respect. But it was worked out in such detail, and so clearly expressed, that it won many converts and for a time diminished the influence of nominalism and transcendent realism among analytic philosophers. As well as being a plausible theory of universals in its own right, the theory had many consequent benefits, as we shall see in the next few chapters. These all add to the strength of the theory. To be able to explain so much surely counts heavily in a theory's favour.

In recent years, however, and after some time lying dormant, a nominalist challenge to Armstrong's realism has resurfaced. This is ably represented, as Armstrong admits, by Rodriguez-Pereyra's *Resemblance Nominalism* (2002). About this book, Armstrong wrote:

> Dan Dennett's *Philosophical Lexicon* contains the entry: "Exhume, *v.* to revive a position generally thought to be humed." This book is the most brilliant philosophical exhumation that it has been my pleasure to encounter. This book argues that our attributions of properties and relations can be given satisfactory truthmakers using no more than resemblances holding between ordinary particulars. Many of us had assumed that this program is bankrupt, but now we must think again. (2003: 285)

Armstrong had conceded early that resemblance nominalism was the strongest form of nominalism (N&R: 44–8), although he still thought that it faced insuperable difficulties. Rodriguez-Pereyra takes on those difficulties and shows how they can be avoided by availing ourselves of Lewis's (1973 and 1986) modal realism. We will encounter modal realism in more detail in Chapter 4. It is the initially astounding thesis that there exist many worlds, more or less like our own, but as real as our own and concrete. Such worlds inhabit a spacetime, but one of their own, spatiotemporally unconnected to any other world. Lewis allows that there can be resemblances between objects in different worlds, hence there could be a man in another world who looked just like David Armstrong, might be a philosopher in a place that resembles our Sydney, and might even go by the name David Armstrong. Lewis had already accepted the nominalistic character of his view (Lewis 1983: 9) but had not shown how his metaphysic could be used to defend an explicit resemblance nominalism.

Some of the traditional difficulties of resemblance nominalism can be avoided if we accept an ontology of concrete possible worlds. Such worlds form a multiverse where every possibility is actual at some world (indeed, we will see that Lewis thinks that this is what it is for something to be possible), so if we allow resemblance across worlds then there is much we can do. We think resemblance nominalism has a problem of coextensive properties, for instance, such as when the class of renate particulars is identical with the class of cordate particulars. As Rodriguez-Pereyra shows, however (2002: 99), if we take the resemblance classes to comprise the renate and cordate things across all worlds, then they will not be coextensive. Similarly, there is a traditional objection that resemblance nominalism cannot account for properties with a single instance, as there is nothing else that they resemble. Clearly, a modal realist will say that there are plenty of other particulars that this particular resembles; it is just that they are not in our world.

There are other problems that a resemblance nominalist would have to solve where a commitment to modal realism is not the answer. Rodriguez-Pereyra does offer solutions to these other problems, however. He disarms Russell's regress by saying that although a and b may resemble, where resemblance is taken as a primitive, he is not ontologically committed to resemblances *as things* (2002: ch. 6). Armstrong had indeed already seen that Russell's regress had no force (U: 55) because resemblance was an internal relation and so required no extra thing or element in order to hold between two resembling particulars. Rodriguez-Pereyra also answers the Imperfect Community objection (2002: ch. 9), to which Armstrong still subscribed (U: 70–71). Particulars a, b and c might form a resemblance class because a is F and G but not H, b is F and H but not G, and c is G and H but not F. Nelson Goodman (1966: ch. 5) had raised this scenario to show that resemblance was insufficient to produce sameness of kind. Rodriguez-Pereyra offers the cleverly simple reply that for a genuine resemblance class, a "perfect" community, it is not sufficient that all the particulars resemble each other, but it is also required that all pairs of particulars resemble all other pairs of particulars and, if there are enough particulars involved, all pairs of pairs of particulars resemble all other pairs of pairs of particulars, and so on. With an imperfect community, resemblance will fail to hold for at least some such level of pairs.

Rodriguez-Pereyra nevertheless concedes that something looks counterintuitive in resemblance nominalism (2002: 201). Armstrong had exploited those intuitions in arguing against the view. In the first place, resemblance is indeed an internal relation (U: 44). The particulars and their natures are enough to make it that the relation of resemblance holds; some additional fact is not needed. But then what is it about such particulars that determines the resemblance? Is it not the properties? Second, does a resemblance class really determine, on its own, a respect in which its members resemble? Suppose I tell you that there are two non-overlapping classes of particulars. One is the class of red things and one is the class of green things. The classes have the same resemblance structure: "If we drew up a resemblance map for either class, specifying the precise degree of resemblance each member had to each other, it could be transferred exactly to the other class" (U: 46). But which class is the class of red things and which is the class of green things? Facts about resemblances between members of the classes seem inadequate to make this determination, which they would have to for resemblance nominalism to be true. Intuitively, sameness of type determines resemblance rather than resemblance determining sameness of type (U: 49). Armstrong has argued this further:

> The resemblances of things, for instance, are not really distinct from the properties and relations of things. We seem to be able to add that the properties and relations of things fail to supervene on their mere resemblances. For a different set of properties and relations might have exactly the same resemblance-structure. If this addition is correct, then it seems that we have here an argument for taking properties and relations to be primary, resemblances to be secondary. (CTP: 7)

Rodriguez-Pereyra nevertheless thinks that resemblance nominalism wins out, all things considered, mainly on the grounds that it avoids additional ontology. Armstrong posits universals to solve the problem of the One over Many, but perhaps the problem can be solved without them. If we can do so in terms of classes of resembling particulars, then our ontology is more economical and so might be preferred on those grounds. An immanent realist could, however, think that a modal realist has some nerve to claim that their ontology is economical. It posits a multiverse of concrete possible worlds of which our own world is just one among very many. Again, Armstrong's naturalism might be brought to bear here. The commitment to but a single world of spacetime rules out the existence of other worlds. If, as Rodriguez-Pereyra concedes, modal realism is the only way of saving resemblance nominalism, then no naturalist can accept it. Immanent realism remains, then, the most attractive theory for the naturalist to hold.

This chapter has been long and the subject matter has been difficult. Universals are, however, the key to understanding many of the positions Armstrong holds elsewhere in metaphysics. The reader who has made it this far should find that things now become a little easier and that the topics to follow fall into place with a little less hard labour.

Chapter 3
Laws of nature

The world is remarkably orderly and predictable. We know that water will boil at 100°C, that the sun will rise every morning, food will nourish us, and that we will be attracted to the ground. If we understand the order of the world, then we will be able to harness it and manipulate it to our own ends.

Before the scientific revolution, such order in the universe was often put down to providence, and it is perhaps from this thought that the original idea of a law of nature originated (see Ruby 1986). Nature seemed so regular and so intricate that it might be compared to a large, accurate clock. God, the creator of all nature, need not keep constantly intervening, winding up his creation to keep it going. God is perfect, so his creation would also be perfect. When creating the universe he might have determined that there be laws of nature that dictate or govern how nature behaves. The order and predictability of the world is good *prima facie* evidence that it is so governed. Such laws imposed necessity on the world: necessary connections between one kind of thing and another.

Armstrong aligns with a naturalism in which there is no supernatural realm that God may inhabit. The theological explanation of nature is no longer available, therefore. Nevertheless, the notion of a law of nature has not been left behind, with scientists and philosophers looking for a down-to-earth account of laws. Since at least Hume, however, and continuing into the twentieth century, naturalists were sceptical of necessary connections in nature. Those inclined towards empiricism think that there is no adequate experiential evidence of such necessity, so cannot accept it as a legitimate idea. Many naturalist philosophers before Armstrong held, therefore, to what is usually called the regularity theory of laws. A law of nature is just some regularity that holds true in nature. There is no explanation of why such a regularity holds, if it is a fundamental regularity. When we get to the most basic regularities, we just have to accept them as a true but contingent feature of the world. This broad view is usually called Humeanism after Hume, the great denier of necessary connections.

The regularity theory

Naturalists have often been empiricists, following Hume's lead. This is the classic empiricist position that all knowledge comes from experience. For our concept of a law of nature to be legitimate, it must have some empirical basis. What then do we know of laws? A typical naturalist answer is that we know only of regularities among events. This was the orthodox view that faced Armstrong when he began to think of laws.

A regularity, which constitutes a law, can be thought of in terms of a universally quantified conditional, $\forall x\ (Fx \to Gx)$, which says that anything that has the property F has the property G. For example, all ravens are black, all electrons are negatively charged, all unsupported objects fall to the ground, all humans are mortal, any charge repels its like and attracts its opposite, and so on. As stated here, there are no explanations of such regularities, except where one regularity is explained by another. Regularities that explain others are regarded as more fundamental. All animals are mortal, for example, and given that a human is an animal, then all humans are mortal too. But for some regularities, there is no further explanation. The regularity theory was defended, for example, by Hempel and Oppenheim (1948), but it was a widely accepted view.

It is worth noting that the form of a law statement, $\forall x\ (Fx \to Gx)$, is here taken to be expressed adequately in an extensional form. The conditional being used is a material conditional. That this is extensional simply means that the truth of the whole is determined by the truth of the constituents, Fx and Gx, as outlined in the truth table for material implication ($\to$). This shows us that $P \to Q$ is true where P is false or when Q is true and it is false only in the situation where both P is true and Q is false. A material conditional is widely regarded as inadequate in many contexts. We often assert counterfactuals and subjunctive conditionals, for instance, where it is assumed that the antecedent, the first term of the conditional, is false. Material conditionals with false antecedents are automatically true in virtue of that fact. But some counterfactuals seem true and some seem false. Consider the difference between "if I had won the lottery I would be rich" and "if I had won the lottery I would be younger". The former seems true while the latter seems false, although both have false antecedents. However, a regularity theorist has good reason to say that material conditionals are adequate to represent laws. Regularity theorists deny necessary connections in nature, so all they are saying when they state a law is that all things that are F are also G. They are not saying that something being F *makes* it be G, or being F *necessitates* being G. They are simply saying that the things that are F are within the extension of things that are G, or things that are F are a subset of things that are G. (They are not committing to the opposite, however, as there could be some things which were G but which were not F.)

Restrictions are often placed on such material conditionals, if they are to express regularities fit to be laws of nature. As well as being true, the statement that $\forall x\ (Fx \rightarrow Gx)$ must also be contingent. Some analytic truths may also have this form, such as that all bachelors are unmarried men. On the widely held assumption that *bachelor* means *unmarried man*, this could not fail to be true. Laws would be the contingent regularities only. They have to be discovered empirically, whereas I can know that all bachelors are unmarried men just from knowing the meaning of the word bachelor. A second restriction is that the predicates used in the law, F and G, be completely general or non-local. They cannot mention a particular. *All ravens are black* might be a law but that all ravens in London are black, or that all ravens in 2007 are black, are not possible laws. "Local" predicates would place restrictions on the generality of the law and allow us to manufacture limited or local regularities, such as that all persons in this room wear wristwatches. Laws should be of genuinely universal scope.

Against the regularity theory

Armstrong's theory of laws is naturalistic and yet is a rejection of the regularity theory. Just as he had done with universals, he manages to forge a naturalistic yet metaphysically realist account. He begins *What is a Law of Nature?* with a detailed and sustained critique of the regularity theory, thereby motivating the need for a new account. His objections fall into three categories. First, there are cases where there can be a regularity that is not a law. Secondly, there can be laws without corresponding regularities. Thirdly, even where laws and regularities coincide, there is reason to think that the regularity and the law are distinct.

It is easy to find cases where there are regularities that do not seem to be laws of nature or should not be accepted as laws of nature (WLN: ch. 2). A common such example is the so-called accidental uniformity. A famous case, which comes from Popper (1959: 427–8), is that of the New Zealand moa bird. All moas died, let us suppose, before becoming 50 years old. Let us assume they died before 50 because of some virus that wiped them out. They are now extinct. Without the virus, they might well have lived longer in so far as there was nothing in their genetic make-up that prevented them from having a longer life. Perhaps one such moa avoided the virus and was in good health, only to be eaten by a predator on the eve of its fiftieth birthday. Nevertheless, in this situation, it is a truth that if x is a moa, then x dies before 50. But do we really think that this fact about the moa is a law of nature?

We might note that the fewer instances there are, then the more likely it is that there be an accidental uniformity. Suppose there are only three things that are F in the entire history of the world. They may all also be G. If you think that a law is simply a regularity then you have to say that it is a law that everything that is F is a G, whereas we feel intuitively that this might just be a coincidence. Extreme examples of this kind are *single-case* uniformities, where only one thing is F, and is also G (WLN: 13–15), and *no-case* uniformities that have non-existent subjects. $\forall x \ (Fx \rightarrow Gx)$ is true when nothing is F, from which it would follow that it is a law that all centaurs are adept at philosophy (WLN: 19). Is it not more plausible to say, having considered this case, that $\forall x \ (Fx \rightarrow Gx)$ is insufficient for a law? One may try to refine the regularity account to avoid this objection, by saying that laws are only the well-confirmed regularities. But this would be to introduce an epistemic factor and this goes against a realist understanding of laws (WLN: 61–4). A law should be understood as a law regardless of our state of knowledge about it. Indeed, wouldn't there have been laws of nature before minds were even created?

Second, we can see that there can be laws without corresponding regularities (WLN: ch. 3). Many laws that are currently invoked in science are irreducibly probabilistic in nature. All particles of a certain kind may have a $\frac{1}{2}$ probability of decaying within a certain time, for instance. But this does not entail that exactly half of those particles will have decayed within that time. Probabilistic laws state only what is most likely to happen, from which we cannot infer what actually does happen. A regularity is not, therefore, a necessary condition for a law. There is a further case that illustrates this. Many laws are functional in nature, such as that F = ma or that F = GM_1M_2/d^2. The regularity theorist would have to say that there are multiple regularities concerning the determinate values of such functions, and that this is all that such a functional law consists in. But it is a feature of such laws that they hold even if some of the values are uninstantiated. One of the masses covered by the gravitational law may be more than the mass of the universe, for instance, or the distance may be greater than the distance across the universe. Nevertheless, the law's generality is supposed to cover even these cases.

Perhaps the most damaging arguments against the regularity theory, however, come when we consider cases where a law and a regularity do indeed coincide (WLN: ch. 4). Regularities do not have the inner connection that we think there should be in a law. We should have a law only when there is a connection between something being F and something being G, and not just when the class of things that are F is a sub-class of the things that are G. Consequently, being F is not an explanation of something being G, on the regularity theory, which it would be if there were a genuine law of nature that makes everything that is F also G. Because of this, regularity laws do not sustain counterfactual claims, which we think real laws should. Suppose a, which is not actually F, were F. Would it also be G? The regularity theorist has no reason to say that it would be. If one thought there was a genuine law that made everything that is F also G, then we would have to say that if a were to be F, it would also be G. As a result of this, as Hume recognized, regularity theorists are left with the problem of induction. Because they grant no inner connection between being F and being G, they have no basis on which to infer from observed cases to unobserved cases. All known things that are F may be G, but that does not support the inference that all things that are F, whether observed or not, are G. In contrast, a realist about laws might claim that there is an inner connection, which provides a reason to think that unobserved cases will be like the observed cases.

This all mounts up to a pretty devastating case against regularities as laws. Such inadequacies have been known for some time (for example, Molnar 1969) but, until the late 1970s, no one had produced a convincing alternative. There had been one attempt, by David Lewis, which was known as the Best Systems account.

The Best Systems account

In *Counterfactuals*, David Lewis revived the Best Systems account of laws that had previously appeared in work by Frank Ramsey (1928) and John Stuart Mill (1843: III, iv, 1). As Lewis states this view:

> a contingent generalization is a law of nature if and only if it appears as a theorem (or axiom) in each of the true deductive systems that achieves a best combination of simplicity and strength.
>
> (1973: 73)

Laws are not simply regularities, therefore, but must form a coherent set of generalizations, from which as much of the world's history as possible could be deduced if they were the assumptions in a systematization of that history. We should take the world as a vast collection of facts. The laws would be the best set of assumptions from which that collection of facts could be derived. What counts as the best set of assumptions is the balance between the two factors of simplicity and strength. A systematization is simpler the fewer axioms it contains but it is stronger the more of the world's history it can generate. It might be possible to deduce 95 per cent of the total world history from only five axioms and this could still come out as the best system if adding a whole new axiom generated only 1 per cent more.

Armstrong questions this balancing act, which seems to introduce an element of subjectivism about the laws of a world: "A Rationalist temperament might value simplicity where an Empiricist valued strength" (WLN: 67). But, furthermore, this theory is a coherence response to the question of what is a law of nature and it is this that offends against Armstrong's realist sentiments (WLN: 70). Whether A is a law of nature is not simply a matter intrinsic to A. A must cohere with others of its like, which form together an integrated system: one which is better than all rival systems. But, in contrast, we might think that the gravitation law is a law simply because of its own truth, irrespective of what the other laws are. This is not to deny that laws can be interconnected and can stand in explanatory relations. Nevertheless, the truth of any particular law ought to be individually evaluable. Like any coherence theory, the Best Systems view also has the implication that there could be two equally good systematizations of the world that were tied for first place but which contained different and inconsistent sets of axioms. Added to that, the axioms of the Best Systems account are themselves regularities and many of the objections to the naive regularity theory carry over. There is no inner connection in such regularities, so they will not support counterfactuals.

Lewis's position is a part of a programme he has called Humean supervenience: the view that all there is in the world is a mosaic of unconnected events (1986a: ix). Anything else either supervenes on this mosaic or is denied. We will encounter Humean supervenience again as an alternative to Armstrong's metaphysics, but now it is time to turn to Armstrong's own theory of laws of nature.

Higher-order universals

We left Armstrong's theory of universals, in Chapter 2, when he had reached the topic of higher-order universals. These now play a central role in Armstrong's theory of laws. A higher-order property would be a property of a property. For example, *being complex* is a second-order property instantiated by some first-order property (ToU: 135). Elementarists claim that only first-order properties are real but the problem they face is that no reductive analysis of *being complex* to first-order properties seems possible. We cannot analyse:

P is complex

as:

For any particular x, if x is P then x is complex

because x might be complex in virtue of others of its properties rather than in virtue of P. Armstrong concludes, therefore, that there are higher-order universals. However, we must again reject the argument from meaning so there is not automatically a property of a property just because we predicate of a property. We say that red is a colour, which grammatically is predicating *being coloured* to *being red*. But *being coloured* is not a genuine universal as it will not be identical in all its instances, whereas *being complex* will be a genuine One over Many. We must apply scientific realism, therefore, and decide carefully what the real second-order universals are. The only higher-order properties are second-order, however. There are no third-order properties. These would be pseudo-properties (ToU: 145). One might think that there is a third-order universal of being a second-order universal, but really this would be some determinable of which the determinates would be *being complex, being conjunctive* and so on.

So much for higher-order properties. As one might expect, by parity of reasoning, Armstrong allows higher-order *relations*, which is the place we will find laws of nature. A first-order relation, R(a,b), is one that takes (first-order) particulars as its relata. A second-order relation would be one that had (first-order) universals as its relata: R(F,G). A first-order universal can also be understood as a second-order particular, fit to partake in relations. Again, Armstrong urges that we can determine only *a posteriori* whether there are any actual second-order relations, but he thinks there are and produces the following, exhaustive, list: nomic necessitation, nomic exclusion and nomic probabilification (ToU: 158). These may, however, resolve to the one relation as nomic necessitation is a probabilification to degree 1, while nomic exclusion is probabilification to degree 0. Nomic probabilification is thus where the degree of probabilification is between 1 and 0, inclusive. For ease of exposition, however, I shall outline Armstrong's theory in terms of nomic necessitation only.

The nomic relation

Armstrong is attempting to give a realist theory of laws, which will distinguish sharply between laws and law statements; it will also be counter to an instrumentalistic theory of laws (WLA: 8). Laws are not, therefore, a merely linguistic item or a useful fiction (see Musgrave 1981). Armstrong is looking for what in the world is a law, which would then serve as a truthmaker for a true law statement (WLN: 77).

The solution was discovered simultaneously by Armstrong, Dretske (1977) and Tooley (1977). Although there are differences of detail, all argue that laws are the holding of a relation between universals, most easily understood as a relation of nomic necessitation. Armstrong represents this as N(F,G), as explained in the previous section, and thinks of laws of nature as the only irreducibly second-order relations (WLN: 84), that is, relations holding between universals.

The relation of nomic necessitation must hold primarily between universals rather than particulars. If we said just that a being F necessitated a being G, b being F necessitated b being G, and so on for various particulars a to n, then a law would be nothing more than a strengthened regularity. It would face the usual problems of any regularity view. It would not support counterfactuals: there would be no reason why z, which is not F, would necessitate G if it were F. What we need to see, therefore, is that the primary nomic necessitation relation holds directly between the universals involved. This idea makes much sense anyway, on independent grounds, as the laws articulated in science do seem to connect universals rather than the particulars that instantiate those universals. The gravitation law, for example, relates mass and distance, rather than things that have mass and things that are distances apart. If a necessitation relation holds directly between universals, then given the identity that runs through all instances of a universal, it will be ensured that every instance of F will necessitate an instance of G. Armstrong provides the following explanation of this:

> If F and G are related by a dyadic relation, a relation whose two terms are confined to these two universals, then it cannot be that they have this relation at one time or place yet lack it at another. The universals F and G are exactly the same things at their different instantiations . . . If it holds in one instance, then it holds in them all, because it is the one identical thing in all the instances. (WLN: 79)

N(F,G) thus ensures the corresponding regularity $\forall x \, (Fx \to Gx)$, but it is not itself entailed by the regularity. As we have already seen, there could be accidental regularities, where it is the case that $\forall x \, (Hx \to Ix)$, but there is no law N(H,I). In such a case, everything that is H just happens to be I but there is no necessitation relation holding between the universals H and I.

Realism about universals is thus an essential part of Armstrong's theory of laws. One reason Armstrong gives ultimately for rejecting trope theory, is that only a realism about universals can provide a robust explanation of laws of nature (see U: 138–9 and 1992: 172). Universals, as a One running through the Many, ensure that if N(F,G) is true for one particular that is F, it is true for all particulars that are F, and thus that N(F,G) entails $\forall x \, (Fx \to Gx)$. N(F,G) can therefore be understood in words as: "Something's being F necessitates that same something's being G, in virtue of the universals F and G" (WLN: 96). This is not yet, however, to explain how N(F,G) holds in any particular case, nor how it holds between universals. Such a necessitation, Armstrong concedes, has to be accepted as a primitive and inexplicable (WLN: 92). We will see that this turns out to be a key bone of contention for Armstrong's opponents.

Another point about this relation that opponents have challenged is how the relation N can be at once necessary and contingent (see Swoyer 1982). If N(F,G), then it is necessitated, for any x that is F, that it also be G. But, insists Armstrong, it is contingent which universals are so related. It may be the case that N(F,G), but it is possible, albeit a *mere* possibility, that N(F,G) is not. Similarly, it may be possible that N(F,G) even though it is not the case that N(F,G). This certainly fits with a long-standing tradition that has taken the laws of nature to be contingent, though we will also see in due course that even this assumption is now challenged.

In Chapter 4, we shall consider what it means to say that something is possible. The statement that it is possible that a law of nature be otherwise can only really be evaluated once we understand what we mean by *possible*. But it will be helpful at this stage if we illustrate the contingency of laws of nature as in Figure 3.1. Taking the vertical axis to represent the first term of the ordered

	A	B	C	D	E	F	G	...
A	–						N	
B		–	N		N			
C		N	–				N	
D				–				
E					–			
F					N	–	N	
G				N			–	
...								

Figure 3.1 Grid of laws

nomological relation (because N(F,G) has to be distinguished from N(G,F)), we can see that, in this example, there is a law of nature N(C,B). Although an N appears in this cell of the grid, it could instead have been empty. Similarly, there is no N on the grid representing a law that N(A,B), but there could have been.

Figure 3.1 illustrates some of the other restrictions that Armstrong imposes. He had already noted, in his work on universals, that there are no genuine reflexive relations that relate a thing to itself (ToU: 91–3). Hence there are no genuine laws that relate a universal nomologically to itself: it cannot be a law that N(F,F). Further, according to one criterion Armstrong mentions for being a universal (see Chapter 2, p. 32), every universal on the grid must figure in at least one law, which would be shown on a grid that was extended to include every universal. The nomic relation is also non-symmetrical. This means that if N(F,G), then it could also be N(G,F), although it need not be. There are also a couple of restrictions that follow from Armstrong's rejection of negative universals (ToU: ch. 14, II). Laws do not contrapose: at least fundamental, underived laws do not contrapose. By this we mean that when it is a law that N(F,G), it will not be a law that N(¬G,¬F) because neither ¬G nor ¬F are genuine universals (I use the negation stroke, ¬, here to mean *not-*). We may *deduce* from the law N(F,G) that if ¬G, then ¬F, and we may speak of this as a derived law, but it is not in the proper sense a law of nature in its own right. For similar reasons, Armstrong rejects exclusions laws (WLN: 143f.). If these are cases where having one property F excludes having another property G, then we saw (ToU: 158) that Armstrong initially accepted them. But how can they be instantiated when it would mean that if something is F it is necessitated that it is not-G? Clearly Armstrong will not permit N(F,¬G).

A long list of advantages can be produced for this theory of laws (WLN: 99–107). It can distinguish, as we have seen, between lawlike and accidental regularities. Although all moas have died before the age of 50, there is no law connecting being a moa and dying before 50, so the regularity is accidental. It can explain why laws cannot be spatiotemporally limited: a law is a universal so is identical in every instance; therefore it cannot hold in one place or time and not in another. The inner connection between being F and being G is explained: with a law we have more than just that every *x* that is F is also G. We can now say that such an *x* is G because it is F, and this "allows us to understand, and to sympathize with, the notion that laws of nature govern particular states of affairs" (WLN: 106).

N(F,G), in contrast to the regularity theory, sustains counterfactuals, being true not just of everything that is F but also things that are non-F. Were those things to be F, and it is a law that N(F,G), then we can say that they would be G. Also, if laws are understood as universals, then we have an explanation of why induction is rational: there is good reason to expect the next case to be like the previous ones.

Unlike the regularity theory, the universals view can also produce accounts of functional and probabilistic laws. In functional laws, one magnitude varies with, or is a function of, another magnitude: $Q = f(P)$. Such functions can be analysed as conjunctions of the form $N(P_1,Q_1)$ & $N(P_2,Q_2)$ & . . . & $N(P_n,Q_n)$, where P_{1-n} and Q_{1-n} are specific magnitudes of P and Q (WLN: 111). Armstrong raised the problem, against the regularity theory, that not all values need be manifested, so there might not be every corresponding regularity. Does his account do better? Where a value of P is uninstantiated, P_0, there will be no law $N(P_0,Q_0)$ but there would nevertheless be a counterfactual, $P_0 \rightarrow Q_0$ (WLN: 112). What sustains such a counterfactual? Armstrong's answer is that there is a higher-order law governing and uniting all the values of P and Q. He represents this law as N(P, a Q such that $Q = f(P)$), and it is instantiated in those cases where P and Q do have instantiated values. This is a higher-order law governing all the conjoined lower-order laws for the specific P and Q values. But it is not clear why such a higher-order function should be taken as a universal if only some of its values are instantiated, and Armstrong admits (WLN: 116) that the account still has problems.

Next an account of probabilistic laws is produced. The proposal is to allow a class of laws of the kind Pr:P(F,G), where $1 > P > 0$. There are verdicts to be produced on a couple of problem cases, however. First, what of a very low-case probability in which, although many things are F, and there is a law Pr:P(F,G), none of those things are also G. Armstrong rules that there is no such law (WLN: 129). Probabilistic laws are instantiated only in their positive instances, that is, where something instantiates both F and G. This is not a comfortable position to hold, however. Some physicists now say that nothing is physically impossible, though some things have an extremely low probability. Hence there may be a law that there is a very small probability of a writing desk turning into a raven. Armstrong will have to deny that this is a law if it has no positive instance at any time. A second kind of case is the reverse of this problem. Suppose there is a law that there is a high probability linking universals H and I. Not many things are H, and all of them are I, but the nomic relation between them is less than necessitation. Is such a case possible? Armstrong allows that it is (WLN: 131). We may not be able to know that the law is Pr:P(H,I) rather than N(H,I), but it may nevertheless be Pr:P(H,I) as a matter of nomological fact. Is it right that Armstrong gives different kinds of response to the two cases of very low probability and very high probability?

We can note that all probabilistic laws are ultimately interpreted in line with Armstrong's standard theory. What they are really about is the probability of necessitation (WLN: 132). Wherever being F does bring about being G, it does so by necessitating it. A probabilistic law merely states that there is a less than 1 probability of one universal necessitating another.

Causation

Earlier (N&R: 115n), Armstrong had thought of a relation R holding between universals F and G to be a particular, on the grounds that "It cannot be repeated". But in formulating his theory of laws he sees that his original verdict was a mistake (WLN: 88). N(F,G) is indeed repeatable and has numerous instances, so it should be understood as a universal. But now bear in mind that Armstrong's realism about universals is an immanent realism where the universal exists only in its instances. There are no uninstantiated universals, therefore no uninstantiated laws. This is one way in which Armstrong's version of the theory differs from Tooley's. Tooley takes a broadly Platonist view of universals and so is happy to allow uninstantiated laws (1977: 671). But for Armstrong, each law of nature, *qua* immanent universal, must be instantiated to be real (WLN: 100).

This raises the question of what instantiates the law. We have already seen that Armstrong speaks of a law having instances. Where there genuinely is a law, N(F,G), it is not instanced simply in some particular *a* being F and G. Where there is such a law, *a* being F necessitates *a* being G. One state of affairs will necessitate another in virtue of the universals involved. Could we find a name for such a necessitation between individual states of affairs? *Causation* is the relation staring us in the face. In a move that unites the notions of universal, law and cause in one neat and elegant theory, Armstrong declares that laws are instanced in particular causal transactions in virtue of the universals that are nomically connected (CTP: 99). There is effectively an identification of singular causal sequences with the instantiations of laws (see Heathcote and Armstrong 1991). This is not a conceptual truth. It need not be. It is an empirical, *a posteriori* identification, like the one between heat and molecular motion (WSA: 218).

Among other virtues, this view of the relationship between laws and causes shows us what is right both about singularism and about the covering-law model of cause. There is a strong intuitive attraction to the view that for A to cause B, there must be a law stating that anything like A will cause something like B. This follows from Hume's own account of cause (1748: §VII). Yet there is also a strong attraction to the singularist intuition that whether A causes B is a matter intrinsic to A and B and cannot be determined, even in part, by what happens at other places and times (Anscombe 1971). Armstrong is now in a position to reconcile the seemingly irreconcilable (WLN: 98). When Fa causes Ga, it will indeed involve nothing more than the states of affairs, Fa and Ga. But the universals F and G are fully present in their instances, and the law N(F,G) will be fully present in this instance of Fa causing Ga. Indeed there will always be a covering law where we have causation, rather than just a coincidence of states of affairs. But the singularist intuition is satisfied because the instances alone contain the fully present law (WLN: 102). That Armstrong's theory of causation is able to satisfy both intuitions at the same time is a major advantage of it and counts heavily in favour of it as at least close to the truth of the matter.

What knowledge do we have of laws? We know of laws through knowledge of causes, which Armstrong takes to be direct and non-inferential: "there is direct awareness of nomic necessitation. Indeed, the cases I have in mind are familiar ones. I refer to the direct perceptual awareness which we appear to have of the operation of causes" (ToU: 164). This is a claim Armstrong had made as early as his work on bodily sensations (see Chapter 7, below), drawing on the work of the psychologist Michotte (1963). We have direct bodily awareness of causes in our own bodies, which is awareness of the operation of laws. Detailed arguments for the direct perception of causation can be offered (WSA: 211–19).

Problems

The neat interconnection between laws, universals and causation looks very promising. The account has, nevertheless, faced serious criticism. In this section I shall draw attention to two major concerns.

In the first place, there has been a long line of criticism on the nature of Armstrong's nomic relation N. It has been called *ad hoc* and *sui generis* (Mellor 1991: 168), it has been lampooned in a famous joke (Lewis 1983: 40), and it has been charged with falling into vicious regress (Bird 2005). The problem is how the relation is supposed to fulfil the role Armstrong requires of it. Its role is to entail the corresponding regularity: if N(F,G), then $\forall x$ (F$x \rightarrow$ Gx). But does Armstrong have any explanation of how it does so? If not, it looks merely to be stipulated that it entails the corresponding regularity. Calling the nomic relation one of necessitation does not, on its own, make it so. Bird's charge of regress is that there would have to be some relation between N(F,G) and $\forall x$ (F$x \rightarrow$ Gx) that made the former necessitate the latter. But this is just to face the same sort of problem with which we began. Is there merely a constant conjunction between N(F,G) and $\forall x$ (F$x \rightarrow$ Gx)? Surely Armstrong should not say so, because if constant conjunctions are permitted, then why not, in the first place, be content with the constant conjunction between F and G? Armstrong almost certainly needs something stronger. So is there a necessitation relation between N(F,G) and $\forall x$ (F$x \rightarrow$ Gx)? If there is, then Armstrong has a choice between saying that the relation between N(F,G) and $\forall x$ (F$x \rightarrow$ Gx) is one of absolute necessity between distinct existences, but we will see that he rejects such strong necessity, or he can say that the relation is one of contingent necessitation. This latter option looks to be his only choice. It is, however, to employ the same relation N that we have already encountered, now using it to connect N(F,G) with $\forall x$ (F$x \rightarrow$ Gx). At the risk of overcomplicating, we would have to represent the necessitation as N(N(F,G), $\forall x$ (F$x \rightarrow$ Gx)). And here, of course, we can ask the very same question of how this further N necessitates the connection between N(F,G) and $\forall x$ (F$x \rightarrow$ Gx). To give the same answer is to show that we have embarked on an infinite regress. The nomological relation looks, therefore, to be in serious difficulty.

Armstrong has steadfastly defended nomic necessitation, however. His explanation of how N ensures the corresponding regularity remains based in the theory of universals. More recently, he has preferred to articulate this in the language of states of affairs (WSA: 225–6). Universals are types of states of affairs, instantiated in token states of affairs. They are that which is the same in the many different tokens. Universals are, then, just tokens of the same type. If it is true of one token, Fa, that it stands in a certain causal relation to another, Ga, then it has to be true also of all tokens of that type:

that is, any token involving F must cause a token involving G. But this seems only to lead to further difficulty. It looks as though the fundamental necessitations occur at the level of tokens, and the types, as Armstrong says, are abstractions from such tokens and exist only in such tokens. But then what justification is there for Armstrong's claim that the connection between the types, the universals, is the direct or primary connection, which then governs the connection between the tokens or instances? How can the law govern its instances if it is only an abstraction from them? The answer Armstrong offers makes use of Wittgenstein's so-called ladder, which we ascend and then throw away. We start by understanding the causal relations between particulars, then rise to the level of universals by seeing that A causes B only in virtue of the universals instantiated in A and B. We then realize that "The fundamental causal relation is the nomic one, holding between state-of-affairs types, between universals" (WSA: 227).

Clearly we could pursue this last point further but there is a second issue that demands attention. Armstrong has said that the nomic relation N is a contingent relation (WLN: ch. 11). The nomic relations that universals bear to each other could vary across possible worlds, although we shall see in Chapter 4 that Armstrong does not take possible-worlds talk literally. Even if N(F,G), it is at least possible that N(F,G) not be a law. This respects a long-held intuition that although laws of nature hold for every time and place in the universe, they could have been otherwise. The inverse square law of gravitation, for instance, could have been an inverse cube law.

If laws are contingent, however, there is a consequence that many philosophers find hard to accept. Assume that F, in our world, is nomically related by N to G. If F and G are only contingently related then it is at least a possibility that *not*-N(F,G). But this means that the universal F would still be F even if it were not nomically related to G. Some have objected to this. What, they wonder, is it that makes a universal the universal it is? An answer that has some attraction is that it is the nomic role of a universal that makes it what it is, that gives it its identity. That would have the consequence that if the nomic relations of F were different, then F would be different: it would cease to be F. In other words, the nomic relations of a universal are essential to it, which means that the laws of nature are not contingent.

The only way to resist this argument is to say that the nature and identity of a universal is determined by something else. No serious alternative to nomic role has been adequately advanced. But perhaps a universal has its identity primitively, dependent on nothing else, and thus remains what it is even if its nomic role varies. This is a view that has been labelled quidditism (Black 2000), meaning commitment to the primitive identity of properties (as opposed to haecceities, which are primitive identities for particulars). Quidditism is usually taken to be a desperate measure. David Lewis, nevertheless, accepts it as a requirement of his Humean metaphysic (forthcoming), even though he rejects haecceities. Remarkably, however, Armstrong seems willing to entertain both quiddities and haecceities in the following passage:

> But why need properties have essential features at all? Perhaps their identity is primitive. To uphold this view is to reject the Principle of the Identity of Indiscernibles with respect to properties. Properties can just be different, in the same way that, many of us would maintain, ordinary particulars can just be different although having all their features in common. . . . Swoyer objects to this view that the "primitive" difference of ordinary particulars is grounded in something: their distinct spatio-temporal locations. But suppose, as seems thinkable, that there are particulars which are not spatio-temporal. *Pace* Aquinas, may not two angels simply be different from each other while having all the same properties? Apparently they would be primitively different. And why should not the same be true for properties? We might put the matter this way: properties can be their own essence. (WLN: 160)

There is much in this paragraph that the reader of Armstrong will find startling. But it does concern one of the deepest questions of one of the deepest parts of philosophy. What makes two properties distinct? What, for that matter, gives a property identity? In the case of particulars, we have already seen that we can at least say two particulars are distinct when they have different properties. Clearly this same answer is not available for properties themselves. We cannot say that properties themselves are distinct when they have distinct properties. Either that answer is circular or it just pushes the problem on to the distinctness of the other properties invoked. Having rejected essentialism, the view that there is something, such as nomic role, that is essential to a property, Armstrong is left with the conclusion that different properties are just numerically distinct, having their identity primitively.

David Armstrong

Other realist accounts

Armstrong argued that the inference from regularities to the existence of laws was an inference to the best explanation. But he did not show in any detail why laws were the best explanation of regularity. He merely issued a challenge to anyone who disagreed: "'Produce a better, or equally good, explanation'. Perhaps the challenge can be met. We simply wait and see" (WLN: 59). Perhaps, then, there is a better explanation of the world's regularity.

It is one thing to criticize a theory and another to produce a rival that has at least the same degree of rigour and plausibility. Very recently, however, a rival to Armstrong's account of laws has developed in the shape of Brian Ellis's Dispositional Essentialism (Ellis 2001, 2002). This account is based on a metaphysic of causal powers, with which Armstrong ultimately disagrees (see Chapter 5, below). It also invokes essentialism, as the name indicates, with which Armstrong disagrees (see Chapter 4). It does, however, avoid the two problems mentioned in the previous section. Laws of nature will not be contingent, on this view, as they concern the essential properties of natural kinds. Such properties will be the same across all worlds. They will always play the same nomic role so there will be no appeal to quidditism. Furthermore, the nomic relation becomes an internal one, which exists just when the universal exists. It can be part of the essence of F to be related to G, hence we do not need some additional relation N to make F and G nomically related. F would not be F unless it were G-related. This, too, is unacceptable to Armstrong as he rejects internal relations as genuine relations (WLN: 84). They are not genuine because they are not anything over and above the related universals themselves. They are "not an addition to the world's furniture" (WSA: 87). But this seems to be a conclusion the essentialists want. If the nomic relation is something over and above the related universal, then it becomes logically possible for it to vary independently of those universals, which is how the problem of quidditism arises.

The role of laws does, however, become controversial in this dispositional essentialist alternative. Ellis presented the theory, among other things, as an account of laws of nature. But such laws seem entirely reducible to natural kinds and their essential properties. And internal relations, as we have seen, are nothing at all. The charge has been brought, therefore, that such laws cannot govern their instances (Mumford 2004: §9.7) and that laws of nature therefore disappear in an essentialist metaphysic as they play no role. Despite in places speaking of laws governing their instances, Ellis (2006) has since made it clear that he does not see natural laws as playing a substantial role. They may, therefore, disappear from our metaphysic or be eliminated. In contrast, Bird, another essentialist (2007), has tried to defend a role for laws even within this framework.

Given that Armstrong rejects essentialism, however, and an ontology of causal powers, it is clear that he still needs laws. There is something that laws do, or are at least required to do, in his metaphysic. Without them, one universal would not be related to another and we would have no explanation of the evident regularity of the world. The properties F, G, H, and so on, are insufficient on their own to necessitate any other property. They are, as Armstrong calls them, categorical, so would not, without laws, endow their possessors with any causal powers. To get causes, therefore, we need an additional element, a necessitation at the level of universals, and this is what Armstrong's laws provide. It is a theory with a high degree of consistency and coherence. It is certainly a tenable view, if one is willing to accept all the consequences.

Chapter 4
Possibility

We saw in Chapter 3 that Armstrong thinks of the laws of nature as contingent. They could be otherwise. But what does it mean to say that something could be otherwise? In answering this we shall also have to consider what it means to say that something could not be otherwise or, in other words, that something must be a certain way. To say that something could be is to say that it is possible. To say that something must be is to say that it is necessary. Necessity and possibility are the two basic modal notions. They are the so-called modes or modifications of propositions. Thus, where we have some proposition, p, we can modify it by saying possibly-p or necessarily-p, which are represented as ◇p and □p respectively. Where it is both possible that p and possible that not-p, we say that p is contingent. Modality is about more than just propositions, however, as it is that denoted by the proposition which is usually regarded as possible or necessary. Hence it may be possible that I go to Buenos Aires and necessary that if I do go, I will have to change my current location. Our modal beliefs seem to be about the world itself and the way it could be or the way it must be.

At first sight this might seem a rather arcane and abstruse subject, but the more that one reads of philosophy the more one will come across modal notions. Philosophers want to understand modality for its own sake as they want to understand how it can be true that George Bush might have lost or that an electron must be negatively charged. Some modal statements seem true and some seem false, so we want to understand why they are true and false. But philosophy also itself invokes modal notions perhaps more than any other discipline. Much of philosophy is concerned with arguments, for example,

David Armstrong

but a valid argument is said to be one where the premises cannot be true while the conclusion is false. To say what *cannot be* is to make a modal claim. Armstrong makes a modal claim when he says that there cannot be uninstantiated universals. One view of substance defines it as that for which it is possible that a single individual of that category exists. In more recent times it has been realized that the fundamental notion of identity is inextricably tied up with modality. If mental states are identical with brain states, for example, is that identity contingent or necessary? We will see that Armstrong has pondered this question in his work on philosophy of mind (see Chapter 8). An orthodox view now, taken from Kripke's lead (1980), is that identities are necessary. If water is identical with H_2O, then it is necessarily so and could not be otherwise. It is probably David Lewis, however, who has done more than anyone else to put the topic of modality at the centre of contemporary philosophy. We shall see shortly that he has produced a systematic, all-encompassing theory of what modal truths consist in. It is primarily this account of Lewis's for which Armstrong is offering his own combinatorial theory as an alternative. At the end of *What is a Law of Nature?*, Armstrong expressed the hope to give a combinatorial account along the lines of Wittgenstein's *Tractatus* (WLN: 163). He also gave a further clue to this theory when he rejected the doctrine of essential properties (WLN: 166). We cannot say, for instance, that Socrates is essentially human, as that would impose a restriction on what could be recombined with what. We will see that Armstrong wants no limitations on recombination.

An adequate theory of modality is usually seen as constrained by the axioms and theorems of modal logic. We intuitively take certain modal inferences as valid, for example:

$p \rightarrow \Diamond p$ (if p, then p is possible)
$\Box p \rightarrow \Diamond p$ (if p is necessary, then p is possible)
$\Box p \rightarrow p$ (if p is necessary, then p).

We also accept the equivalences:

$\Diamond p \leftrightarrow \neg \Box \neg p$
$\Box p \leftrightarrow \neg \Diamond \neg p$,

which means that the two basic modal operators are interdefinable. One need accept only one of them as primitive and then define the other using an equivalence. Modalists take at least one modal notion as primitive and then just accept that we employ modal claims and modal logics in our reasoning (see Melia 2003: ch. 4). Unlike modalists, both Lewis and Armstrong are attempting to get at the metaphysics that lies beyond the logico-linguistic reality. They are concerned with what it is that makes it true that ◇p and □p. They will respect the constraints of modal logic and discourse, but they are looking for a metaphysical theory of its grounding. We shall see that they offer widely differing accounts.

Possible and other worlds

David Lewis in *On The Plurality of Worlds* (1986) presents his most thorough account of modality, although it builds on the notions he first employed in his theory of counterfactuals (Lewis 1973). The central idea is that taken from Leibniz of a possible world.

Various things are true in our world, the actual world, but sometimes we say that p is possible where it is not true in the actual world. This would be a case where p is false but ◇p is true. Everything that is actually true is also possibly true, but more interesting to philosophers are the cases where something is possibly true, but not actually true: the truths of "mere" possibility. Lewis's explanation of such mere possibilities is that there are some other worlds, or at least one, at which they are actually true, and these worlds are distinct from ours. Necessity is explained using the same possible-worlds apparatus: p is necessarily true if and only if it is true at all worlds, which will, of course, include the actual world.

There is a surprising, some think startling, twist to Lewis's theory. Lewis thinks that all these worlds are concrete existents. They contain physical objects, just like our world. They may even contain people, or at least things that look a lot like our people. They can contain planets, water, gases, suns, rocks and living creatures. Such worlds are not like distant planets, however. They are not spatiotemporally connected with our world at all, nor with any other, so it would not be possible to visit such a world no matter how powerful one's space rocket. Being spatiotemporally discrete could be understood as part of what it is to be a world: if it would be possible to travel to any location L, then L is part of our world. Worlds are then like island universes: isolated but complete totalities. Lewis called his view modal realism in an attempt to convey his realism about possible worlds, although he later admitted that the name was not entirely appropriate. Lewis is a Humean, believing in no necessary or modal connections within any one world. The apparatus of possible worlds provides a reductive analysis of modal notions into non-modal notions. They are instead understood in terms of truths in other worlds and relations between such worlds. But each world is understood as a Hume-world, containing within it no necessary connections. Lewis is not a modal realist, therefore, in the sense of believing in intra-world modal truths. All modal truths have to be understood as inter-world. The label *modal realism* is not entirely apt; therefore, and *other-worlds realism* would have been better.

One might think that there is something special about our world, the actual world, which this account does not explain. We may have thought that ours was the only *real* world or at least the only one containing concrete particulars, located in space and time. But Lewis tells us that each world has its own spacetime with its own concrete particulars therein. Our world is not, after all, special or in a privileged position. It seems special to us only because it is our world. But Lewis urges that we should understand the notion of the actual world not in absolute terms but as an indexical, which changes its reference according to the context of use. Indexicals such as *I*, *here* and *now* gain their reference by the situation of utterance. *Here*, for me, is Nottingham, UK. For Armstrong it is Sydney, Australia. We do not feel that there is a dispute between us over where *here* truly is. Lewis thinks we should employ the same account for the reference of *actual* in respect of worlds.

The ontology of modal realism may seem extravagant, positing numerous concrete worlds just like ours, but Lewis thinks he has good reasons for holding this view. One reason, as will be explained below, is that any weaker notion of a possible world faces a charge of circularity and leaves modal notions unanalysed. Another reason, however, is that modal realism explains and unifies so many different issues in metaphysics. We have already seen (Chapter 2, pp. 37–40) how a nominalistic account of properties can be got from modal realism. Lewis also thinks it provides an account of counterfactual truths. *If P, then Q* will be true, where P is not true in our world, if and only if Q is true in all the closest worlds to ours (understood in terms of overall similarity) in which P is true. This generates a theory of causation as counterfactual dependence between events. We have also seen (Chapter 3, p. 46) how an account of the laws of nature can be delivered: laws will be the axioms of the best possible systematization of the total history *of a world*, and thus may vary from world to world. Modal realism is no mere folly, therefore. It is a serious attempt to explain modality, and the fact that it can also explain many other troublesome phenomena counts strongly in its favour. Armstrong has a very conciliatory view of method in metaphysics (recall the quotation from Chapter 1, p. 13) so is unlikely to dismiss such a productive view out of hand.

Armstrong has furthermore been willing to articulate claims of possibility in terms of other worlds (WLN: 163) but he is careful, when he does so, to say that such talk is not to be taken literally. His talk of them, at least in his early theory, is a form of fictionalism (CTP: 4n): they are useful fictions for our modal discourses (for how Armstrong changes his view from this, see Chapter 6, p. 109). Any theory that invokes real other worlds contradicts Armstrong's central commitment to naturalism. We have already seen from Armstrong the statement that:

> Every systematic philosophy must give some account of the nature of possibility. The main constraint I wish to place on such an account is that it be compatible with *Naturalism*. The term "Naturalism" is often used rather vaguely, but I shall understand by it the doctrine that nothing at all exists except the single world of space and time. So my objective is to give an account of possibility which is in no way other-worldly.
>
> (CTP: 3)

The argument for the rejection of possibilia, alleged possible objects, is the causal argument: such things make no causal difference to the world of space and time – certainly not our space and time – so "we have no good reason to postulate such entities" (CTP: 7). This causal argument is a development of the Eleatic principle – that to be real is to make some causal difference to the world – and it is here that Armstrong mounts one of his most detailed defences of the claim. Are there things such as mathematical entities that are real but make no causal difference? No, says Armstrong. Sets, for example, make no causal difference. Members of sets might make a causal difference to the world but the sets themselves are no more than those members (CTP: 11).

Even if one rejects the causal argument, however, there are still some very serious difficulties for any non-natural theory of possibility. In Lewis's modal realism, individuals are world bound. Because each world is concrete but spatiotemporally isolated, each particular exists only at one world. But this raises problems for modal realism *qua* an analysis of possibility. One might say

Humphrey could have had six fingers on his left hand. This is a statement of mere possibility because the real Humphrey had only five fingers on each hand. Lewis's analysis of this case cannot be that there is another world that contains a six-fingered Humphrey. There is only one Humphrey: the one in our world. Instead, Lewis says that there is a counterpart of Humphrey, in some other world, who has six fingers. A counterpart resembles our Humphrey closely; he may even be called Humphrey in that world. But there is no identity of particulars across possible worlds. Lewis's theory exploits the fact that there can nevertheless be resemblances across worlds. As Armstrong grants (CTP: 15), resemblance is an internal relation determined by the nature of the resembling particulars, so can hold across possible worlds even if they are spatiotemporally unconnected. But this still leaves Lewis with what looks like an inadequate theory. Humphrey, it seems, could not have been six-fingered because the six-fingered counterpart is not him (CTP: 19). Similarly, I sometimes wonder whether I could have been a pro-fessional footballer. It does not help me determine the answer if I know that there are some counterparts, with whom I am not identical, who are professional footballers. All that tells me is that I resemble other people who are professional footballers, which I knew already as people have told me I bear a passing resemblance to David Beckham. Lewis has tried to argue that this issue is not a big problem for modal realism (1986: 195–6), although I must say that I find his response unsatisfactory.

Further difficulties accompany modal realism. What guarantee is there that there will be a world for every possibility (CTP: 20)? Lewis admits that there is none (1986: 1.8). What is to stop there being duplicate worlds that resemble each other in every detail? Apparently nothing. It is hard for us to find constraints that neatly fit our modal logic. It would be convenient if there were just one world for every possibility. But these worlds are concrete existents. They are real things. How, then, could something prevent there being two the same, and what would guarantee that there be a world for everything that logic tells us is possible? That the nature of the pluri-verse would neatly match our modal logic sounds like a fantastical hypothesis.

Some philosophers have been attracted to the apparatus of possible worlds and have tried to use it without committing to their real existence. Instead, they have tried to form something akin to worlds from elements that they think are already actual. Lewis calls this ersatz realism. A world could be understood, for example, as a set of propositions that can represent possibilities (CTP: 31). Adams (1974) speaks of a world as a maximally consistent set of propositions. Plantinga (1974: ch. 4) calls such a world a "book" of propositions. Such sets or books must be maximally consistent in order to be a credible world with no gaps. A set of two propositions would in most cases be considered insufficient to form a viable world.

Armstrong sees such accounts as preferable to modal realism as they invoke only actual entities without any reified possibilia or possible entities. He accepts eventually that there are propositions, as we shall see in his work on truthmaking (Chapter 10), although he was initially concerned that they would be outside the causal order (CTP: 32). Ersatz theory would have an account of why we could not have two exactly resembling worlds: sets are identical if they have the same members. And there would be a world for every possibility as nothing further is required for a set to exist other than that its members – the constituent propositions – exist. But Armstrong does not accept ersatz realism and he agrees with Lewis's reasoning. Ersatzism is "paradise on the cheap", with all the advantages of theft over honest toil. A consistent set of proposition is one where it is *possible* for all the propositions to be true together. To account for consistency one needs a modal notion, therefore, which it seems in the final analysis must be taken as primitive.

This point shows why Lewis thinks one must opt for the strong version of modal realism and accept something as counterintuitive as concrete possible worlds. If one says that for p to be possible is for p to be true in some possible world (and that for p to be necessary is for p to be true in all possible worlds), one is clearly invoking the very same concept that one is seeking to explain. Instead, if one accepts the reality of the plurality of worlds, then modal notions do not have to be taken as primitive but are grounded in non-modal terms. In modal realism, for p to be possible is for p to be true at some world (to be necessary, it is true at all worlds). If one is going to use the apparatus of possible worlds, therefore, one might as well opt for full-blooded realism.

But this offends deeply Armstrong's naturalist instincts, so he has no option but to look for an account of modality that is not in terms of possible worlds and he will speak of such worlds only as fictional entities. His combinatorial theory is intended, therefore, as an acceptable naturalist alternative to Lewis's modal realism.

Combinatorialism

Armstrong got the idea of combinatorialism from Wittgenstein, via Skyrms (1981). In the *Tractatus*, Wittgenstein had said: "A proposition determines a place in logical space. The existence of this logical place is guaranteed by the mere existence of the constituents" (1921: 3.4).

These constituents fall into three kinds in Armstrong's metaphysics. They are the constituents that were found in his immanent realism about universals. He uses them to outline a "Wittgenstein world" (CTP: 38), the key features of which are that all the constituents are atomic or simple and that they are logically or "Hume" independent. The constituents are the simple particulars, properties and relations. As we saw in Chapter 2, all real relations will be external, thus something over and above the particulars and their properties. These constituents are simple in the sense that they do not have further constituents as parts. A particular may be complex in the sense of having numerous properties, but it is counted as simple if and only if it has no further particulars as constituents. Similarly, a property is simple when it has no further properties as constituents; it is not, therefore, a conjunctive property.

	A	B	C	D	E	F	G	...
a	✓		✓		✓	✓		
b		✓				✓		
c	✓						✓	
d				✓	✓			
e		✓		✓		✓	✓	
f	✓						✓	
g			✓	✓		✓		
...								

Figure 4.1 Combinatorial grid for instantiation of properties

Where a is a simple particular and F is a simple property, then Fa would be an atomic state of affairs (represented by the "tick" of instantiation in Figure 2.1, reproduced here as Figure 4.1) (CTP: 41). The usual immanent realist constraints apply to such constituents, however. Every particular instantiates at least one property (there are no bare particulars) and each property is instantiated by at least one particular (there are no uninstantiated universals). The basic entities are states of affairs ("States of affairs rule!" – CTP: 43), from which bare particulars and properties are abstractions. Molecular states of affairs might be built out of these simple ones, where these are conjunctions of states of affairs (CTP: 45). There are no negative or disjunctive states of affairs.

What, then, are "mere" possibilities? Simply, they are the blank cells on the grid. The existing elements create all the logical spaces by the combinatorial principle that all the simple elements are compossible. Compossibility is the thesis that any particular may occur with any property or stand in any external relation to any other particular. To represent all the possible relations we would need a separate grid (see Figure 4.2). Everything that is actual will indeed come out as possible, on this view. It is simply that these logical spaces are filled by states of affairs. The merely possible logical spaces are empty. Unlike Lewis's account, therefore, Armstrong's mere possibilities do not exist, in any sense, at any place or time. They have no being whatsoever (CTP: 46). A possible world is a fiction, as Armstrong initially depicts it, constructed from these merely possible states of affairs. This shows the difference between Armstrong's fictionalism and ersatz realism. Ersatzism identifies possibilities with actually existing components, such as groups of propositions. The fictionalist sees the mere possibilities as nothing at all.

There is one additional state of affairs that would be needed to form a world, however, namely a higher-order state of affairs that makes it that these are all the first-order states of affairs (CTP: 48). This complicates the theory somewhat, as a world can no longer be understood as a totality of first-order facts. But at least since Russell (1918: 93) it has been recognized that the fact that we have all the facts, of a world for instance, must be an additional fact about that world. This further "totality fact" will also be of use elsewhere, as we shall see in Chapter 10 when we consider negative truths (Armstrong first offers a solution to this problem at CTP: 96). We have already seen that, quite apart from these considerations, worlds are likely to contain

	a	b	c	d	e	F	g	...
a	–	R			R		R	
b		–		R				
c	R		–					
d				–				
e	R	R			–			
f					R	–		
g							–	
...								

Figure 4.2 Combinatorial grid for instantiation of external relations (Note that nothing bears a real relation to itself)

higher-order facts. Laws of nature were accounted for by Armstrong as higher-order relations. There is no reason why such relations must exist at every world, so some world might be lawless. But it seems pointless to rule out such higher-order facts just in order to retain a world solely of first-order facts, as Wittgenstein and Skyrms wanted. Our world looks to many people to be one that is law-governed, so at least in ours it seems that there are these higher-order states of affairs.

It has to be conceded that the world may contain infinite complexity (CTP: 66), in which case there would be no atomic, first-order states of affairs. (This would contrast with a world that had atoms but an infinite number of them.) Whether a universal is simple or complex, Armstrong now thinks, is a necessary matter (reversing a decision in ToU: ch. 15, I), but we have to allow that it is *doxastically* (i.e. as far as we know) possible that a universal be either simple or complex. What we have to do, therefore, is accept a notion of relative atoms that, as far as we know, may or may not be real atoms. Relative atoms must nevertheless meet the requirement that they be wholly distinct from each other, and thus be available for free recombination.

Once this basic picture is accepted, with the few required modifications, we can put it to use. Not only does an account of possibility come from it, but much else will follow simply by supervenience. Supervenience is taken to be a dependence relation, although Armstrong commits only to a very weak version of it, which is that entity or entities S supervenes on entity or entities R if and only if S exists in all the worlds in which R exists (CTP: 103). Internal relations would clearly be supervenient as they exist simply if their relata exist. Thus they are not understood to be "real" relations, as they require nothing more for their existence than their relata. Similarly, conjunctive states of affairs would supervene on their conjunct states of affairs.

Aliens

There nevertheless remains an apparent advantage that Lewis's modal realism has over combinatorialism. It seems plausible that there could have been more basic elements than there are. There could, perhaps, have been a simple universal that is not instantiated in our world. Lewis is able to allow this. Such a universal might not be instantiated in this world but it would be instantiated at some other. Similarly, might there not have been more individuals than there are in our world? Isn't it a contingent matter that there is not just one more individual than actually exists in our world? Again, Lewis would allow that it existed in some other world. Universals that do not exist in our world are called alien universals. Particulars that do not exist in our world are called alien particulars. It should be clear, however, that there may be some molecular universals and particulars that are not instantiated in our world but are nevertheless possible on combinatorial principles. All the basic elements for generating them are there, but it is just that they never come together in actual fact.

There are a couple of reasons why aliens create a difficulty for Armstrong's theory of possibility. First, combinatorialism seems to rule counterintuitively that a non-actual universal is not even a possible universal. Possibilities are just recombinations of the actually existing elements. If a simple universal does not exist, it is not available for recombination. But does it not make sense to speak of a possible universal: a *merely* possible one? According to Armstrong, there is no such thing. He accepts some intuitive appeal of such aliens, for instance: "one thing that seems to keep a theory of uninstantiated universals going is the widespread idea that it is sufficient for a universal to exist if it is merely possible that it should be instantiated" (U: 80). To concede that uninstantiated universals are nevertheless genuine universals, however, is to concede Platonism. More importantly here, it is also based on a view of what is possible. If combinatorialism is the best account of what is truly possible, then we might have to reject some of our uninformed modal intuitions.

Secondly, however, Armstrong faces what looks like an uneasy asymmetry in his account. Contracted worlds are possible, that is, worlds with fewer basic elements than ours (CTP: 62). Not every possible world has to have all the elements that our world has, although a completely empty world is not possible as it is constructed from no elements (CTP: 63). But it does not seem possible to construct an expanded world from the actual combinatorial elements. Lewis can generate both contracted and expanded worlds. If Armstrong cannot provide the latter, then it looks like a weakness of combinatorialism as a modal theory; namely, it cannot generate enough possibilities. Why could not the world have contained more things – more elements – than it does? Is not Lewis's theory more intuitive here?

Armstrong discusses this problem and comes up with a compromise solution. His view is that there are no alien universals although there are alien particulars (CTP: 54). How does he justify treating universals and particulars differently in this respect? The basis is that he rejects haecceitism for individuals while he accepts quidditism for universals (CTP: 59). Haecceitism, we saw, is the idea that individuals have a primitive essence or identity, not defined in terms of anything else. Lewis rejected haecceitism in making his case for counterpart theory. Were there haecceities, there would be more possibilities than allowed by anti-haecceitists. The haecceitist might accept two very simple but different worlds, one consisting solely in the states of affairs Fa and Gb, and the other consisting solely in the states of affairs Fb and Ga. The problem for haecceitism is that these look like the same states of affairs by different names, so not really distinct worlds. Both contain a thing that is F and a thing that is G, and only if there are primitive identities for a and b can we say that they differ. Armstrong makes a surprising move, which compromises the combinatorial theory, when he accepts quiddities: primitive essences for properties. The acceptance of quiddities means that nothing in the natures of the existing properties can combinatorially generate the new primitive natures, so alien universals are denied. But in the case of haecceities, the parallel argument is not used simply because of the (non-combinatorial) intuition that alien individuals are possible. The intuition comes from "analogy" with existing individuals but, again, it is not clear why alien universals cannot also by inferred by analogy. Overall, this looks like an unsatisfactory account and it is arguable that Armstrong should have opted for one of two preferable options. He might have rejected quiddities as well as haecceities, and then he could have permitted alien universals by analogy and created more possibilities. Alternatively, he could have retained his combinatorial theory, and then he should have rejected both alien universals and particulars. His compromise solution looks both messy and undermotivated and indeed, as we shall see, he does come to revise it in later work (see Chapter 6).

Incompatibilities and necessities

We have seen the criticism that combinatorialism fails to deliver enough possibilities. Even after admitting alien individuals, modal realism delivers more possibilities by also admitting alien universals (Lewis 1986: 91–2). But combinatorialism can be criticized from the opposite direction, namely with the charge that it admits too many possibilities. The basis of combinatorialism is the Humean distinct existences principle, which permits that all atomic states of affairs are compossible. But is this obviously the case? Does it not appear that some states of affairs exclude each other and does it not appear that some states of affairs necessitate each other? Some philosophers think that there are *de re*, in the world, incompatibilities and necessities. For example, we have already seen (Chapter 2, p. 35) that only one determinate under the same determinable can be instantiated at the same time by the same thing in the same respect. Nothing can be both one metre long and two metres long at the same time, so these two universals are incompatible. This is a failure of compossibility. On the other hand, where R is a transitive relation, the two states of affairs Ra,b and Rb,c seem to necessitate the distinct state of affairs Ra,c. Here there seems to be a necessary connection between distinct existences.

The first kind of case, failures of compossibility, Armstrong concedes but he invokes an earlier strategy to show that such incompatibilities are consistent with combinatorialism. It may be recalled that determinables are to be understood as structural, extensive properties. The reason that nothing can be both one metre long and two metres long is because one metre is a proper part of two metres (CTP: 79). A requirement for compossibility is, of course, that the two elements be wholly distinct. Being one metre and being two metres are not wholly distinct, so they cannot be freely recombined. This account would not apply to determinables that were inherently qualitative. Colour incompatibilities are the obvious case. But here (CTP: 82), Armstrong repeats his conviction that the real structure of the colour properties is likely to be quantitative after all, even though this structure does not present itself to perception. Our colour experience may be caused by something that is in a sense not coloured, such as the quantifiable length of a light wave. Incompatibilities are thus accountable by the combinatorialist.

What of necessities? Similarly, Armstrong accepts them but does not concede that they are a threat to the theory. In particular, he thinks that the alleged cases can be explained without having to forego the distinct existences principle. In the case of a symmetrical relation, for example, where Ra,b it is necessary that Rb,a. But these states of affairs are not distinct, claims Armstrong; they are in fact identical (CTP: 84). In the transitivity case, there is also a lack of distinctness. Ra,c would supervene on Ra,b and Rb,c, where R was a transitive relation (CTP: 85). There may be some necessary connections, therefore, but they again do not hold between distinct existences. The principle of recombination still holds for all distinct existences.

Armstrong's response to this issue is, of course, conclusive only if all incompatibilities and necessities can be treated this way. There yet remain a couple of threats to the account. One is from essentialism and one is from an ontology of causal powers. Some people, such as Ellis (2001), think that these two issues are related.

According to essentialism, certain properties have to go with certain particulars or kinds of particulars. There is a clear sense in which the particular and the property are distinct things – after all, one is a particular and one is a property – and yet there is a necessary connection between them. We might say, for instance, that Bertrand Russell is essentially human. This would mean that the state of affairs of Russell instantiating humanity must be the case and that his being some other, non-human, kind of thing is impossible, such as being an alligator or even a poached egg (CTP: 51). One other way of understanding this claim is to say that Russell would not be Russell if he were not human. There are some things about him that might have been different, and yet he remain the individual he is. We might plausibly say that he could have had five wives instead of just four. But could there be a poached egg that was also Bertrand Russell? Surely not. There is an even simpler example from science, where it is plausibly claimed that electrons are essentially negatively charged. If a particle is not negatively charged it is not an electron. It would have to be something else instead, perhaps a neutron or a positron.

Although these claims have a strong intuitive appeal, Armstrong effectively rejects them all when he rejects essentialism. For one thing, Armstrong thinks that it is notoriously difficult to pick out a subset of a thing's properties as being essential to it (CTP: 51) and this is indeed a real difficulty (see Mumford 2005). The ordinary particulars, with which we are surrounded, are "thick" particulars: particulars instantiating many properties, as Russell clearly does. On what basis can we say that some of his properties are more special to him and make him the thing he is? If we take away any of his properties, fictitiously, then he is not quite the Russell we knew. But if we are engaging in a fiction, the only limit is our imagination. The "thin" particular is the abstraction out of states of affairs that is bare particularity, just as the universal is an abstraction. Now Russell is undoubtedly a complex particular, as he has many parts, so he consists in many thin particulars together. There is no reason in principle why the "thin" particulars that constitute the complex particular Russell could not fictionally instantiate the properties of a poached egg (CTP: 53). Were they to do so, it is unlikely that we would call this poached egg *Russell*, but it is nevertheless combinatorially possible that the "thin" Russell be such an egg. But there is a clear problem, here, of whether Armstrong's account, and the verdict he pronounces on Russell, strains credibility beyond its limit.

Essentialism has, however, seen a revival of late and may be able to provide a response. Humans are a biological species. Might it be that only natural kinds have essences and biological species are not natural kinds (Ellis 2001)? With a genuine natural kind such as electrons, there is an exact identity of the non-relational properties of all kind members. Could something really be an electron if it were not negatively charged? Could it still be an electron even if it instantiated the properties that are instantiated by protons? Perhaps I cannot even imagine that it is so because whatever it is I imagine in a fictional world and that is positively charged, it is not an electron, says the essentialist.

The other source of necessary connection between distinct existences comes from an ontology of powers or, as some prefer to say, dispositions. If these are real properties, then they necessitate other properties in certain situations. More is to be said about powers shortly, but it should be noted here how their existence would affect the combinatorial principle. According to the powers theorist, if something has a disposition of brittleness and it is suitably struck, then of necessity it must break. This sets up a necessary connection between the distinct existences of the disposition *brittleness* and the manifestation *breaking*. For this reason, Armstrong thinks that the combinatorialist is compelled to reject pure powers, dispositions and propensities (CTP: 117). The powers ontology is inconsistent with the idea of free recombination of distinct existences. Armstrong does not, however, deny that there are dispositions. What he does instead is give some account of them that is consistent with combinatorialism, and this is the subject of our next chapter.

Armstrong thinks, overall, that combinatorialism is protected from the various lines of attack that say that there are incompatibilities and necessities, and that his principle of recombination can be upheld. He either denies that there are the alleged necessities or that they involve distinct existences. He also argues that incompatibilities are consistent with the combinatorial principle because they do not involve distinct existences but, rather, quantities that stand in part–whole relations.

Mathematics and other *a priori* truths

There are no necessary connections between distinct existences but there are nevertheless necessary truths. The combinatorial theory is primarily, and is presented as, a theory of possibility. But what about necessity? Lewis's modal realism is a unified modal theory in which the accounts of necessity and possibility involve the same device: the possible world. Such unity is no doubt an asset, especially as we grant the interrelatedness and interdefinability of possibility and necessity.

Armstrong does not present a combinatorial theory of necessity because the principle of free recombination tells us that there are no necessities, at least not *de re* necessities in the world between distinct existences. There are necessities such as identities, but these do not, of course, involve the wholly distinct elements that are required for recombination.

It cannot be denied, however, that there are some necessary truths involving distinct objects. Armstrong takes such things to be a problem of truthmakers rather than a problem of combinatorialism (see Chapter 10). He nevertheless indicates what the combinatorialist should say about such necessities. In short, they are to be treated as *a priori* truths, such as the truths of mathematics (CTP: 119). Being *a priori* does not, however, entail being known with certainty. A mathematician could have doubts about their proof and whether all the correct *a priori* steps have been taken.

Mathematical truths are true "solely by reference to the content of the concepts involved" (CTP: 121). Like other necessary truths, they have a hypothetical character. For example, we may say that if there are seven objects and five further objects, then they would make twelve objects. The truths of mathematics basically supervene on the things, the numbers. They involve the internal relations of the numbers. Thus it is necessary that three is smaller than four simply in virtue of the numbers. What we need then is a naturalistic theory of the existence of numbers. Armstrong thinks that he has such an account (Forrest and Armstrong 1987), in which numbers are internal relations between structural universals and unit-properties. This will be elaborated in Chapter 10 (pp. 180–81).

Consideration of the combinatorial theory will end for now, although I shall return to the theme in later chapters. Armstrong himself seems now to admit something that would make combinatorialism false (see Chapter 11). Despite such criticism, however, it does remain an attractive account of this world and of what we mean by another possible world. Its allure is illustrated superbly by a pegboard analogy that Armstrong presents (CTP: 64–5), to which the interested reader might turn straightaway.

Chapter 5

Dispositions

Armstrong's work on universals offers a thorough and detailed account of properties but, as he recognizes, there is a distinctive class of properties that bring with them some very particular problems. These are the dispositional properties, and we shall come to see that they play a crucial role in Armstrong's philosophy of mind. Dispositions are, in any case, often considered as a subject matter in their own right and any naturalistic metaphysics needs to say something about them.

As well as something being square or one metre thick, it may be soluble, volatile or elastic. None of these are likely to be the sparse properties invoked in a final physical theory. But the properties that currently are described in fundamental physical theory, properties such as spin, charge and mass, at least appear to have the same dispositional character as solubility and elasticity. What is this dispositional character that some properties seem to have? This very question is one of the main problems that metaphysicians consider when they look at dispositions. We can offer an initial characterization. What seems most remarkable about dispositions is the way they point towards or make possible other properties or states of affairs. When something is fragile, it bears a special, intimate relation to the property of being broken. It is distinctive of dispositions, however, that this further property or state of affairs need not occur. A fragile object might be handled carefully throughout its existence and might never break. What this shows is that while dispositions have an intimate relation to these further states, the presence of the disposition does not depend on the presence of the further state. These features make dispositions puzzling.

Since Armstrong began discussing dispositions, some terminology has become well entrenched. The terms *disposition* and *power* are usually taken to be equivalent (Mumford 2007). A disposition is said to have an actual, or merely possible, *manifestation*. Brokenness is, or would be, the manifestation of fragility. The manifestation of solubility would be in being dissolved. It is also now orthodox to think of the manifestation being *conditional* upon some antecedent or *stimulus* conditions being realized. Hence that which is soluble will dissolve *if* it is placed in the right solvent. Something is considered fragile when, *if* dropped, it breaks. This immediately suggests an account of what it is to have a disposition. Something might be said to be soluble, for example, precisely when it is true of it that if it is in liquid, it dissolves. Such a view is known as the conditional analysis of dispositions.

Conditionals

The view that a disposition ascription is equivalent to a conditional statement is advanced by Gilbert Ryle in his book *The Concept of Mind*. For Ryle, to have a disposition is not to be in any particular state or change, it is to be bound or liable to be in a certain state or change when some other condition is realized (1949: 43). Armstrong calls this the phenomenalist view, although it is now more frequently called the simple conditional analysis. Hence we might ordinarily think of a disposition ascription to be a property ascription, to be understood in logical form as Da. But Ryle tells us that when we seemingly ascribe D to a we are instead really asserting some conditional such as Sa → Ma: for example, if a is dropped then a will break, where Da means that a is fragile. The simple conditional analysis tells us, therefore, that for any thing x that has disposition D, if x is S then x is or will be M. Logicians will formulate this in the following way:

$$\forall x\,(\mathrm{D}x \leftrightarrow (\mathrm{S}x \rightarrow \mathrm{M}x))$$

This is a reductive account, indicated by the biconditional if and only if, ↔, which is intended to mean that there is nothing over and above Dx than the conditional Sx → Mx. The account is of particular interest, therefore, to those who wish to avoid postulating fundamental dispositions, as the properties S and M can be perfectly "respectable" categorical or non-power properties. Armstrong himself wishes to avoid fundamental powers because, as we saw in Chapter 4, they would introduce necessary connections between distinct existences. Yet he does not follow the phenomenalist conditional analysis. He finds it implausible as a reduction, for reasons he learned from Charlie Martin concerning truthmaking.

As Armstrong tells the story (1989: 8–11), Martin's concern was with phenomenalism in its more traditional guise as a theory about the existence of objects. The phenomenalist takes objects to be constituted by the mental states we usually think of as the perceptions of objects. But what of unobserved objects of which, by definition, there is no perception? Do they not exist? There is a table in my office that no one is observing, for instance, as there are no people in the room (I will set aside Berkeley's rather special solution to this problem). The standard phenomenalist answer is that the unobserved table's reality consists in the true counterfactual that if someone were in the room then they would experience table-like sensations. But Martin wondered why we should accept such a conditional to be true. If such a conditional is true, what is its truthmaker? It is a contingent truth, not true in virtue of logic alone, so it must be true in virtue of something in the world. Ordinarily, I would think that the object – the table – makes it true that if I enter my office I get table-like sensations. But for a phenomenalist, the table is nothing more than our sensations of it. Without a mind-independent object that causes the sensations, there seems nothing making the conditional true that I would have those sensations if I entered the room.

Exactly the same problem strikes Ryle's phenomenalist theory of dispositions, as Armstrong saw in his work on philosophy of mind (see Chapter 8). Ryle takes it that there is nothing more to having a disposition than for a conditional to be true, such as that if this thing were in liquid, then it would dissolve. But this true conditional is contingently true only; indeed there are many actual things for which it is false. So in virtue of what is it true? Ryle offers no answer.

In a couple of places, Armstrong tries to present this truthmaker objection in the form of a rigorous *a priori* argument (1969: 23 and DaD: 15). It is intended to be not only destructive of the phenomenalist view but also supportive of his so-called realist view, which is a view of what the truthmakers are for such conditionals. We will see his answer to that question shortly. Here is the argument. Dispositions can be possessed between their manifestations, indeed this is a necessary condition of being a disposition (MTM: 86). This means that the disposition attribution licenses certain counterfactual conditionals (1969: 23). We assume that such conditionals can be true or false (they are not mere material implications, true whenever the antecedent is contrary to fact) and we assume that they are contingently so. The realist has an explanation of why a conditional will be true, and specifically why it is true when it is not being manifestated. They can allow that the true conditionals have truthmakers in the non-dispositional states or properties of the object (see also 1969: 23 and DaD: 15).

There could be other candidates for the truthmakers. A bad one would be to allow counterfactual states of affairs (DaD: 15) but these would be mysterious, non-natural entities. Or the phenomenalist could try to say that this thing, the subject of ascription, is identical with a thing that has so behaved on other occasions (MTM: 87). But what is so good about this answer? It just depends on identity through time, which does not explain why the conditional is true now. The phenomenalist seems reduced to scepticism about dispositions except when they are manifested. But dispositions can be gained and lost over time, so a certain conditional (if dropped, breaks) might have been true before time t and false after t, although the conditional was never put to the test. How can we account for the change in truth-value of the conditional? The realist has an answer: some actual, non-dispositional property has been acquired or lost at t that is the truthmaker for the conditional (1969: 24).

The truthmaker argument shows, in sum, that for a disposition-conditional to be true, it must be made true by the presence of a non-disposition property in the subject of ascription. There will be much more to say about Armstrong's account later. For now we can just note his finding that the conditional analysis, the so-called phenomenalist account, is to be rejected. The conditionals invoked for dispositions, on the phenomenalist theory, seem to be true without having truthmakers, which amounts to them being primitively true. It is just not believable that such conditionals are primitively true. What other views are on the table?

Dualism

We may have to take dispositions seriously as properties after all, if we cannot reduce them to conditional sentences. A further view is property dualism, which is an acceptance that there are distinct dispositional and non-dispositional properties inhabiting the world.

This would take at face value the disposition ascriptions that we make and would treat them as ascriptions of real properties, on a par with any other. It would be a denial of the conditional analysis that attempted to reduce dispositions away.

It is now standard in the literature to refer to non-dispositional properties as categorical properties. This is mainly down to Armstrong, who took the term from H. H. Price (1953: 322). Typically, categorical properties are supposed to be properties of shape or structure, especially the microstructure of an object. Sometimes they are said instead to be the spatiotemporal properties of an object. The dualistic view, that there are both dispositional and categorical properties, can be found in Molnar (2003), Ellis (2001) and Place (Crane 1996). Some of the arguments produced in favour of dualism are the arguments from ordinary usage, from knowledge, and from the multiple realizability of dispositions. We speak as if a disposition and its base are distinct. We may know that something has a disposition without knowing of its base. And the same disposition looks as if it can be realized by different categorical bases. A naturalist like Armstrong is unlikely to be impressed by these arguments, however (DaD: 33–48), which look to be more about what we know and how we speak of dispositions, which might not be a guide for how they really are.

Are there arguments against dualism? As Armstrong notes (2005a: 313), any dualist has to explain how the categorical and dispositional properties relate. This is not as easy as it sounds. Can categorical properties do anything; specifically, do they have a role in causation? If they do, then it looks as if they are powerful and so it is not clear why they are being classed as categorical rather than dispositional properties. But if they play no role in causation, then they look to be mere epiphenomena. Epiphenomena are things that have, and can have, no effects at all and the usual concern with them is what reason we have to posit them in our ontology. Properties should do something to earn their keep and if categorical properties are epiphenomenal, then it seems they do not. To jettison them, however, is to abandon dualism.

Dualists have, therefore, looked for some role that categorical properties can play and that justifies their inclusion in our account of the world. Molnar tries to maintain that spatiotemporal properties, although not causally active, like powers, are nevertheless causally relevant (Molnar 2003: 162–5). But it is not clear that this distinction can be defended (Mumford 2004: 188). Place argues that the categorical property in a sense causes the disposition, as when we say that

David Armstrong

the glass's microstructure *makes* it brittle. Any resultant manifestation would then be attributed to both the disposition and the microstructure. The manifestation is caused both by the disposition (directly) and the categorical microstructure (indirectly) as a cause of the disposition. But this account does not impress Armstrong, who has a different interpretation of the relation between the disposition and the microstructure, as we shall see.

Two-sided view

An improvement on dualism, Armstrong thinks (2005a: 314), is the view Martin urged for some time: the two-sided view. On this account there is just one kind of property, so the position could be called a property monism. But while there is no division in kinds of property, properties nevertheless have two sides to them. They have a qualitative side, which roughly corresponds to what Armstrong calls the categorical. But they also have a power side. Martin sometimes called this theory the limit view because he saw the purely qualitative and the purely powerful as two artificial limits – two ends of a spectrum – where in reality all properties had both a qualitative and power side. Some properties may be more obviously powerful than qualitative, or vice versa, such as squareness, which falls more towards the qualitative or categorical end of the spectrum than the power end. But no property is entirely qualitative or entirely powerful. As Martin says, all properties are Janus-faced, like two sides of the same coin (Martin 1984). This will get us over some of the worries about property dualism because each and every property will now be powerful as every property has a powerful side. We do not have to worry, therefore, about finding a role for the causally inert or epiphenomenal categorical properties.

Similar theories have been advance by Heil (1998) and Mumford (1998), under the name of neutral monism, and supported by Mellor (2000). This view is stated in a slightly different manner: the world does indeed consist in just one kind of property and the dispositional and the categorical are merely two ways of talking about the same thing. In reality the properties are neither dispositional nor categorical. In other words, there are no dispositional or categorical properties as such – hence the neutrality of the view – but there are valid dispositional and categorical ways of talking about properties. Armstrong himself once said something along these lines:

84

What then is the disposition, the brittleness? It is the "categorical base", the microstructure, but it is this property of the object picked out not via its intrinsic nature, but rather via its causal role in bringing about the manifestation.   (DaD: 39)

While Armstrong appreciates the strength of a two-sided view, however, it is not one with which he is ultimately satisfied. The crucial difficulty for such an ontology, as he sees it, is to explain the link between the two sides of the property. Specifically, he wants to know whether the connection between the two sides of the property is contingent or necessary. If it is contingent, then it implies that the same qualitative side to a property could occur with a different power side. But this makes it look as if the two sides are distinct existences, and part of the appeal of the two-sided view seems to slip away. The view is supposed to overcome the problems of property dualism by saying that the qualitative and the power are just two sides of the very same property. But if we are talking about one and the same property, could we really have the two sides of it varying independently of each other? That sounds like a return to dualism. And how would it square with the realist view of universals: that they are identical in every instance? It is difficult, therefore, to maintain the view that the connection between the two sides is contingent. Is it necessary, then? Perhaps it is, but Armstrong finds such necessity inexplicable. The only non-logical necessity he can see in the world is that which springs from identity but Martin is not (at least to begin with) making an identity claim between the qualitative and the powerful. So why cannot the qualitative side and the power side vary independently? If Martin is to go for the necessity option, therefore, it would seem to be an *ad hoc* move that does not appear to have any independent motivation. It should be seen that these difficulties, of accounting for the relation between the two sides of a property, will carry over to the neutral monist version of the theory.

Identity

Armstrong does find worldly necessity in identity. At times he seems a reluctant convert to this view and, as we shall see when we look at his philosophy of mind, he supports a notion of contingent identities in certain circumstances. Following Kripke (1980), however, he now acknowledges that if A and B are identical, then they are necessarily so. Perhaps with this in mind, Martin (1997) and Heil (2003) have both tried to justify the necessity of the link between a qualitative and a power side of properties in terms of identity, and the neutral monist position might also be understood in this way.

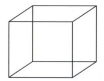

Figure 5.1   The Necker cube

What we are asked to accept is that the power side and the qualitative or categorical side of a property are really one and the same thing, perhaps only viewed in different ways. We might think of the Necker cube as analogous. It is a single line-drawing yet it can be seen in two (if not three) different ways (Figure 5.1). Either way might be thought to be really there, in the object, and yet it is also true that it is still exactly the same object that is seen in these different ways.

There are at least two important problems with this account. One is a complaint from Molnar that this seems to make any dispositional–categorical distinction mind-dependent (Molnar 2003: 155–6). Something is a power only because it is seen as a power by a thinker. Similarly in the case of a Necker cube, what we have is two ways of seeing or understanding the same object rather than two different ways that the object actually is. This itself need not be a fatal consequence because one might accept the mind-dependence of the dispositional (and categorical), which neutral monism seems to acknowledge explicitly. But it is not a position that can be allied easily with a strong realism about powers, which some, such as Martin, want to support. Being a power and being qualitative seem, on this account, to be ways of seeing properties rather than features of the properties themselves, and this just does not seem the right result for anyone with realist inclinations. For the same reason, Armstrong will find this view at odds with his naturalism.

Armstrong himself offers a different objection, however, which is that any putative identity between a quality and a power is "totally incredible". Indeed, we may go so far as to think it a category mistake:

"to identify a quality – a categorical property – and a power, essentially something that points to a certain effect. They are just different, that's all" (2005a: 315). If there is some fact about A that is not a fact about B, then A and B are not identical. But, as Armstrong argues, powers point to certain properties that are outside themselves while the qualitative side does not. They cannot, therefore, be identical.

Pan-dispositionalism

Any theory that tries to defend distinct dispositional and categorical elements in the world will face difficulties in explaining how the elements relate, whether they are distinct properties or distinct sides of properties. It would be natural to consider the alternative: whether there is just one kind of property in the world. That leaves us with two simple options: all properties are dispositional or all properties are categorical. Let us begin by considering the first option, which can be called *pan-dispositionalism*.

Could every property be a disposition? Such a view has an attraction in that it is consistent with the already-mentioned Eleatic principle: that power is the mark of reality. All properties should be powerful, therefore, which is to say that all are dispositional. Sydney Shoemaker (1980) is a contemporary philosopher who has seriously proposed such a view, stating simply that all properties are powers. But Armstrong thinks that there is a very serious difficulty for the pan-dispositionalist to face, which was originally raised by Richard Swinburne (1983). To be dispositions, these things must have manifestations. But what are these manifestations? Of course, they would be understood as further properties. But, on this account, all properties are dispositions so the manifestation of a disposition will be in a further disposition. Armstrong thinks this is very problematic because "Causality becomes the mere passing around of powers from particulars to further particulars" (2005a: 314). The pan-dispositionalist might be happy to accept this, even if they have no other choice in the matter. They might think that such a view makes sense, for does not science see causation as a passing round or redistribution of energies? And when something is affected by a change, do we not see it as meaning that it has acquired a different set of causal powers to the ones it had before?

But Armstrong thinks that there is a deeper problem here, namely: "the world never passes from potency to act. . . . *nothing ever happens*".

Here, there is a real difference of opinion between Armstrong and the pan-dispositionalists over the force of the argument. The pan-dispositionalist will contest the charges. In the first place, they are likely to deny the claim that nothing ever happens. As Armstrong himself characterizes the situation, causality is a "passing around of powers". A passing around sounds like an event so at least *prima facie* something is happening. Armstrong's chief concern, therefore, must be over what it is that is passed around. Indeed, it appears that he thinks that the things that are passed around are not real at all. Pure powers, of the kind supported by the pan-dispositionalist, are thought of by Armstrong as mere potencies: potential rather than actual. This is where there is the second major difference of opinion. The realist about dispositions or causal powers will accept such powers to be real enough. Powers may be an assumption of this metaphysic, but they are certainly assumed as actual in their own right, whether or not they are manifested. For this reason, Martin objects to the term *categorical* for the non-powers. Categorical means *unconditional*, but there is nothing conditional about the ascription of a power; it is the powers' manifestations, if anything, that are conditional. When I ascribe a disposition I ascribe it actually and unconditionally. Passing round of powers would be for the realist, therefore, the passing round of something actual. But Armstrong, who professes to find irreducible dispositions mysterious (DaD: 91), sees them as attaining actuality only in their manifestations. And if, as the pan-dispositionalist has to concede, their manifestations are only further powers, then we reach Armstrong's conclusion that a world containing only powers contains nothing actual.

We reach an impasse at this stage where neither side is prepared to budge from their position (see Mumford 2004: 174–5 and Armstrong 2005b). Some have tried to mediate in the dispute. Molnar, who is not a pan-dispositionalist himself, has said that there is no formal contradiction in the "shifting potencies" position. It does not involve, for instance, an infinite regress of powers (Molnar 2003: ch. 11). One way of avoiding such a regress would be to have a finite number of powers each of which is a manifestation of one of the others in the finite set, giving us what may be called a circle of dispositions (Holton 1999). While this may halt a formal contradiction in pan-dispositionalism, it will still not address Armstrong's chief concern that nothing in this circle of powers can move from potency to act. Hence Armstrong reasserts his view:

The power is constituted the power it is [*sic*] by the *sort* of actualization it gives rise to in suitable *sorts* of circumstance. But what are these sorts of actualization and sorts of circumstance? They themselves can be nothing but powers, and so again they can only be constituted by the sorts of actualization which they give rise to in suitable circumstances. The power to produce A is nothing but the power to produce the power to produce B . . . and so on. Nor will the situation be relieved by bringing the powers around in a circle.   (WLN: 123)

If pan-dispositionalism were the only offer on the table, then maybe we would have to pursue these issues until we found a resolution. That is not the case, however, as we still have to explore the possibility that all properties are categorical. If this view has none of the problems that beset the rivals, then we might see, without the need for further argument, that it is the view we should hold. This is indeed Armstrong's claim.

Categoricalism

Armstrong dislikes irreducible dispositions or causal powers among other reasons because he thinks they do not have adequate actuality. This is explained in the following:

I assume the truth of what may be called Actualism. According to this view, we should not postulate any particulars except actual particulars, nor any properties and relations (universals) save actual, or categorical, properties and relations. I do not think this should debar us from thinking that both the past and the future exist, or are real. But it does debar us from admitting into our ontology the merely possible, not only the merely logically possible but also the merely physically possible. . . . This debars us from postulating such properties as dispositions and powers where these are conceived of as properties over and above the categorical properties of objects.   (WLN: 8–9)

The problem Armstrong faces, however, is that he sees dispositionality as an important feature of the world and, as we shall see, of the mind in particular. Armstrong accepts the Rylean insight that many mental phenomena are dispositional in nature. But he cannot accept these as primitive possibilia. Similarly, he cannot accept the kind of conditional analysis that Ryle offers because it has no truth-makers. If we can find truthmakers for such conditionals among the realm of the actual, then we might have the beginnings of a tenable, naturalistic, theory of dispositions.

Armstrong's initial breakthrough came in relation to mind. In contrast with Ryle's behaviourism, Armstrong says that the mind is not to be identified with behaviour, but "only with the inner principle of behaviour" (MTM: 85). He offers central-state materialism as his philosophy of mind, where the key difference from behaviourism is the way dispositions are understood. Opposed to a phenomenalist account, Armstrong offers his own realist theory of dispositions, which is characterized in the following claims (MTM: 86):

1. Each disposition has a categorical basis.
2. The categorical basis is responsible for the behaviour (the manifestation) in the appropriate circumstances.
3. The categorical basis may be unknown.
4. The categorical basis can be a cause or causal factor in the behaviour (not so with phenomenalism) (MTM: 88). It "stands behind" its manifestations.
5. The categorical basis is sometimes identified with the disposition (although the identification is a contingent one – MTM: 88).

What supports this view is the *a priori* truthmaker argument against the conditional analysis. Armstrong identifies categorical properties, such as microstructures or geometrical properties, as the truth-makers for such conditionals and therefore for ascriptions of unmanifested dispositions. This seems naturalistically plausible. It suggests a scientific reduction of dispositions to their categorical grounds or bases. While we may not yet know all the categorical bases of all the dispositions, we have enough plausible examples, such as when we explain the solubility of salt in terms of its molecular structure. We can infer that all other dispositions can in principle be reduced to their categorical bases.

However, we still need to defend the plausibility of the realist position. We must relate dispositions to categorical bases and difference of disposition to difference of categorical basis. We must then also explain how a categorical property can be powerful, that is, how it can produce a manifestation while remaining clearly a categorical, naturalistic property. Armstrong's attempt to develop the theory has gone through two phases, one before and one after he discovered his theory of universals. Indeed it is arguable that he needed the theory of universals in order to make his realist theory of dispositions at all tenable.

To the initial statement of the theory, in *A Materialist Theory of Mind*, Roger Squires (1968) objected that the categorical properties seem to do the causal work, rendering dispositions impotent. This would be a strange position and almost the reverse of what we expect pre-theoretically. Dispositions, which we might have thought of as causal potencies, would now be impotent while categorical properties, the non-power properties, would be causally efficacious. Armstrong's initial response is not convincing. He says that "dispositions are states with causal powers" (1969: 23). But he also admits that "It is this [categorical] state that, if and when the glass is struck, actually brings about the breaking in conjunction with the triggering cause" (1969: 26). How can both the categorical basis and the disposition be the cause of the manifestation? Armstrong thinks they can be because he *identifies* the disposition with the categorical, causally active, state (1969: 26). So if categorical bases are causes and dispositions are identical with their categorical bases, then clearly dispositions are causes.

But this view seems difficult to maintain. Recall that Armstrong now objects to the identity view, saying that dispositions and categorical properties are "just different, that's all". He even says he finds this "totally incredible", despite it being a view he once championed. He further tries to maintain that this is a contingent identity. It is not like Kripke's *a posteriori* identifications, which are identities of property constitution. Armstrong agrees that these are necessary. The disposition is like a causal role and, given the contingency of laws, it is contingent what categorical property is the causal role filler:

> Other microstructures might have played the brittleness causal role in the glass, at least in a world whose laws of nature differ from the actual world. But it is a contingent truth that in this glass the brittleness causal role is played by this microstructure, i.e. that the brittleness of this glass is (is identical with) this microstructure. (DaD: 39)

Since Armstrong developed his theory of universals, from around 1977, he has had a different account to offer. It is still a reductive and naturalistic account but it no longer attempts to identify dispositions with just their categorical bases. That identification still leaves the problem of causation and how the categorical base produces the manifestation. The theory of universals, which as we have seen delivers a theory of laws of nature and causation, explains how manifestations are produced and why the same categorical property will always produce the same manifestation when it is in the same circumstances. Here is how Armstrong presents the simple explanation:

> How can we bestow power on categorical properties? . . . My idea is that this is best done via direct relations between the universals involved. These will give us the laws of nature and the powers will be subsequent to, and nothing more than, these laws. Or as we may put it, the truthmakers for attributions of powers are these laws. (2005a: 315)

This quotation does not fully characterize the new position, however. It emphasizes the importance of laws in the explanation of powers but the view as a whole should be characterized as a categorical properties *plus* laws view, as he makes clear elsewhere (1989: 15; DaD: 17). Powers thus reduce to the instantiation of laws in regular causal sequences. When some particular a has a disposition, what this means for Armstrong is that it has some categorical property that features in a law of nature such that when a certain stimulus occurs, a certain manifestation will result. For example, assume that a is F, and there is some law that N(F&S,G), where S is a stimulus property, in which case a will G. Laws thus provide the kind of necessity we need to get from one property causally to another and that kind of relation is precisely what other philosophers have tried to explain by positing irreducible powers. Armstrong's theory remains perfectly naturalistic because we have naturalistic, categorical properties as the relata of laws and, as we saw in Chapter 3, Armstrong's laws of nature are also perfectly naturalistic.

Problems with categoricalism

Instead of irreducible causal powers, then, Armstrong offers us an ontology of categorical properties plus laws. As he sees it, the existing resources in his metaphysics give him a theory of dispositions at no extra cost. He need posit no extra entities or properties in order to generate a theory of dispositions.

If the account of dispositions rests on the categorical properties plus laws view, then it, of course, suffers from any problems of that view. Indeed, the case of dispositions might make any such problems look more pressing. In Chapter 3, I raised some difficulties for

Armstrong's account. The charge of quidditism will look particularly apposite in the present context. It is clear in this account that a property F could, given the professed contingency of Armstrong's laws, have an entirely different set of dispositions to the ones it actually has, and yet still be F. Moreover, F and G could swap entirely their dispositions and F would still be F and G still G. Armstrong sees the force of the Eleatic principle, of course, and has spoken of the "intimate link" between properties and powers, which looks difficult to square with this account of dispositions. This is not to deny, however, that the Eleatic principle could simply be rejected by someone who wanted to hold a categorical properties plus laws view. But Armstrong clearly is reluctant to make this move.

There is another kind of concern about Armstrong's approach. This is simply the old problem of how laws govern their instances. Armstrong's metaphysics contains a modal domain of natural necessitation containing the laws, and a non-modal domain containing the categorical properties. But how do the laws naturally necessitate their instances? It is arguable that Armstrong must take the natural necessitation relation as a primitive. But this then looks as if the natural necessitation relation is one big disposition, what Handfield (2005) has called an über-disposition. Instead of allowing lots of individual causal powers to G, if F&S, Armstrong seems to posit one big, irreducible causal power, N(F&S,G).

It may further be thought that Armstrong has still not fully justified the notion of a categorical property. He has tried to maintain the Eleatic principle, notwithstanding the aforementioned concerns, but he has only shown that categorical properties extrinsically make a causal difference to the world. Some time ago, Mellor (1974) wrote in defence of dispositions as it was still thought at that time that it was dispositional properties that stood in need of vindication. But now there are just as many concerns about the categorical. The charge against the categorical of epiphenomenalism remains. Intrinsically, categorical properties can have no causal powers and make no causal difference to the world, lest they be dispositional properties. Yet if they are intrinsically powerless, they look epiphenomenal. Armstrong wishes to maintain that being powerful, though only in relation to the laws of nature, is power enough. But because such power is not an intrinsic feature of such properties, he then has to face the objections of quidditism and the problem of how the properties and laws can be said plausibly to relate.

Many of the discussions in this chapter concern contemporary debates that are still points of controversy. If there are problems with Armstrong's theory of dispositions, then it is no worse off than every other theory of dispositions of which we know. He has ably argued that a conditional analysis, if it does not provide a truthmaker, is a form of primitive modality. He has shown that any kind of dualism has great difficulty in explaining how the dispositional and the categorical relate. He has argued that if every property is dispositional, then it looks as if nothing ever happens. Armstrong's preferred view might have problems but clearly it does not have them uniquely. It might, therefore, be a question of which problems we are prepared to live with or which problems might not be as serious as they at first seemed. It is also a possibility that we are all confused and the whole debate has been misconceived. The pure dispositional and the pure categorical seem problematic, as does an ontology that mixes the two, so perhaps the original dispositional–categorical distinction is the problem.

These controversies are still relatively young, so we are far from the "end-game". They are likely to continue long after Armstrong and the rest of us are gone, but it looks likely that Armstrong's development and discussion of the debate will continue to play a role in shaping its future.

Chapter 6

States of affairs

We have seen how Armstrong has developed naturalistic theories of universals, laws and causation, modality and dispositions. What has emerged is a consistent and, to a large extent, systematic view of the world. This may not have been Armstrong's original intention, as he does not present himself as a system-builder, but it seems that he did come to see his work more and more as an integrated whole. Towards the end of his career, he decided to present his philosophy in such a way in *A World of States of Affairs*. This chapter will present the most important ideas of that work and show how the theories discussed in previous chapters all come together.

We can start with the question of what, fundamentally, the world is made of. The philosophical enterprise is to interpret this question in a general and abstract way. What are the general categories of things that exist? A simple answer would be that the world is a sum of particular objects, such as tables and chairs, planets and electrons, dogs and cats. But if this were all there was in the world, something would seem to be missing. Armstrong sees this, and agrees with Wittgenstein, near the start of the *Tractatus* (1921: 1.1), that the world is not just a sum total of things. Another option would be to say that the world is a totality of properties. However, we have seen that Armstrong argues for the irreducibility of both particularity and universality. Neither can exist without the other. So should we then say that the world is a sum of universals and particulars, both ineliminable?

This seems to be the ontology that emerges from Armstrong's early work in metaphysics, from his work on universals and combinatorialism. The world may seem to be built from universals and particulars in various combinations, with other possibilities being recombinations of those same elements. The picture presented in this way remains misleading, however. It was not quite Armstrong's intended view, even in the early work. It suggests that particulars and universals might be free-standing entities that sometimes come together, united by the tie or nexus of instantiation that keeps some, and only some, of them together in a contingently connected parcel. But we can instead look at things from the opposite direction.

Parts of this chapter will be recapitulation of what has gone before. Positions that will be familiar to us will now, however, be recast in terms of states of affairs. The acceptance of a factualist ontology will enlighten many of the claims we have already encountered. But this is also a good place for us to take stock as it can be understood as the final part of Armstrong's core metaphysical project that has been expounded since Chapter 2.

The existents

Instead of the world's fundamental existents being the particulars and universals, that are able to fall into a suitable relation of instantiation, is it not metaphysically more plausible to say that what exist are the particulars-bearing-properties? The properties themselves have no existence apart from the particulars in which they are instantiated. And the particulars themselves have no existence except in so far as they instantiate properties. The "thin" particular, the propertyless substratum, is an abstraction just as much as is the uninstantiated, perhaps transcendent, universal. What are they abstractions from? They are abstractions from the things that are independent existences. The simplest thing that can exist is a simple-particular-possessing-a-simple-property. The key point is that this is not a molecular entity or composite whole made of proper parts. It forms an indivisible package that can be broken down into its component particular and universal only by abstraction, not by any real process. A particular-possessing-a-property is what Wittgenstein calls a fact but what Armstrong prefers to call a state of affairs. A fact sounds too much like a true proposition, for Armstrong, although since he has brought such issues to our attention it is now common again to use the term *fact* to name one of his states of affairs. We can call them *Tractarian* facts if we really need to make the distinction between them and true propositions. A state of affairs is a thing in the world and atomic facts are the fundamental entities of the world. They are the smallest possible units of existence. Atomic facts cannot, therefore, be broken down into smaller facts. They do not have other facts as constituents. Their constituents may be properties, particulars and relations, and while these are real enough, they are not themselves existents because they are not states of affairs. Atomism is assumed, in this theory, but it cannot be known *a priori*. If the world is infinitely complex, we may have to be satisfied with "relative" atoms only.

Armstrong had already noticed the ontological importance of states of affairs and had an account of what they were. As early as *Nominalism and Realism*, he had declared: "A state of affairs I define as a particular's having a certain property, or two or more particulars standing in a certain relation" (N&R 80). In *Universals* (U: 88–94), there is an argument for why they must be taken as the fundamental existents of the world. States of affairs, as Armstrong describes them, are more than their constituents. If we take the constituent particulars a, b, and the non-symmetrical relation R, then R(a,b) and R(b,a) are distinct states of affairs but with exactly the same constituents. The state of affairs is a feature of the world extra, therefore, to the existence of the constituent particulars and universals. Similarly, with constituent particulars a, b and properties F and G, we have two different conjunctive states of affairs made out of the same constituents: (Fa & Gb) and (Fb & Ga). If we were to give a full description of the world, therefore, it would not be adequate to say what particulars exist and what universals exist. I could know that John exists and that tallness exists but I would not know, just from that, whether John is tall. John being tall would be some further fact about the world. (When we get on to the issue of truthmaking, in Chapter 10, we shall see the importance of understanding facts in this Tractarian way, rather than as true propositions, because this state of affairs can be the reason *why* the proposition that *John is tall* is true.)

It was around 1989 that Armstrong first ventured his view of *global factualism*, in his two books *Universals* and *A Combinatorial Theory of Possibility*. Global factualism is the view that the world is a world of states of affairs and *only* states of affairs. Everything else that there is can be accounted for in terms of states of affairs. All that is real is either a state of affairs or else supervenes on states of affairs. Entity B supervenes on entity A if and only if it is not possible that A should exist and B not exist (WSA: 11). But this means that if we have A, and B supervenes on A, then we also have B. B is thus "no addition of being" to A. Supervenience can thus give us an "onto-logical free lunch". *A World of States of Affairs* is an attempt to show just how much that we take to exist supervenes on states of affairs. Armstrong's most systematic work of metaphysics in this way brings together many different ideas into a single theory. That theory is very simple: "the world, all that there is, is a world of states of affairs" (WSA: 1).

The grid of Figure 6.1, that we first saw in Chapter 2, shows those states of affairs as the ticks in the cells where a particular instanti-ates a property (we needed a separate grid, Figure 4.2, to illustrate the case of relations). One might have got the impression that the particulars a, b, c, ... and properties A, B, C, ... were ontologically primary, with the facts or states of affairs, the ticks in the boxes, somehow dependent on them. But it should now be clear that the situation is the opposite way round. In the first place, the particulars and the properties are not existents in their own right. The par-ticular cannot exist without its properties, so what thing would be a in its own right? And a property cannot exist other than in its instantiations in particulars, so what would be A in its own right? But now we have a second and equally important argument. The

	A	B	C	D	E	F	G	...
a	✓		✓		✓	✓		
b		✓			✓			
c	✓						✓	
d				✓	✓			
e		✓		✓		✓	✓	
f	✓						✓	
g			✓	✓		✓		
...								

Figure 6.1 States of affairs

existence of the particulars and properties is not, as we have seen, sufficient for the existence of any particular state of affairs. But if we have all the states of affairs, then that would determine which particulars and properties exist. If a is F is a state of affairs (and we assume that this is an *a posteriori* discoverable, scientifically genuine state of affairs), then a exists and F exists. But if b exists and G exists, that does not entail that b is G is a state of affairs. This shows why states of affairs must be taken as the primary existents of the world. It also explains why the formal restrictions had to be placed on the grid. In Chapter 2 (p. 30), we saw that each row had to contain a tick (each particular had to instantiate at least one property) and each column had to contain at least one tick (each property must have at least one instantiation). It might have been wondered, at that stage, why there were these restrictions and what necessitated them. How could we be sure that A would have an instantiation? But if we now see that particulars and properties (and relations) exist only in states of affairs, then the restrictions become immediately understood. Unless there is a state of affairs involving a, at some place and some time, then a has no existence. Without a tick somewhere in the row for a, there is no a.

Mode of composition

Properties and particulars are depicted as the constituents of a state of affairs. The relation of the constituents to the state of affairs is not simply the mereological part–whole relation, however, as it is a principle of mereology that there is only one sum for any collection of parts. In contrast, many states of affairs could be made out of the same constituents. This shows, therefore, that states of affairs have a "nonmereological mode of composition" (U: 93).

To accept a states of affairs ontology one must be prepared to accept this non-mereological composition. As Armstrong notes, Lewis denies the ontology precisely for this reason as he thinks that the only real mode of composition is mereological (WSA: 37). This is hardly surprising for a Humean, who sees all as loose and separate. With mereological composition, a whole exists if and only if its parts exist. But we have already seen that even where the components exist, a state of affairs that would be composed of those components need not exist. Hence the particular George Bush exists and the property of being female exist. But there is not a state of affairs of George Bush being female. Armstrong requires, in addition to the component particular and universal, that they also have the appropriate non-relational tie before there is such a state of affairs.

Let us now look in more detail at the argument for states of affairs having this special mode of composition. The composition is non-mereological for the following reasons. First, as we have just seen, if the parts exist, a mereological whole exists. It is not the case with state of affairs that if the constituents exist, the states of affairs exist.

Secondly, only one mereological whole can be formed from a group of parts. But *a* loves *b* and *b* loves *a* are distinct states of affairs with exactly the same constituents (WSA: 119). States of affairs can be "non-symmetric" or having a direction. The "order" of their constituents can matter so that, in the previous example, one constituent particular is the lover and the other constituent particular is the beloved. There must be, therefore, some kind of internal organization of the components (WSA: 121). Some states of affairs involve symmetrical relations, of course, such as *a* being one mile from *b*. Here, *b* being one mile from *a* is judged to be an identical state of affairs to *a* being one mile from *b* (namely, *a* and *b* being one mile apart). Thus, only if we have identity of particulars, universals and the same organization do we have identical states of affairs (WSA: 132).

Thirdly, mereological wholes are no increase in being over their parts. This cannot be the case with states of affairs. As the parts can exist without the whole, then the state of affairs must be some further feature of the world over and above the existence of the parts (WSA: 120). The actual situation is that Armstrong is taking the states of affairs as fundamental and the existence of the particulars and universals effectively are supervenient on the states of affairs.

Although states of affairs are not themselves mereologically composed, they can nevertheless partake in some mereological relations. For example, a molecular state of affairs might be thought of simply as a mereological whole whose parts are states of affairs. So where we have atomic, non-mereological states of affairs F*a* and G*b*, there will be a mereological whole: the molecular state of affairs, F*a* & G*b*, that is their conjunction. But this is not to say that all molecular states of affairs are simply merelogically formed. Some molecular states of affairs might be temporally, causally or nomologically conjoined (WSA: 122).

What, then, is the mode of composition for states of affairs? Can we say anything positive about it? Monadic states of affairs are particulars having properties; polyadic states of affairs are numbers of particulars bearing relations (WSA: 113). Our problem is that something more would be needed to "weld" together these particulars and universals. "Non-relational tie" was originally Strawson's phrase for this (1959: ch. 5, secs 2–3). Armstrong speaks instead of *instantiation*. What supports the need for such "welding" between universals and particulars is the truthmaker argument (WSA: 115). If it is true that *a* is F, there must be something in the world that makes it true, "that serves as an ontological ground" (WSA: 115) for the truth. The truthmaker cannot be *a*, the thin particular, alone because *a* might exist without it being that *a* is F. Nor can the truthmaker be *a* and F together because *a* and F might exist without it being that *a* is F. The truthmaker must necessitate the truth and it does so internally; that is, the truthmaking relation is an internal relation where the truth must be, if the truthmakers exist (WSA: 115–16).

However, this now allows us to see that the state of affairs is the most plausible truthmaker and effectively allows the problem of instantiation or tie to disappear. What makes it true that *a* is F is the state of affairs of *a* being F and we thus arrive at a further argument for states of affairs, an argument from truthmaking. But this also allows us to see that no "welding" together of two parts is required because states of affairs are the units or basic building blocks of the world. There is, then, no *relation* of instantiation over and above the states of affairs themselves. That would already suggest two parts that have to be stuck together. The state of affairs has constituents that are not parts. Instead, the components are abstracted from the states of affairs. This allows Armstrong to say, without leaving himself further difficulties, that "States of affairs hold their constituents together in a non-mereological form of composition, a form of composition that even allows the possibility of having different states of affairs with identical constituents" (WSA: 118). This "holding" of the constituents within a state of affairs is not a real relation – not an external relation – so there is no tie as an extra part to the state of affairs.

Understanding states of affairs as the units of our ontology allows us to avoid Bradley's regress. If instantiation were a real relation, then it would itself be a universal that must be somehow instantiated by the particular(s) involved. But then how does a particular *instantiate* this universal of instantiation? The problem has now been dissolved because particulars and universals are not parts that have to be welded, but abstractions from the basic entities that exist.

David Armstrong

Particulars and universals

We have seen that both particulars and universals are abstractions from states of affairs. They can be *considered* apart from states of affairs though they cannot *exist* apart from states of affairs. This gives us a new way of understanding both particulars and universals. Universals can now be understood as state-of-affairs *types* (WSA: 28). The type–token distinction can be applied to states of affairs with a universal being nothing more than a type of state of affairs. We thereby gain some clarification on what the universal element or constituent is of a state of affairs. Armstrong says:

> A universal is a gutted state of affairs; it is everything that is left in the state of affairs after the particular particulars involved in the state of affairs have been abstracted away in thought. So it is a state-of-affairs type, the constituent that is common to all states of affairs that contain that universal.   (WSA: 28–9)

Hence there may be various states of affairs: a is F, b is F, c is F, and so on. If we "gut" these states of affairs of their particularity, we are left with the type: _ is F. This is the F-type of state of affairs, with F-ness not being an existent in its own right. This is not to say that F-ness is not real, however. F-ness is a real feature of these states of affairs. It is real enough that F-ness runs through all these different facts. What the real types of states of affairs are, however, will of course be subject to the constraints of scientific naturalism. We will know what they are only *a posteriori*, and the way it looks to Armstrong at present is that all the fundamental states-of-affairs types are extensive quantities. There are no purely intensive quantities or qualities at this fundamental level (WSA: 64). Hence colours are not fundamental intensive properties but are instead physically reducible to quantities.

The same account can be given of relations. Where $R(a,b)$, $R(c,d)$ and $R(e,f)$ are states of affairs, there is the type $R(\_1,\_2)$. However, many relations will be internal, which means that they supervene on the properties of their relata, as in the case, for example, of the relation of *exact resemblance* (WSA: 87). Exact resemblance is, therefore, no addition of being over and above the things that exactly resemble. External relations are, however, an addition to the world's being, although Armstrong thinks it a plausible *a posteriori* hypothesis that only spatiotemporal relations, causal relations, and facts of totality (a sort of relation holding between facts, see p. 69) are external.

Many philosophers think that in addition to properties and relations, another class of universals is kinds, or *natural* kinds. Ellis in particular emphasizes the importance of natural kinds. But there are no additional natural kinds in Armstrong's ontology. Given all the particulars and universals that compose the states of affairs, kinds, such as they are, would be merely supervenient things (WSA: 68). There is no distinctive metaphysical or explanatory role for them to play. An acceptance of natural kinds often goes along with an acceptance of essential properties, but these Armstrong does not accept at all as they would impinge on combinatorial freedom. While we accept properties and relations, therefore, we need not also accept kinds as a class of distinctive universals.

What of classes themselves? Some have thought that classes were transcendent entities. Armstrong brings them down to earth and treats them also in terms of states of affairs. A class may be understood as a conjunction of units, according to some unit-determining property that makes each a *one* (WSA: 192). These units are singletons or set members that are conjoined to make the set. Just as sets are purported to be, this conjunction of members will be a particular (WSA: 188).

What can we say of particulars themselves? Need we posit them at all? Why do we need property bearers in addition to the properties? Do we know of any such bearer or is it ontologically surplus to requirements? Armstrong argues that we cannot claim to experience only properties (WSA: 96). When we see properties, we see them as properties *of particulars*. It is in metaphysics that this issue is to be resolved for certain, however. Can particulars be replaced in our ontology by bundles of compresent properties? If one is to dispense with particulars, however, one needs to put some bundling relation for properties in their place. Compresence would have to take the place of the fundamental tie (WSA: 97). Are the bundled properties universals or particulars? If they are universals, there is the difficulty of accounting for the numerical difference of things, given that universals are identical in their instances. Two bundles of all the same properties would collapse into the same bundle. Whether the bundles are universals or particulars, there is the basic problem that properties and relations are not entities capable of independent existence (WSA: 99). Properties are ways things are. Relations are ways things stand to each other. One cannot have a *way* without something that is that way or some things that stand in that way.

What more can we say about particularity? In *A Combinatorial Theory of Possibility*, Armstrong had already considered the question of haecceities or primitive essences of individuals. In the simple world with nothing more than two particulars, *a* and *b*, and two properties F and G, there seem to be at least two distinctive possibilities:

(1) F*a* and G*b*
(2) G*a* and F*b*?

Armstrong had said that these were the same states of affairs just described differently. If we thought that these really were distinct possibilities, we would be haecceitists. But now he has changed his mind (WSA: 108). There can be, after all, distinct particulars that are indiscernible. Haecceitism is now accepted, in which "the particularity of a particular is fundamental and unanalysable" (WSA: 109). This particularity is only the "thin" particular – the abstraction from states of affairs. Particulars themselves will all be "thick". They will also have temporal parts (WSA: 100). These parts are connected (WSA: 105) by causal relations, what Russell called a causal line (Russell 1948: Pt VI, ch. V). This is immanent causality, meaning earlier stages of a thing causing and supporting later stages of the same thing.

The abstraction that delivers the thin particular is what Locke calls "partial consideration", where "we consider the particular only in so far as it is a particular, we consider it only in its particularity" (WSA: 123). But when we refer to a particular in ordinary discourse we include with it its properties. This is the thick particular (WSA: 124), which includes all and only the non-relational properties of the particular. There is no reason to favour some privileged class of a particular's properties, which is why Armstrong does not accept essentialism. There is a further particular, however, which is the state of affairs itself. It is a particular. This exemplifies the victory of particularity, where a particular + a universal = a particular, a state of affairs (+ represents the appropriate non-mereological composition, WSA: 126).

A worry remains, however, concerning the realist and naturalist credentials of universals and particulars in the states of affairs ontology. What really exist are the states of affairs. Particulars and universals exist only as abstractions from states of affairs. Does this not, however, look as if particulars and universals are mind-dependent? Would not a nominalist be encouraged by the idea of universals being mere abstractions? The only counter seems to be that particulars are also abstractions, so the nominalist has no reason for favouring particulars over universals. But does the whole idea not seem unsatisfactory in some way for someone professing to be a realist about both universals and particulars? Armstrong protests that his account does not make universals and particular unreal, even if they are abstractions (1984: 43). The mind is not justified in making any abstractions it chooses. The abstraction has to fit the real features of the states of affairs. But what is clear here is that it is the states of affairs that rule. Armstrong really does have a states of affairs ontology. Such Tractarian facts are what do all the work. Universals and particulars both then seem to fall foul of the naturalist commitment. Nothing, said Anderson, was constituted, wholly or partly, by its relations to anything else. Both abstraction and partial consideration sound too much like mind-dependence. If one really is to hold to a states of affairs ontology, it might be that universals and particulars will have to be sacrificed.

Higher-order states of affairs

There are some higher-order states of affairs that are non-supervenient. They are, therefore, an increase in being. A higher-order state of affairs is a state of affairs that has lower-order states of affairs as constituents (WSA: 196). For example, laws of nature are higher-order. They are relations that hold between state-of-affairs types and they do not exist just because those states-of-affairs types exist. Hence there could be states-of-affairs types F and G without there being a law that N(F,G). Higher-order states of affairs presuppose the existence of their constituents, although their constituents do not presuppose the higher-order states of affairs. There are two main types of higher-order states of affairs that Armstrong endorses: totality facts and laws of nature. The former also show why further negative states of affairs need not be admitted.

What a totality state of affairs actually is, is an aggregate or conjunction of states of affairs standing in a relation of *alling* or *totalling* (WSA: 199). The totality fact T "constrains" the facts under it (WSA: 199) such that there cannot be more. But the totality fact T is not constrained by the facts under it.

We have already encountered the necessity for totality facts. They are needed because the conjunction of all the first-order facts cannot entail that they are all that there is. In the *Tractatus*, Wittgenstein depicted the world as a world of atomic, first-order facts only. But Russell saw a problem with this (1918: V). Consider a room that contains three people, A, B and C. What makes it true that A, B and C are all the people in the room? It cannot be just A, B and C. They cannot entail that they are all the people in the room. It is logically possible that another person, D, also be in the room. Now if A, B and C entailed that they were all the people in the room, they would still do so even if D were also in the room, which would lead to contradiction.

Instead of considering a fact about the totality of people in the room, we might consider the totality of all the facts in the world. It is clear that exactly the same argument can be brought to bear on this totality and any other. Indeed, any time that we invoke the word *all* – any general claim – it requires a totality fact among its truth-makers. In formal terms, $\forall x\,(Fx \rightarrow Gx)$ cannot be entailed by the particular states of affairs that a is F and is G, b is F and is G, c is F and is G, . . . n is F and is G, even if a to n are all the particulars that are F (and G). That they are *all* such particulars is an irreducibly higher-order fact.

The totality fact, while being contingent, entails the truth that there are no more facts within the relevant domain. Does this produce a regress? If A, B and C are the first-order facts, and T the totality fact that these are all the facts, do we have to add a new totality fact, T′, that A, B, C and T are all the facts? But then we would need a further totality fact, T″, that A, B, C, T and T′ are all the facts. There is not an infinite regress in this case, however. The addition of the first totality fact, T, is a contingent fact and an increase in being. But any further truths of totality would be merely supervenient on T, so no increase in being.

Once totality states of affairs are admitted, there need be no further negative states of affairs allowed in our ontology (WSA: 135). There may be negative truths but we do not require negative states of affairs as their truthmakers. This is because, as we shall see in Chapter 10, the admission of such general facts will suffice as the truthmakers for negative truths on Armstrong's theory.

Laws of nature are the other main class of higher-order states of affairs. Laws are best understood as causal connections between states-of-affairs types (WSA: 228). Understanding them in this way solves some difficulties with Armstrong's initial formulation in *What is a Law of Nature?* Armstrong had previously ruled against a law relating a universal to itself: N(F,F). But "like sometimes causes like in a law-like way" (WSA: 228). If we now understand universals as states-of-affairs types, it becomes clear how there can be such a law for like causing like. One thing being F can cause another thing to be F, in which case the law should be represented as (WSA: 230):

($-_1$ being F) causes ($-_2$ being F).

We cannot have a relation between universals as there is only one universal involved, and it cannot have a relation to itself. But we can have one state of affairs involving a universal causing another state of affairs that involves that very same universal.

It will also be recalled from Chapter 3 (p. 52) that functional laws were problematic because some of the values of their functions might be uninstantiated. Functional laws were depicted as determinables for which the determinates were specific laws concerning necessitation relations between specific values of the magnitudes P and Q. It can now be seen that a functional law itself will be an even higher-order state of affairs than a non-functional law of nature. It will be a state of affairs that has states of affairs as constituents that themselves have states of affairs as constituents. The functional law is "the law that determines and unifies the determinate laws" (WSA: 243). Regarding the uninstantiated values, we should accept, instead of uninstantiated laws, that we have only a counterfactual whose truthmaker is in the higher-order functional law (WSA: 244). A higher-order state of affairs, it will be remembered, "constrains" the states of affairs "under" it. Effectively, a functional law is "a determinable law that governs a class of determinate laws" (WSA: 245). How does it do so? It is a law that relates "real" determinables, in the sense that there is a real and *"strictly* identical property that is a property of all and only the determinates that are the members of that class" (WSA: 247), that fall under the determinable. Mass and distance, which are related in the law of gravitational attraction, are real determinables: there is something strictly identical in all their determinate values. They are fit, therefore, to partake in a genuine functional law. Only *a posteriori* can we know which laws are genuine in this way.

The general lesson to learn of this section, is that although the world is a world of states of affairs, it is not just a world of first-order states of affairs. Some of the states of affairs will have to be higher-order: facts about the (first-order) facts. As Armstrong is a naturalist, these states of affairs, lower- and higher-order, are all that there is (WSA: 135–6). They constitute the whole of spacetime.

David Armstrong

Atomism

Armstrong thinks that not all states of affairs can be atomic. We have just seen the necessity to posit higher-order states of affairs and these are molecular. It is an *a posteriori* matter whether there are *any* atomic states of affairs (CTP: ix). Armstrong maintains talk of atomism, even though he cannot be sure that there actually are any atoms. He retains atomism because atoms convey the idea of Humean distinctness. States of affairs are "logically independent of each other" (CTP: ix).

Each state of affairs is a contingent being (WSA: 139). Not only their constituents need never have existed, even if they did exist, the states of affairs made from them need never have existed. And each first-order state of affairs is independent of all others that are entirely distinct, where one state of affairs does not contain another (WSA: 139–40). Higher-order states of affairs entail the lower-order states of affairs that they are about. With these exceptions, Armstrong thinks, or rather hopes, that independence holds between one state of affairs and another. He only "hopes" it holds because he admits that it is a matter to be decided "as a result of scientific investigation of the fundamental universals, the fundamental quantities, relations, etc. that are to be found instantiated in the world" (WSA: 146). There are some difficult cases, such as transitivity where two states of affairs seem to entail a distinct third one. If a is before b and b is before c, it is entailed that a is before c, which seems to violate independence. But an analysis of such cases reveals that there are chains of relatively atomic *before* relations and a, b and c have their place within such a chain (WSA: 142). a being before c is ontologically supervenient on a being before b and b being before c.

With independence established, or at least a commitment to independence being made, the way is open for a combinatorial theory of possibility as outlined in Chapter 4. Merely possible states of affairs as existents would violate naturalism, and are ruled out (WSA: 148–9). The truthmakers for modal truths are thus all to be found among the actual states of affairs of this world (WSA: 151). States of affairs will be the logical atoms that, taken with a principle of free recombination, yield all the possibilities. "Possible worlds" would be constructed from the simple particulars and simple universals, producing many different possible states of affairs (WSA: 161). All these "worlds" are to be understood in a deflationary way. Armstrong is no longer a fictionalist about possible worlds (WSA: 172). Instead, he has deflated that discourse. He prefers to express the combinatorial theory in terms such as the states of affairs being adequate truthmakers for all modal truths. These modal truths are in no sense fictions. The actual is adequate to determine the possible (WSA: 173). Possible worlds are not required at all, whether understood as real, as in Lewis, or as fictional, as in the Armstrong of *A Combinatorial Theory of Possibility*.

There, Armstrong had accepted alien particulars but rejected alien universals. These are alleged to be possible particulars and universals that are simple but are not real in our world. Might there have been just one more simple particular than our world contains or one more universal? It seemed an asymmetry of the combinatorial theory that it allowed the contracted world but not the expanded world. But there was a further asymmetry in accepting alien particulars while denying alien universals. He uses this opportunity to correct both asymmetries, now permitting alien particulars and universals and thereby allowing the expanded world. This means that our own world is no longer combinatorially inaccessible from a contracted world (WSA: 170). We can construct expanded worlds from relatively smaller worlds, which seems to be a strengthening of the case for combinatorialism.

Humean distinctness is a key commitment of Armstrong's theory, but he does not deny that the world is united or held together in various important ways. Not everything is entirely "loose and separate", as Hume had maintained. For one thing, every particular is linked to every other particular by some external relation (WSA: 263). Given that every particular is spatiotemporal, it will bear a spatiotemporal relation to every other particular. Furthermore, every state of affairs will bear at least some causal relation to every other state of affairs. This may be via many other causal relations in a chain or down and then back up various causal branches. But it is highly plausible that everything in the world is a part of the same causal net (WSA: 264–5). The idea of there being some isolated state of affairs, or set of states of affairs, causally unrelated to anything else in the world, is highly implausible. Next, we can note that realism about universals brings unity to the world. Universals bring an identity that runs through many distinct states of affairs, uniting them into various types (WSA: 265). The totality fact offers further unity in the world in that it limits the lower-order states of affairs. In a sense, it makes them a complete whole (WSA: 266). Let us not also forget that there are laws of nature, as higher-order states of affairs, that relate various universals nomologically.

Such factors impose limitations on the degree of independence between states of affairs. There is some independence, though not as much as the Humean would grant. There is, nevertheless, a strong inclination among those other than Humeans that Armstrong has the balance just about right. Some features of the world exhibit independence but some exhibit unity and connectedness. It should be clear by now that Armstrong has offered us a general, coherent and all-encompassing account of the world. It is compelling enough that it cannot be dismissed lightly. His opponents will have much work to do before they have offered anything as good.

Chapter 7
Sensations and perceptions

There is a distinctly philosophical problem of perception that would remain even if we knew all the facts of physics and biology. Suppose we knew all the science of what happens when we see something. We know that light waves enter the eye. We know how they land on the retina and how a corresponding stimulus is sent down the optic nerve. We even know the physical facts, or most of the physical facts, of what happens when the signal reaches the brain. We know that certain neurons move in a certain way, firing and sending a signal to a connected neuron. But, even if we understand all this, do we still really understand what perception is? Do we even know what it is that we see? Do we see physical objects in the world? Do we see light? Do we see the contents of our eyes? Or do we see our own ideas in our minds, at the end point of the causal process of perception? In philosophical terms, this is the question of the *object* of perception and science does not answer this question nor even attempt to answer it. Here is a case where it is philosophy, and philosophy alone, that allows us to understand some aspect of the world. It is a case where we need to get our thinking in order to grasp the way some portion of the world works. One might have thought that our own perceptions were that part of the world with which we are most familiar, but philosophy shows us how little we may understand ourselves.

The case of sight concerns just one faculty of perception, of course. The same questions can be asked of hearing, taste, smell and touch. We know that sound waves stimulate small bones inside the eardrum. Does this mean that we hear our ears, or the sound waves, or the mental impressions of those sound waves? We have to understand which of these options is tenable, if any. Taste and smell raise similar questions. Touch, as we shall see, is a distinctive and exceptional sense faculty and, as Armstrong recognized, it has some entirely distinctive features that are unlike those associated with the other four senses.

Armstrong's first philosophical interests were all concerned with this branch of epistemology. He would later expand on these interests, after his first three books, and study the mind–body problem and the notions of knowledge and belief. Having presented his core metaphysical work, we now go back to the epistemology with which he began. We shall see, however, that it was some of the outstanding problems of epistemology that led him to be a metaphysician. Specifically, we shall see that he invokes dispositions, universals and laws in several places in his accounts of sensation, knowledge and mind. It was thus his need to understand these things further that led to his move to metaphysics.

Berkeley on touch and sight

Armstrong began his academic work as a Berkeley scholar and his first book, *Berkeley's Theory of Vision*, was a study of the bishop's *Essay Towards a New Theory of Vision*. The book was thus concerned largely with details of Berkeley interpretation and I shall not linger on such details. As a contribution to the philosophy of perception, however, the book has its own interest. Berkeley had made a claim that the immediate objects of sight and touch are numerically different (BTV: 38), contrary to common opinion. One might think that one can both touch and see the same object, as when I see myself holding and feeling a billiard ball. But Berkeley's surprising conclusion is effectively that we cannot do this. We see one object in a *visual space*, the experience of space delivered by sight, and we feel another object in a *tangible space*, the experience of space delivered by touch. Berkeley argues that these two spaces cannot themselves be spatially connected. They are independent or discrete; hence we cannot say that the visual object is in the same place as the tangible object.

Armstrong admits the possibility of multiple, unconnected, spatiotemporal systems. He says "The idea of spatial objects which have *no spatial relations to each other*, which are not merely distant, but really spatially unrelated, does not seem to be an incoherent conception" (BTV: 34). Such a possibility sounds remarkably like the discrete, spatially disconnected worlds of Lewis's modal realism, although *Berkeley's Theory of Vision* pre-dates Lewis's work by some time. While Armstrong admits this logical possibility, however, he does not think that Berkeley has demonstrated in the case of perception that visual and tangible space are indeed distinct.

One of Berkeley's chief reasons for taking visual and tactual space to be unconnected was his commitment that distance cannot be immediately seen. What we see immediately is nothing but a two-dimensional manifold, he contends. The judgement that one thing is nearer to us than another comes only from some kind of inference, not usually a conscious one, based on other features and sensations we have when we see. A close object strains the eye to see, for example, and can become blurred if we cannot focus. Such sensations are extra cues that we use to estimate distance. If we do, however, see only in two dimensions, then our idea of a three-dimensional space must be gained by touch (barring any other explanation), which is why Berkeley thinks visual and tactual space are distinct. One is two-dimensional while the other is three-dimensional.

Against such a view there is a weight of argument, however, which Armstrong introduces, considers and judges. Can we not really see in three dimensions, as just a brute phenomenological fact, and do we not really see tangible objects? Berkeley would say that we have a mere association of ideas: we learn to associate visual and tangible spaces even though they are distinct. But can we really develop the notion of distance by the sense of touch alone? How would I judge that an object was one hundred metres away when my hand cannot reach that distance (BTV: 71)? I could move towards the object but how do I do that, and how do I know that I am doing that, without my sight? From the mere bodily sensations alone, I can tell that my body moves but I cannot tell that it moves across space, as I might be on a tread-mill. This book, however, is unlike Armstrong's others. He is not so much concerned with advancing his own thesis. That would be inappropriate in a book that is a work of scholarship. Instead it is a collection of discussions and arguments: a survey of all the available points pro and con.

There is consideration of Warnock's claim, for example, that tactual perceptions are felt entirely in the body (Warnock 1953). To feel something rough, for instance, is to feel that my skin is irritated in a certain way. But if these sensations are within my body, how can I know that they are caused by three-dimensional physical objects outside my body? It seems I can only know of the causes through

113

visual perceptions and any associations I make between them and my bodily sensations. But sight, according to Berkeley, gives us only two-dimensional knowledge. The conclusion, therefore, must be that Berkeley has given us no plausible account of how we acquire three-dimensional knowledge of the world (BTV: 74). We evidently do have three-dimensional knowledge, so Berkeley must be wrong some-where. But Armstrong cannot endorse this view of bodily sensations, as he thinks they can give us some immediate knowledge of the world, so the argument is not decided. He does not proceed to present his own general theory of bodily sensations, but we shall see in the next section that he did produce such a theory shortly thereafter.

Berkeley's contention that there are no relations between visible space and tactual space is certainly counterintuitive and it is a view that Armstrong finally rejects (BTV: 102). We believe that the place at which we see water is the same place at which we feel wetness, for example (BTV: 86). And Armstrong goes on to argue that taste, smell and sound are also located in space. There could, for instance, be two olive tastes inside two olives at different ends of a table (BTV: 99). A smell could fill a room and a sound can reach out from its source and have a spatial extent, beyond which it cannot be heard. Instead, then, of accepting five different spaces, of which we are aware, should we not accept that there is a single space and that we have five different ways of sensing it? Armstrong can see, however, the need for a general theory of perception, and this is what he presented in his next two books. I shall begin by looking at his detailed case study of bodily sensations before going on to the broader theory of perception in which it sits.

Bodily sensations

It may be a surprise to hear that bodily perception, the sense of touch, is unlike perception from any other of the four remaining senses. Armstrong saw that the sense of touch deserved a book-length study all on its own in which he could demonstrate this claim. In the first place, and very obviously, there is not a single sense-organ associated with the sense of touch, as the eye is the organ of sight or the tongue the organ of taste (BS: 9). One's whole body can feel, by which we mean not just the surface of one's body but the whole thing. I can feel nausea inside my body, a headache inside my head, or arthritis in my joints.

Second, bodily perception differs from the other senses in that one has to be in physical contact to perceive something by touch. In contrast, one's eye does not have to be in contact with something in order to see it. Nor does one have to touch something with one's ear to hear it. In the case of heat, it may be thought that one can feel heat from a distance and one does not have to touch fire, for instance, to feel that it is hot. But in this case, what one feels is the hot air that touches one's body or one may just feel one's body heating up (BS: 11). Perception of heat would not, in that case, be perception at a distance.

Third, bodily perception involves perception of some relation holding between our body and that with which it is in contact (BS: 14). We think of something as hot when it is hotter than our bodies or, more strictly, hotter than that part of our body with which it is in contact. Similarly with cold, rough and smooth, hard and soft, pressure against our bodies, heaviness and lightness, and even with large and small. When we perceive by touch, we are always in contact with some object and aware of that contact. Where I am touching something I do not feel that it is 4°C, for instance. Instead, I would feel that it is colder than my hand, or whatever body part it is touching. When I judge something cold through perception of it, my judgement has this relational nature. Even shapes can be perceived this way (BS: 18). When a round object presses against me, it produces a concavity of my flesh. By moving the object around I can feel the various relations it bears to my body as it presses into my skin. By feeling our way around, employing "active exploration", we can usually detect the shape of the object fairly easily and would be able to distinguish without great difficulty a sphere, cube and pyramid while blindfolded. To do this, then, I must be perceiving some part of my body. For perception of touch to have a relational nature, the sense-organ itself must be at least a part of the object of sensation.

This feature offers a major contrast with other sense faculties. When I see that something is large, as opposed to feeling that it is large, I am not seeing that it is larger than my eye. Indeed, my eye is no part of the visual sensation at all. I do not see my eye when I see; hence my visual perception is not a comparison between the sight of some object and the sight of my eye. Similarly, when I hear, I do not hear my own ear. I do not compare the sound of a trumpet with the sound of my ear; indeed it is most unusual for my ear to make a sound at all. When I smell, I do not smell my own nose and compare it to some other smell. And when I taste, I do not taste my own tongue but some object or substance upon it. Touch is therefore the sense that uniquely has this relational nature and it is the only case of sensing where the "organ" of perception – the body, or a part of it – is immediately perceived.

The subject of pressure on the body is worthy of note. Pressure is a causal concept, concerning one thing making another thing happen. But we can perceive pressure when it is applied to our own bodies and so this is a point where we can have immediate perception of a causal connection (BS: 23). We now know that Armstrong was to go on to make much use of this view. Causal relations will be understood as instantiations of laws and through experiences of causation, in the cases of our own bodies, we gain a foot-hold that allows us eventually to understand higher-order relations between universals. In *Bodily Sensations*, however, we find this thesis as purely a claim about our experiences, not yet put to any metaphysical use.

On the central claim, however, it is not clear that touch *alone* requires the perceived object to be in contact with the sense-organ. Certainly the sense of taste looks exactly like the case of touch in that I must touch with my tongue the object that I taste. Are sight, hearing and smell different? One can only see what strikes one's eye, smell the particles that enter one's nose and hear the sound that enters one's ear. In that case, perhaps the response that Armstrong gives to perception of heat should apply here. While one may not be comparing the smell of one's nose with the smell that enters it, it seems that one certainly needs some kind of contact with that smell. But here we might think that the object of the sense of smell is not the thing that is in one's nose but some more distant object that is emitting the smell. To sort out this question, we will need to consider issues of representationalism and direct realism, for these are attempts to defend a theory of the objects of perception. We will come to these issues shortly.

Intransitive sensations

A distinction can be drawn between transitive and intransitive sensations. Transitive sensations are of such qualities as warmth, pressure and motion: qualities that could exist without minds. Intransitive sensations, such as pains and tickles, are things that can only exist if there are minds. Thus, if the world contained no minds, there might still be things that are warm or are in motion but there would not be any pains or tickles (BS: 1). Armstrong deals with the transitive sensations quite quickly. They are identified with bodily sense impressions, such as that a part of the body is warm or under pressure (BS: 39). More difficult are the intransitive sensations, such as pains, tickles, itches, stitches, nausea, erotic sensations and aches, and most of Armstrong's book is devoted to these cases. We can refer to these simply as bodily sensations for ease of reference. He discusses and dismisses four theories about their nature before presenting and defending a revised version of one of the theories.

Can we say the intransitive sensations are (i) *qualities* of portions of the body? Just as I might say that my hand has a quality of being warm, can I say that my hand has a quality of being itchy? I cannot. Intransitive sensations cannot exist unfelt (BS: 49). While my hand could be hot though I do not feel it – because I am distracted or unconscious – itches, pains and tickles cease to exist when they are not felt. When I am distracted from the itch, it ceases to be, even though I may later think it the same itch, back again, when I can again feel it. Further, we cannot be *good or bad* at feeling bodily sensations (BS: 52), although we might be good or bad at sensing qualities in the world. I might be good at distinguishing shades of colour if I work in a paint shop, for example. But to be bad at detecting my own bodily sensations, or characteristics of them, is simply not to have those sensations or those characteristics to them. We would not say, in contrast, that if I was bad at detecting the quality of green, perhaps because I am red–green colour blind, that green did not exist. Also related to this same point, bodily sensations cannot be misfelt (BS: 54). There is no possibility of error. I cannot say that I feel at itch in my hand but might be mistaken and there might be no such itch. In contrast, we can say that we feel a pressure on our hand when there is no such pressure.

Are bodily sensations (ii) bodily *sense-impressions*? Not quite, although this is the theory that Armstrong revises and supports eventually. There are two serious difficulties with the simple version of this account. First, bodily sensations neither correspond, nor fail to correspond, to physical reality, as the transitive sensations do (BS: 63–4). "It feels itchy, but is it really itchy?" makes no sense. Only phenomenalism or a representative theory of perception would avoid such problems, and Armstrong rejects both, as we shall see below. Second, bodily sensations have a physical location, whereas it makes no sense to give sense-impressions a physical location (BS: 71). Later in his book, Armstrong will overcome both these difficulties.

Are bodily sensations (iii) *irreducibly themselves*? Are they irreducible non-physical events or items? Are they *sui generis* (BS: 75)? No. If it is said that these items are located in our bodies, then there are problems. How could a physical substance – the body – be the place where a non-physical item was located? Further, bodily sensations entail a mind. But if sensations are located items, it seems logically possible that they could exist in a body-part that is unconnected to a mind, such as a severed hand. Perhaps, then, these irreducible items are unlocated. Some sense would then have to be given to why we ordinarily think and speak of sensations as located. By the sensation's location, might we mean the location of the cause of the sensation? This would be to ignore the fact that sensations are not always felt where their cause is, as shown by the cases of amputees feeling pains to be located in their missing limbs. Might we mean by the sensation's location merely the place where we believe the cause of the sensation to be? No, as a doctor can convince me that the cause of the pain that I feel in my toe is a trapped nerve in my back. Do we mean by the location the place we are inclined to believe the cause of the sensation to be? This is the best formulation, but at this point Armstrong simply rejects as entirely implausible any attempt to equate a sensation and the cause of that sensation, no matter how the details of such an identification are spelled out. For want of any further account of sensations as unlocated items, we must accept them as intrinsically located and accept that this counts against their existence as non-physical items.

Might a sensation be simply (iv) *to take up a certain attitude* towards a portion of the body? Perhaps having the desire to rub or scratch actually constitutes the itch. The *attitude theory* could give an account of the location of a sensation: it is simply the place we are impelled to rub or scratch. This theory exploits the point that we do take up attitudes to sensations. We want to stop pains, while we want erotic sensations to continue as long as we enjoy them (BS: 90–95). But there are again serious difficulties with this account. What do we say of sensations such as tingles, to which we seemingly have no attitudes? And it is difficult to describe the attitudes that are supposed to constitute pain or erotic sensations, other than that they are con- or pro-attitudes. Further, when sensations are scarcely felt, there may be no con- or pro-attitude to them at all.

We come at last to Armstrong's own account of bodily sensations. Intransitive sensations differed from transitive sensations in neither corresponding nor failing to correspond to reality and in not having a physical location. Hence they did not seem simply to be sense-impressions. Can these difficulties be overcome? Armstrong offers an account in which intransitive sensations that apparently do not correspond to reality and apparently do not have location might be understood as cases that do. To have a pain is to feel a disturbance in one's body at a certain location and to have an immediate dislike of that feeling (BS: 106). As well as having a location, this can either correspond or fail to correspond to reality depending on whether there is actually the bodily disturbance. We typically have two components: a sensation of disturbance and a con-attitude to the sensation. But it is possible that the sensation occur without the attitude, as in the case of a mild pain. In the case of amputees, the feeling of disturbance may fail to correspond to reality when there is no such place on one's body. Armstrong offers accounts of tickles, erotic sensations, nausea, hunger, thirst and tingles along these lines.

It turns out that all bodily sensations, whether transitive or intransitive, are simply bodily sense-impressions (BS: 127); hence the distinction between transitive and intransitive, with which Armstrong began, turns out not to be so important. Bodily sensations can after all correspond or fail to correspond with reality. With a bodily sensation, it feels as if something is going on in our bodies and it is at least possible that this be an error, as in the case of phantom limbs. Nevertheless, a distinction between transitive and intransitive bodily sensations still can be made. The intransitive sensations differ in the relatively indeterminate nature of the impressions involved and in that some characteristic attitude is typically evoked.

Sensible qualities

What is the status of sensible qualities? In his main book on perception, *Perception and the Physical World* (PPW), Armstrong tackles this question in detail. In the first instance, he rejects the Berkeleyan arguments that purport to prove that the sensible qualities of things – such as their shape, colour, smell and taste – exist only in the mind. Berkeley was seeking to reduce sensible qualities to sensations. But Armstrong rejects any such reduction. We perceive the sensible qualities of things but we cannot say that we perceive our sensations. We *have* or *feel* our sensations but we do not perceive them (PPW: 5). Sense-impressions can also be distinguished from sensible qualities. Sense-impressions cannot be the same as the qualities of things as I can say that something looks blue to me (I have a blue sense-impression) when it is not really blue. These sense-impressions, sometimes called *sense data*, exist only when persons have them (PPW: 37), which is quite unlike physical qualities of objects.

Now if there are sensible qualities and sense-impressions, how does perception occur? There is an entrenched distinction, which Berkeley defended, between immediate and mediate objects of perception. I hear a coach on the cobbled street around the corner. Do I perceive the coach immediately? No: immediately I hear only the sound. I perceive the coach mediately in that I perceive its presence only indirectly from the sound that I hear immediately. My perception of the coach is then mediated via the immediate perception of sound.

There is a powerful and resilient kind of argument that often follows on from such a distinction. It is known as the argument from illusion. It is possible, when I have perceived something, that I could have had exactly the same kind of sense-impressions but that they were hallucinatory. The argument is supposed to suggest that the immediate objects of perception are sense-impressions, which can be had whether or not there are things in the world causing them and to which they correspond. If there is credibility in this view, then it seems we must accept either an indirect realist theory of perception, sometimes known as the representational theory, or we accept phenomenalism. Armstrong proceeds to argue that both theories face problems and so he will return to the original argument and offer instead a naturalistic account of illusion. This will clear the way for a form of direct realism, which states that the immediate objects of perception are sensible qualities.

Indirect realism

Indirect realism, or representationalism, is the theory that the direct objects of perception are sense-impressions that represent the sensible qualities of the physical world. The theory has a number of well-known and serious problems. In the first place, we cannot say that our sense-impressions resemble the objects in the physical world. A vital platitude about perceptions cannot, therefore, be accounted for by indirect realism. We may think, for instance, that we perceive a square object by having immediate awareness of a sense-impression of squareness. But what is the basis for saying that our sense-impression *resembles* the quality we are perceiving? All our experience is, on this theory, of our own sense-impressions. We do not have independent access to the world of objects and their qualities that we can somehow hold up to the world of sense-impressions in order to perform a comparison. Our entire experience is of sense-impressions, if indirect realism is true, so we are epistemically incapable of any such comparison.

Berkeley pushed this problem even further (in an attempt to show that if our experience is limited to sense-impressions, we should be phenomenalists). Physical objects cannot have the qualities of our sense-impressions. If they did, then they would be immediately perceivable too. So it is not just accidental but necessary that physical objects and sense-impressions do not resemble. Armstrong accepts this as a consequence of the view (PPW: 31) and it shows what is so perilous about indirect realism. It is also called the representative theory of perception because the idea is supposed to be that while we cannot see the world directly, we can nevertheless see it indirectly by seeing a representation of it in our sense-impressions. But if we cannot say that our impressions resemble the physical objects (or, on the stronger version, we must say that our impressions cannot resemble the physical objects), then how can we say that our impressions *represent* the physical objects? Representation usually requires some correlation or analogue between the representation and the thing represented. We cannot claim any such correlation or analogue on this theory of perception, so the representative claim must fall by the wayside. The physical world therefore becomes an unknowable thing-in-itself.

To take the critique as far as possible, might we say that we have no good reason to posit any physical world at all? There is no direct awareness of the world. Any such knowledge is inferential and, it seems, such an inference looks far from safe. Given that we cannot see such a world directly, why claim that it is there? Is it a mere hypothesis or inference to the best explanation? But surely our knowledge of the world is more than just hypothetical. Can we not know directly that physical objects exist?

Phenomenalism

If we are concerned about the question of resemblance and of our evidence for the existence of a physical world we might, like Berkeley and A. J. Ayer (1954: ch. 6), attempt to take a phenomenalist line. If all our immediate experiences are of sense-impressions or sense-data, why not allow that the physical world is nothing but a construction out of sense-data? Thus, when I talk of the cat in my room I am actually talking about a set of sensations – cat-like sensations – that you or I have. In a way, this could be understood as an acceptance of the criticisms of indirect realism. Instead of trying to reject them as counterintuitive, phenomenalists embrace them as consequences of their position.

But we have some very serious difficulties to face if we try to defend phenomenalism. The main one is familiar to us (from Chapter 5). It is one thing to construct a "physical" object from some set of actual experiences, but we usually take unobserved physical objects to be at least possible. What can the phenomenalist say about them? Berkeley urged us to accept that God perceived everything so that there were, strictly speaking, no unobserved physical objects. But we might find this move desperate unless we are theists and have rejected naturalism. If we try to get by without God, then we may have to say that an unperceived cat consists only in the possibility of sense-data when it *is* being observed. This, however, gives unobserved objects a merely hypothetical existence. The physical world is supposed to consist in nothing more than sensations. We cannot, therefore, say what we ordinarily would say, which is that there are mind-independent physical objects that make sensations of them possible. If sense-data are the beginning and end of physical objects then nothing makes such sense-data possible when they are not occurring.

This problem is serious enough, although it is still open to the phenomenalist to accept it as a consequence of their position. But it is not their only problem. For one thing, Armstrong accepts the indeterminacy of our experiences. I can have sense-impressions of a group of strewn matchsticks. There may actually be 63 matchsticks though my sense-impression can be indeterminate in respect of the number (PPW: 40). I see the collection just as a collection of quite a few matchsticks and have no definite view as to their exact number. We would say ordinarily that although my sense-impressions can contain such indeterminacy, physical objects are nevertheless determinate. There may be exactly 63 matchsticks regardless of my sense-impressions. Similarly, I may be unable to discriminate between two lengths when one is in fact longer than the other. The phenomenalist, however, who says that the physical world is actually constructed from sensations, has great difficulty according with common sense on this. The pile of matchsticks is constructed from sense-impressions which, if indeterminate as to number, seems inevitably to mean that the number of matchsticks is indeterminate. If the two lengths cannot be distinguished in sense-impressions, then they cannot be distinguished at all.

Further difficulties include how a phenomenalist can construct a public space and time from the experiences of individual minds. I might be able to construct a "subjective spacetime", based on the order of my own experiences, but I cannot compare these or locate them with respect to yours. Further, how can we judge that minds are distinct when they have no location in an objective spacetime? But minds in general become a problem and we would seem forced to accept the Humean view of them that they are nothing more than bundles of sensations. A consequence of this, and Humean distinctness, seems to be the possibility of sensations that are a part of no bundle, existing apart from a mind, which Armstrong judges an absurdity (PPW: 78–9).

Although Armstrong has subsequently expressed reservations about the force of his arguments against the representative theory and against phenomenalism (1984: 16), it is clear that both positions face major difficulties.

Direct realism

Armstrong finds problems for indirect realism and phenomenalism so he considers the alternative, a form of direct realism. This is the view that the immediate objects of perception are physical objects and their qualities, rather than sense-data. Such a view of perception certainly accords with Armstrong's naturalism but for it to be even a starter we would need to tackle the argument from illusion. That was an argument purporting to show that the immediate objects of perception were sense-impressions and is a conclusion that indirect realism and phenomenalism can accept but direct realism cannot. What we need therefore, to prepare the ground for direct realism, is a naturalistic account of what occurs during hallucinations and other illusions.

Armstrong offers an explanation in terms of belief. We shall learn more about belief in Chapter 9, but for the moment we can see how important the notion is in Armstrong's theory of perception. Simply put, this is because illusions and hallucinations are accounted for in terms of false beliefs. To say that I hallucinate a pink elephant is not, as other theories would insist, to say that I see a real pink elephant sense-datum, although one for which there is no corresponding physical object. Armstrong wants an explanation that is free of sense-data. Instead, to hallucinate a pink elephant is merely to have a false belief that one is perceiving a pink elephant. One cannot be perceiving a pink elephant if one is not really there when, as direct realism would have it, the immediate objects of perception are physical. But one certainly might believe that one is so perceiving, although this belief is false.

This account will have to be complicated slightly, however, as the relationship between illusion and belief is not quite so straightforward. Were I regularly to "see" pink elephants whenever I wanted alcohol, I may well stop believing that I am perceiving pink elephants even though I have the hallucination. I may reach a state where I know the elephant is hallucinatory. In such a case, I have the hallucination without forming the (false) belief. Similarly, I might one day coincidentally come across a real pink elephant and dismiss it as a hallucination when it is in fact a case of veridical perception. Here I have perception without forming the (true) belief. Armstrong amends the account, therefore, in terms of *inclination* to believe: "when we suffer sensory illusion, it is a mere matter of falsely believing or being inclined to believe that we are perceiving something" (PPW: 93). An inclination, it might be noted, is a disposition, so his account of hallucinations will rest on the account of dispositions he was later to give (see Chapters 5 and 8 on mental dispositions). Even where I withhold the belief that I am perceiving a pink elephant, because past experience has taught me that I merely need a drink, I am still disposed to believe there is such an elephant. I resist or hold back the inclination to believe because of other, countervailing beliefs (PPW: 106). The inclination must still be there, however, for it to be something that can or cannot be resisted. Thus we arrive at a naturalistic account of illusions and hallucinations that does not invoke sense-data or sense-impressions as the immediate objects of perception. A major motivation for representationalism, the argument from illusion, is thereby disarmed. And if we no longer accept that our perceptions are of ideas, impressions or sense-data, then the motivation for phenomenalism also vanishes. The path is clear for direct realism.

So much for illusion. What can the direct realist say about veridical perception? Continuing in the same vein, perception can be

accounted for in terms of knowledge. To perceive is to acquire knowledge about the world (PPW: 110). This is an idea that Armstrong
got from discussion with Ayer, deciding to answer in the affirmative
Ayer's question "Do you want to treat veridical perception as a
form of knowledge?" (1984: 16). *Perceive* is what Ryle called an
achievement word, hence if one fails to acquire knowledge about
the world one at best misperceives. Note that adding "veridical" to
"perception" is effectively redundant on this view. But the account
is subject to the same *inclination*-proviso that was added before: to
perceive is to acquire knowledge or to have the inclination to acquire
knowledge. We can imagine cases where one might resist holding
the relevant belief, belief being taken usually as a prerequisite of
knowledge (as we shall see in Chapter 9).

The main objection to this kind of account is that it seems to leave
something out. Perceiving seems to involve more than just believing.
Is it not tempting to say that one believes because of the sensations?
Does it not seem as if there is a raw feel, a qualitative *sensa*, to
perceptual experience, for which Armstrong has not accounted?
Armstrong concedes that there is a major difference between acquiring a belief through one's senses and acquiring it in some other
way, perhaps from a trusted friend passing on information. But the
difference may still be explicable in terms of belief. In the first case
I believe that something is the case and I also believe that I have
seen it with my eyes, for example. When I perceive something, I am
frequently aware that I am perceiving something and believe that
I am doing so (PPW: 113). These extra beliefs about perception
clearly are absent in the cases where I trust the testimony of a friend,
even where that source is reliable and believed.

While the theory may stand in need of a defence against the charge
that sensations are more than beliefs, a point that Armstrong later
concedes (1984: 17), there are also noteworthy points in favour of the
proposal. There are some significant similarities between sensations
and beliefs that might, upon consideration, make the theory look
plausible after all (PPW: 129). Our sense-impressions are not under
our direct control – we cannot choose what we see – but neither are
beliefs under our direct control. We cannot choose what to believe. We
cannot be mistaken about what sensations we are having but nor can
we be mistaken about which beliefs we are holding (we shall see in
Chapter 8 that Armstrong backed away from depicting the mind as so
transparent). The indeterminacy of belief might also explain the
indeterminacy of our sense-impressions. I can sometimes see that

something is red without seeing it as being a specific shade of red. But, on Armstrong's view, this would be explained as a case of believing that something is red without having a belief about its specific shade.

Something else significant comes out of this direct realist account. Perception of the world can give us immediate knowledge of physical reality. By immediate knowledge, Armstrong means knowledge that rests on or presupposes nothing else. It is based on no other reason or justification. Knowledge is often understood as justified true belief. But Armstrong follows Plato (*Theaetetus*: 206e–210b) in rejecting this definition. To have a justification of one's belief is to know something, so the account would be incomplete. Only if something can be known directly or immediately can we know anything, and Armstrong allows this in his theory of perception (PPW: 120). We do not, therefore, require sense-data as a foundation or justification of our knowledge about the world. Our knowledge is, in a sense, direct, though this is not to deny that there are cases where we are mistaken in thinking we have attained knowledge. This last theme is considered again in Chapter 9.

Science

One big problem remains for direct realism, however. Russell summed it up in the following, initially puzzling, way. He said "Naïve realism leads to physics, and physics, if true, shows that naïve realism is false. Therefore, naïve realism, if true, is false; therefore it is false" (Russell 1940: 15). (This was one of the first philosophical arguments I was asked to consider as an undergraduate so I know how confusing it can seem.) We can explain the argument in a little more detail. According to direct realism, the objects of perception are things like tables and chairs and cats, or the sensible qualities of such things. They are the ordinary physical objects. But that is to say that the objects of perception are the objects described by physics. It is to grant that physics has a right to tell us about these perceived objects. But what does physics tell us about them? It tells us that they are nothing like the things we think we see. I see and feel a table in front of me that looks brown and feels solid. But physics tells us that the table is mainly empty space and that it consists of tiny moving particles that, when viewed under the most powerful microscope, have no colour at all. How, then, can the direct realist square the perceived world with the world of physics when they have such different properties? Is the brownness of the table really there or is it a subjective phenomenon? This is what Armstrong calls the problem of science.

There are various ways we might approach this difficulty, and Armstrong's solution is rather startling. He has already given an account of illusion as false belief. In the case of colour, and some of the other qualities we think we see in the world, he is prepared to offer the same explanation: an error theory (PPW: 164). Our belief that things are coloured is illusory. It is a false belief, in which case it is literally false to say that we perceive colour: we only misperceive it. This is a systematic error and it arises because "language follows perception" (PPW: 168). Blood appears a continuous red to us in ordinary conditions, although our scientific knowledge tells us that it is not in reality. There could, though, still be truth in saying that blood is red if by that we mean "presents that appearance to normal observers under standard conditions" (PPW: 169). To say this is to concede a limited form of phenomenalism, where the redness of blood is more a report of our experience than a fact about the physical world. We can easily enough qualify this by speaking of the *sensible* qualities of things and their *true* qualities, as discovered by science. But this would not be a lapse back into representationalism, he contends, with one world of our sense-impressions and another of the objects represented. This would be merely a linguistic concession, not an ontological one. It has been established for centuries that blood is red. Scientific discoveries, which are comparatively recent, tell us otherwise. But rather than overthrow centuries of ordinary linguistic practice, it is better just to distinguish between how things appear to our senses and what they are truly like according to science.

All this does, however, raise some serious ontological questions about the status of the secondary qualities in general. While length and shape may still appear in a physical theory of the world, it seems that there will be little or no place for colours, sounds, smells and tastes. Should we say that no such qualities are among the true qualities? Armstrong considers but rejects the Lockean answer, as defended by J. J. C. Smart. The secondary qualities do exist in objects, in Smart's account, though as powers that cause us to make certain discriminations (Smart 1959: 150). The problem with this, as Berkeley had already argued, is that primary qualities are also powers that cause us to make discriminations. Instead of seeking to reduce the secondary qualities to the primary ones, Armstrong bucks the popular conception of the scientific view and argues that the world cannot contain only primary qualities. The primary qualities, as we have understood them from Descartes and Locke, are not sufficient to make a thing substantial. Descartes thought that extension was the essence of matter, but this is clearly inadequate as a volume of empty space can be extended. Aware of this, Locke tried to add the qualities of solidity or impenetrability. These do not solve the problem as they are relational. One material object is impenetrable only in relation to another. If we have not yet already grasped what a material object is, then we will not understand impenetrability. *Perception and the Physical World* ends in rather unsatisfactory fashion, however. At least some other qualities must be added to those invoked by physics for our world to be substantial. But Armstrong has no definite conclusion about what those other qualities are. It may be that they are secondary qualities. Until he can add this detail, the case for direct realism seems not proved as it is at odds with the scientific view of the world that it supposedly supports, thus at odds with the core commitments of naturalism and empiricism.

This completes the survey of Armstrong's main ideas on perception. The faculty of perception is just one aspect of the mind, however. A systematic philosopher such as Armstrong was bound to want to know more about the mind in general, and that was the next problem to which he turned his attention.

Chapter 8
Metaphysics of mind

Human beings have bodies. These are physical things made of matter. We have no special worries about how they fit into the natural world described by science. Our bodies would fall under the general problem of characterizing matter, although we may feel that we would have to investigate biology if we wanted to understand living matter in detail.

As well as bodies, however, it seems apparent that we also have minds. These have some very special abilities. I can think thoughts, which are private and may remain so. I can have beliefs and knowledge. As we saw in Chapter 7, I can feel sensations. I can feel pain, see colours and hear sounds. Such sensations exist, if they exist anywhere, in my mind. Other people may look at the same patch of red and experience their own sensation of red. Although there is a perfectly respectable sense in which we see the same thing, there is also a tempting thought that I see only my own sensation of red and you see only your own sensation of red. Sensations are part of a wider phenomenon that we attribute to mind: consciousness. This will include sensations, perceptions, thoughts, dreams, imagination, after-images and so on. It is a kind of general awareness of the world and of the state of my own mind that purely physical things, such as rocks and chairs, do not have. Only animate matter is capable of consciousness, but not all animate matter. Plants and vegetables are alive but not, we are pretty sure, conscious.

A conscious being has another remarkable ability. Their thoughts can be *about* things in the world. They can make a pencil drawing that is of Winston Churchill. I can have a belief about Sydney, Australia. I can fear an intruder in my living room (even if there is no such intruder) and I can see that the cat is on the mat. This mental phenomenon has been named intentionality, though some call it directedness or about-ness. One may think it a very special ability of minds that allows them to *mean* things (Searle 1991). My thoughts and statements are meaningful – they have a meaning – because they are about something.

The problem for any naturalist, such as Armstrong, is how such mental phenomena fit into the natural world of science. These are very special and intriguing phenomena. A traditional view, which comes to us from Descartes, is that as well as having a body, I also have a mind in which my thoughts and experiences take place. The mind–body problem is the problem of how these two parts relate. Are they completely distinct things, perhaps even made from different types of substance? But if they are, how is it that they seem to interact so easily? Physical causes can have mental effects, as in perception, and mental causes can have physical effects, as in action. This suggests a very close connection rather than a wide separation. Can we, instead, account for the mind in entirely physical terms, as physicalists or materialists maintain? Or might we even account for matter in entirely mental terms, as idealists such as Berkeley try to do? Such questions are old, yet philosophers are far from agreeing on the answers. Speaking of the mind–body problem, Armstrong in one place asks "How did we get into this mess?" (MBP: 1).

We have already noted, in Chapter 1, that as well as being a naturalist, Armstrong is a physicalist. This commits him to the view that the mind, and all its special abilities, must be given a purely physical explanation. The problem to be dealt with here, therefore, is how to give an account of the mind in such physical terms. Other Australians had already begun the work when Armstrong came to the problem. In particular, Ullin Place (1956) and J. J. C. Smart (1959), who both worked at the University of Adelaide, had proposed physical theories of the mind, or at least of parts of the mind. Armstrong at first resisted the view but in time came round to it (1984: 21). With the addition of his contribution, these three are sometimes known as the Australian materialists.

This chapter will be concerned primarily with Armstrong's position in *A Materialist Theory of The Mind*. While he continued to work on the mind–body problem, and in some places revised his view (see the essays in *The Nature of Mind and Other Essays*), it was for this materialist solution to the mind–body problem that he was most famous for much of his career. It represents an authoritative statement of Australian materialism and was, and still is, a seminal piece of philosophy.

Dualist theories

By the time that Armstrong wrote *A Materialist Theory of The Mind*, it seemed that there were only two remaining viable theories: dualism and materialism (bearing in mind that Armstrong had already studied Berkeley's idealism quite closely). Each of these could be developed in two ways, however. Dualism could be divided into substance dualism and bundle dualism. Materialism could be divided into behaviourism and the view that Armstrong would defend: the central-state theory.

A bundle dualist would be someone who "conceives of the mind as a temporal series of non-physical items . . . The mind is a succession of such things as thoughts, feelings, desires, mental images, sensations, and, above all, sense-impressions or sense-perceptions, all conceived of as non-physical particulars" (MTM: 15). There are two main problems with this view. First, there is no uniting principle that makes such a bundle the unity that is a mind. Second, such experiences are not the sorts of things that can have independent existence so they are ill prepared for the requisite bundling.

Should we then be substance dualists, as Descartes famously recommended? While substance dualism does not suffer the problems that beset bundles, however, it still faces the same notorious difficulties of any dualism. Perhaps most significantly, substance dualism cannot account for the unity of mind and body. Clearly, our minds and our bodies are closely interconnected. There are at least two aspects to this and dualism struggles to explain either. First, if mind and body are entirely distinct things, then it seems that I have no assurance that my mind will inhabit the same (my) body tomorrow. How, then, can these be both *my* mind and *my* body? Second, my mind and body are, as we have already seen, causally interconnected. Physical occurrences can have mental effects, such as when bodily damage causes an experience of pain or when physical phenomena affecting the ear cause a sensation of sound. The dualist divides the mind and the body into distinct substances with their own characteristics. The physical is spatiotemporally located and extended while mental substances are not. Where one thing causes another, we usually think of the cause and effect as being proximate – close together – and the cause passing on some movement or energy to its effect. But if minds are not spatiotemporal, it would not even make sense for them to be spatiotemporally close to any physical event and it would make no sense to speak of them gaining any movement or physical energy. I cannot even say that my mind is in my body (MTM: 25) as that would be ascribing it spatiotemporality. Dualism struggles, therefore, to make even basic sense of the commonplace of mind–body interaction.

That is not all, however. Physical objects are differentiated by their locations. We can know that we have two things by seeing that they are far apart and separated. But these are physical features. In the case of immaterial objects, Cartesian minds, how would we differentiate them numerically? How can we know when we have one mental substance, two mental substances or more? This might be a key issue for us. One putative attraction of substance dualism is that it can at least make sense of the idea of the mind surviving the death of the body. The mind might be our eternal spirit that lives on once our bodies have died. But if it is to be *my* afterlife, there must be some way in which my spirit has numerical identity through time and is numerically distinct from all the other spirits. It is not clear what this numerical identity is for an immaterial thing.

Suppose one tried to retreat to a position in which all substances were physical but in which there were both mental and physical properties of those substances. This could be a dualism of attributes where there was still a substantial grounding for persons. But other problems would remain with this view. Disembodied existence would be impossible as a property must be instantiated in a particular and all such particulars, in this view, are physical. We would also need to explain how mental properties could emerge from otherwise entirely physical things. This weakened form of dualism certainly does not solve all the problems, therefore. Furthermore, any form of dualism faces the problem that it is scientifically implausible. We are biological creatures and we now understand biology to be reducible to chemistry, which is in turn reducible to physics. A completed science would explain everything about human beings, including their mental lives. What place in this would there be for things like eternal souls? Probably there would be no place at all.

Although Armstrong dismisses dualist theories of the mind, his discussion has nevertheless thrown up some crucial features of mind such that any plausible theory must be able to explain them. An acceptable theory of mind:

a. should allow for the logical possibility of disembodied existence
b. should not treat mental happenings as capable of independent existence

c. should account for the unity of mind and body
d. should provide for the numerical diversity of minds
e. should not be scientifically implausible
f. should allow for causal interaction of mind and body.

Behaviourism

In the middle of the twentieth century, there was a radical challenge to the appeal of dualism. Philosophical behaviourism had foundations in empirical psychology but also in Wittgenstein's later work. The clearest and best statement of it as a philosophical position is to be found in Gilbert Ryle's (1949) book, *The Concept of Mind*.

Descartes was led to a dualist position from a certain way of viewing the mind and mental phenomena. The mind was understood as a private, inner theatre of consciousness. The contents of the mind were all seen as events or occurrences that took place on the stage of this inner theatre. The mind was the thing that contained all such mental events. Just as I had a body, I also had a mind, and it then seemed natural to think of human beings as being composed of two parts: one made of physical substance and the other made of mental substance. To avoid being drawn to this conclusion, Ryle wanted to rethink the starting assumptions.

Mental phenomena were not to be thought of as occurrences. That just did not make sense in many cases. To have a belief, for instance, is not to be in a conscious mental state. There need be nothing going on in any inner theatre. Rather, to have a belief is to be disposed to do something: to be disposed to be in a state or disposed for something to occur. We have already seen (Chapter 5), however, that to have a disposition does not mean that the disposition must be manifested. Thus I can believe that zebras have black and white stripes for a long time – many years – without the belief manifesting itself. I very rarely think anything about zebras at all. It could nevertheless be true of me that I have for many years believed that zebras have black and white stripes because throughout that time I have been disposed to behave in certain ways. I have been so disposed even if I have never behaved in any of those appropriate ways. What, however, have I been disposed to do? Had anyone asked me whether zebras had black and white stripes, I would have answered affirmatively; had I ever been drawing a zebra, I would have drawn black and white stripes on it, and so on. Dispositional accounts can be given of other types of mental phenomena such as emotions. To be in love is to be disposed to behave in a certain way. A man may be in love when he is thinking of something else altogether and even when he is asleep. We might even be able to say something similar of sensations. To be in pain, for instance, is to be disposed to cry out. I can be in pain without actually crying out, if I am self-controlled, but I will always be at least disposed to cry out even if I resist the urge.

The most significant feature of such a view of mind is that it allows us to offer a purely physical theory (MTM: 54). It can offer an account of what it is to have a mind in terms of physical behaviour and dispositions to behave. Having a mind does not mean that one has a thing made of some peculiar non-physical substance. When we say that someone has a mind we simply mean that they behave or can behave in a certain, sophisticated way.

Why, then, is Armstrong not a behaviourist? The main reason is that it is an evident datum that we are able to think privately to ourselves (MTM: 70). If Ryle is claiming that there is nothing "inner" occurring in our minds, only outward behaviour, then he has surely gone too far. We can go through thoughts without any revelation of them in behaviour. Of course, we may well be disposed to behave when we have these thoughts, and they may even issue in some actual behaviour. But behaviourism seems to be missing something out of the story if it tries to maintain that there is nothing more to such mental phenomena than our behaviour and dispositions to behaviour. It seems that as well as that, there is some specifically mental activity that often accompanies the disposition. When I am in pain, for instance, I certainly may be disposed to cry out, but that does not seem to be all that there is to being in pain. Accompanying my disposition is a *feeling* of pain. Indeed we might think that the connection between the feeling and the disposition is closer than mere accompaniment. We might think that I am disposed to cry out *because* of my feeling of pain. I am not feeling pain because I cry out; rather, I cry out because I am in pain. This way of conceiving the relationship of mind to body is the basis of Armstrong's causal theory of mind.

The central-state theory

Behaviourism does not entail materialism or physicalism – that everything is made of physical matter – although it would be usual for only materialists to defend behaviourism. But there is a different form of materialism that Armstrong defends at length in *A Materialist Theory of The Mind*. This theory is that the mind is identical with certain physical states of the central nervous system. We might say that the mind is identical with the brain, although that would not be strictly accurate as often more than the brain is involved in our mental states (MTM: 73). That can be left as an empirical matter for the biological sciences to determine, however. A state, it ought to be said, is something that "endures for a greater or lesser time, but it exists entire at each instant for which it endures" (MTM: 130).

Behaviourism had allowed only stimuli and responses in its account. Dispositions were characterized by their stimulus conditions and their manifestations. Indeed, Ryle had offered a conditional analysis of dispositions where there was nothing more to a disposition than the truth of some conditional, "if F, then G", where the antecedent F named the appropriate stimulus and the consequent G named the appropriate manifestation. What the account omits is that, in the case of dispositions, there is some state – some central state – that causally mediates between the stimulus and manifestation. When something has a disposition it is in some condition that, when caused by the right stimulus, in turn causes a specific kind of manifestation. It may be recalled, from Chapter 5, that Armstrong understands such states as the categorical bases of dispositions and he thinks that all dispositions must have categorical bases. Seeing dispositions this way allows us to find an improved theory of mind. Ryle was keen to deny the existence of any central state because he did not want to allow the possibility of the state being mental. He did not want to allow the Cartesian inner theatre made of mental substance. But he had stretched the credibility of the theory to the point where he implausibly denied anything in the mind. Instead, Armstrong allows that there are inner states that causally mediate our behaviour but he argues that, as a matter of empirical fact, such states are physical. The categorical bases of all mental dispositions are states of the brain or central nervous system. The basics of his position are stated as follows:

As a first approximation we can say that what we mean when we talk about the mind, or about particular mental processes, is nothing but the effect within a man of certain stimuli, and the cause within a man of certain responses. The intrinsic nature of these effects and causes is not something that is involved in the

concept of mind or the particular mental concepts. The concept of
a mental state is the concept of that, whatever it may turn out to
be, which is brought about in a man by certain stimuli and which
in turn brings about certain responses. What it is in its own
nature is something for science to discover. Modern science
declares that this mediator between stimulus and response is
in fact the central nervous system, or more crudely and inaccur-
ately, but more simply, the brain.   (MTM: 78–9)

That the mind is the brain is, therefore, an empirical matter.
Armstrong takes it to be an empirical truth that is already near-
enough established.

What we have here is a two-stage argument (MTM: 90–91).
Armstrong presents the sort of view that David Lewis had also
supported shortly before (Lewis 1966). The first stage of the argument is the conceptual part. Using conceptual analysis we can
conclude that "the concept of a mental state is the concept of a state
of the person apt for the production of certain sorts of behaviour"
(MTM: 90). This is the causal theory of mind. The second stage is the
empirical part. We have to look for what it is in the world that fills
this role, that of producing certain sorts of behaviour.

Not just any old behaviour will do. My leg might jerk by reflex
action but "behaviour proper" would be behaviour that relates to my
mind (MTM: 84). We will of course also have to exclude behaviour
such as the ordinary operation of the liver. In order to do so, we will
need a conceptual analysis of what behaviour counts as mental
behaviour, and Armstrong provides this in Part II of his book. The
general answer, however, accords with a famous claim made by
Brentano. Mental states are typically *directed at*, "point to", or are
about something. When I believe, I believe *that p*, where p is some
statement or proposition. When I am afraid, I fear *something*. When
I am in love, I love *someone*. This is intentionality and the thing to
which the state is directed is known as the intentional object.
Armstrong revises his account, therefore, to say that a mental state
is an *intentional* state that is apt for the production of behaviour
(MTM: 120). This leaves him with further work to do, however. He
will need to offer a physicalist account of the somewhat puzzling
phenomenon of intentionality (see p. 146, below).

There are two technical points that need to be made clear. First,
while Armstrong calls his account of mind a causal theory, it is clear
that this is an early form of what is now known as functionalism.

He makes this clear in his 1993 preface (MTM: xiv). This now quite popular view has it that mental states can be characterized by their functional role. A functional role is usually defined in terms of its typical causes and typical effects. That mental state which is typically caused by bodily damage and can typically cause avoidance behaviour will be pain. That mental state which typically is caused by seeing a cat on a mat and can typically cause one to assert that the cat is on the mat will be *the belief* that the cat is on the mat. Functionalism is, thus, Armstrong's theory of mind, derived by conceptual analysis. The exact nature of the thing that occupies that causal role is the empirical part of the central-state theory and here there is the second point to be clarified.

At first, both Lewis and Armstrong went for what is now called a type–type identity theory. In Armstrong's case, this was largely because he was insensitive to an issue that later came to the fore. The hypothesis was that for any mental state, such as pain or the belief that today is Wednesday, there was a physical state, probably a brain state, to which it was identical. Pain might be identical to C-fibre firing, for example, where this is a physical process in the brain. The belief that today is Wednesday might be identical to the firing of xyz-neurons. But this is not, on further reflection, very plausible. Is it not possible that a different person believe that today is Wednesday but that they have a different brain state at that time? Perhaps their abc-neurons are firing. Or the same person at different times may have different patterns of neuron firings at the times that they believe the day to be Wednesday. Similarly, is it not possible that a cat can feel pain even if it has, let us suppose, no C-fibres? Might there not be a different physical state that realizes the functional role of pain for them? If that is the case, then one cannot say that pain is identical with C-fibre firing nor, in the other case, that the belief is identical with xyz-firing. But this need not lead us to jettison physicalism. What it means is that we cannot identify a whole mental type, pain for instance, with a physical type. But we might, nevertheless, move to what is called a token–token identity theory. This states that each token or instance of pain will be identical with some physical-state token. Many different types of physical token might realize the functional role of pain in different people, in different species, or in the same person at different times. While Armstrong did not explore the distinction between type–type and token–token theories to begin with, he did later indicate his preparedness to move to a token–token theory (1984: 32 and MTM:

xiv–xv). In that case, I might say that while pain tokens are identical with C-fibre firings in humans, a pain token in a cat might be identical with a D-fibre firing, or some such other physical state.

The fundamentals of the central-state theory are now in place. Regarding the demands of an acceptable theory of mind, Armstrong thinks that the central-state theory fares well. In particular, that a theory

c. should account for the unity of mind and body

is obviously a requirement that is met. Mind and body will be part of a unified whole as the mind is identical with some part of the body (MTM: 75). It is unlikely to be identified with the whole of the body, including parts such as the feet or the navel, but it will be identified with those parts that biologists pick out as the central nervous system.

In addition, central-state materialism will allow for:

d. the numerical diversity of minds

Minds will be distinct when they are in different places. They will be able to have locations because they will be physical things, or identical with physical things, which is to say the same.

f. Causal interaction of mind and body

faces no special difficulties of the sort generated by dualism. Both mind and body are made from material substances so their interaction will be just like that between any other physical substances.

In addition to meeting some of the already-mentioned desiderata for a theory of mind, we can also note a further advantage. Unlike behaviourism, the central-state theory need not deny that there are inner mental states that exist whether or not accompanied by behaviour (MTM: 75). I may have a feeling that I keep secret from everyone else. Perhaps I want to be brave, so do not reveal that I am in pain. Perhaps I am in a state of paralysis and unable to display any physical behaviour at all. While behaviourism has difficult work to explain such cases, the central-state materialist can accept them at face value. They can be real, inner mental states but also be identical with brain states.

The causal theory of mind

The understanding of the mind in causal terms is supposed to be proved through philosophical analysis. It is supposed to be analytic that my beliefs are causes of my behaviour, understood in terms of disposition and manifestation. It is helpful to understand the mind in this way. We exhibit lots of different kinds of behaviour, including twitches, deliberate actions and automatic responses. Within the causal theory, behaviour that is purposive can be defined as behaviour that has a mental cause (MTM: 131–2). This is a simple and compelling claim but it faces a philosophical objection. It is often said that there is a causal relation between A and B only if there is not a logical connection between them. The reason for this is that causal relations are classically said to hold only between distinct events or existences. When one billiard ball causes another to move, the two events can be characterized or described entirely independently of each other. Suppose now I claim that my intention to raise my arm caused my arm to rise. The problem here, it seems, is that I cannot specify the first event, an intention to raise my arm, without reference to the second event, my arm rising. The first kind of event makes sense only if there is the second kind of event, so the former is logically dependent on the latter. The objection to the causal theory is, then, that "There seems to be some logical bond between the intention and the occurrence of the thing intended that there cannot be between ordinary cause and effect" (MTM: 134). This problem has led other philosophers to ask questions such as whether reasons are causes and whether my intentions cause my intentional actions (Davidson 1963).

Armstrong has an answer to this kind of objection, however, which allows him to uphold the causal theory. Beliefs, intentions and so on are mental dispositions. On Armstrong's theory, as we saw in Chapter 5, to have a disposition is to be in some categorical state that, in suitable circumstances, will cause the manifestation. And while there may be an analytic connection between the disposition (specified as a disposition) and its manifestation, there is not an analytic connection between the categorical basis of that disposition and its manifestation even though, as we saw, the disposition and its categorical basis are identical. What we must have in this case, therefore, is one and the same state that can be picked out in either dispositional terms, which makes essential reference to its manifestation, or in categorical terms, which does not make essential reference to its manifestation. The connection between the categorical state and the manifestation is contingent only and there is no objection, therefore, to the positing of a causal relation between the two (MTM: 134).

Mental states can, therefore, be causes of our behaviour, as seemed intuitive in the first place. My intentions can cause my intentional actions. But the reason this is plausible is because the workings and mechanisms of my mind are to an extent hidden from me. I can know that I have an intention to raise my arm without knowing the causal mechanism involved in my doing so. I have no idea, just from introspecting on the contents of my own mind, what categorical state is the cause of my arm rising. I know that state only as an intention. I do not know it as a physical, categorical base for the disposition. According to central-state materialism, however, that is what, as a matter of fact, my intention really is. While my mental states are identical to physical states, usually in my brain, no materialist has ever claimed that this could be known through introspection alone. The materialist is effectively, therefore, rejecting certain key Cartesian claims about the mind. Cartesians typically uphold a thesis known as *transparency*, which is that everything in my mind can be known by me. Materialists hold that many parts of the mind may be hidden from introspection. A causal account of the mind is offered but where such causal mechanisms are hidden.

This point explains away one frequently raised objection to materialism. When I look inside my own mind, I do not find physical states. I find only my thoughts and experiences. So how can the mind really be a physical thing? In answer to this, Armstrong (1968) raises a seemingly obscure reference to the Headless Woman illusion. This is a carnival trick in which a woman stands in front of a black background wearing a black cloth over and around her head. From the lack of a perception of a head, our minds move to the perception of a lack of a head. Clearly this is not a valid inference, but one that we are inclined nevertheless to draw. Armstrong thinks things are the same in respect of the physical states of our minds. We introspect and cannot find physical states in our minds. But it would then be invalid to infer that we had seen that our minds were non-physical.

Contingency and identity

There are a number of outstanding problems and possible objections to a materialist theory of the mind. It is Armstrong's contention that they can be dealt with adequately such that the materialist theory remains tenable. It was suggested that an adequate theory of mind

a. should allow for the logical possibility of disembodied existence.

If minds are identical with brains, how can disembodied existence be possible? According to Armstrong, however, the theory is indeed compatible with the logical possibility of disembodied existence. While it was claimed that mental states were identical with brain states, this was not taken to be a logically necessary truth. The only necessity in the theory is in the causal theory of mind, which Armstrong takes to be analytically true. But the truth that brain states play that causal role, are the categorical bases of behaviour, is only an empirical and allegedly contingent truth. It is at least logically possible that spirits play the appropriate causal role, although as a matter of empirical fact they do not. Therefore, while it is false that there is disembodied existence, it is only contingently false, hence it remains logically possible (MTM: 91).

It was also said that an acceptable theory of mind

b. should not treat mental happenings as capable of independent existence.

The central-state theory will indeed not allow mental states independent existence. A mental state is (the *is* of identity) a physical state apt for bringing about behaviour. It will, therefore, need to be a state of something that is able to behave. It must be a *state* of something rather than something itself, capable of existing on its own.

There is, nevertheless, now a tension between these points. The former suggests the contingency of identity; the latter suggests there must be something more than contingency. What is Armstrong's view and is it tenable? Many people have thought that Armstrong offers the wrong answer here. He thinks that while the mind and brain are identical, they are only contingently so. He takes it that there are other, uncontroversial cases of contingent identity statements. That the mind is the brain or is the central nervous system should be compared, on Armstrong's theory, to these cases. He assumes that little argument is required to establish this:

> If there is anything certain in philosophy, it is certain that "the mind is the brain" is not a logically necessary truth. When Aristotle said that the brain was nothing but an organ for keeping the body cool, he was certainly not guilty of denying a necessary truth. His mistake was an empirical one. So if it is true that the

> mind is the brain, a model must be found among contingent iden-
> tity statements. We must compare the statement to "The morn-
> ing star is the evening star" or "The gene is the DNA molecule",
> or some other contingent assertion of identity.   (MTM: 76–7)

After Armstrong had published this book, however, the topic of
identity was rethought by Kripke, with an objection to the mind–
brain identity thesis partly in view. If we have a genuine identity,
then we have but a single thing named in two ways. But then how
could this one thing have been two separate things? How is that even
a possibility? It is now standard to speak of some terms as being rigid
designators, which are terms that designate always the same thing
(some like to say that they designate the same thing in all possible
worlds). Names are usually taken to designate rigidly, while if I
designate using a description, I designate non-rigidly. "The next
person to enter my room" could refer to different people in different
situations (or in different worlds). But when I designate using a
name, such as David Armstrong, I always refer to that same thing.
The upshot of this, contrary to Armstrong's analysis, is that "the
morning star is the evening star" would now usually be judged as a
necessary truth. It may be a truth knowable only *a posteriori*, after
scientific investigation, but Kripke has shown that there can be
necessary *a posteriori* truths. Some call these metaphysical necessities. They are necessary but their necessity does not spring simply
from logic. It springs, rather, from the way the world is.

It is then arguable that if materialism really is a claim about
identity, then mind and brain could not be distinct. But this is to say
that it is a necessary truth that the mind and the brain are identical.
Disembodied existence is then not even a possibility. Mind and brain
are either identical, and necessarily so, or not necessarily so and so
not really identical. However, Armstrong still denies the force of the
objection:

> Given the truth of the Causal theory, however, when a mental
> state is identified with a physical state the physical description is
> a *non-rigid* designator of that state, that is, one that fails to pick
> out a mental state "in every possible world". Kripke's argument
> only holds for *rigid* designators.   (MTM: xiv)

There are still problems here. Can it really be maintained that the
physical description of the state refers non-rigidly? Is the point not
supposed to be that *C-fibre firing* designates the same *physical state*

in all possible worlds? Is not the claimed identity supposed to be between one physical rigidly designated state and one mental rigidly designated state? If it is, then Kripke's objection holds.

Suppose, on the other hand, that Kripke's objection does not hold and Armstrong is right that the same mental-state term can pick out different physical states in other worlds. But then what of the original proposed identity? In what way are these two states really identical if it is possible that they come apart? Their association seems to be either contingent, in which case they are not identical, or they are identical and their association is one of necessity. Lewis, however, comes to Armstrong's aid on this point and rebuts the charge (Lewis 1994: 303–4). Pain would still be pain whatever physical state realized it, as long as that state was one that filled the pain-role. That is his intuition, at least. And the principle of recombination suggests that anything can go with anything so why should pain always be the same thing in every world? "Pain" would then designate only non-rigidly and contingent identifications would be permissible in at least these instances. But this remains a contentious issue.

Intentionality and consciousness

A further objection to any materialist theory of the mind is that a purely physical account of persons cannot account adequately for the special mental phenomena of intentionality and consciousness.

A purely physical account may be all well and good from a third-person perspective on other people's minds. But when it comes to our own, we know that there is a first-person perspective that looks quite different to us. I know of pains not just as the causes of my crying out but also as feelings that are intrinsically painful. I know that pleasurable sensations have an intrinsically enjoyable feel. I also know that thoughts are not just causes of my behaviour but also that they are a form of inner experience, as ineffable as it is, that can only be known from the first-person perspective. The problem of consciousness has been nicely captured by Nagel (1974). Nagel asks what it is like to be a bat. We might know every physical fact about a bat, through dissection and close examination. In particular, we could look at its brain and all the parts it uses for sensing. But a bat is able to "see" the world using a form of sonar, emitting a high-pitched shriek and knowing the distance of objects by the time it takes to receive the echo back. This gives them a form of sensing the world, through echo-location, that we simply do not know. Even if we know all the physical facts, we would still not know this "subjective fact" of what it is like to be a bat. What this suggests is that there are facts of experience in addition to the physical facts. How, then, can physicalism be a complete account of the mind?

Armstrong's solution to the problem of consciousness is simple:

> I suggest that consciousness is no more than awareness (perception) of inner mental states by the person whose states they are. ... If this is so then consciousness is simply a further mental state, a state "directed" towards the original inner states.
>
> (MTM: 94)

This further mental state then receives the same treatment as all the others. It is a state apt for the production of behaviour (for more, see *Consciousness and Causality*).

Ryle had been unconvincing, however, when he came to such subjects as mental images. Does Armstrong do better? Suppose I imagine myself being presented with the Nobel Prize for Literature. Is it not possible for me to conjure up some suitable image that exists in my mind only, and not in reality, of some important person handing me the award? Can I not picture all other sorts of situations, including memories of past events that actually occurred to me? I once saw a car crash, for instance, and can picture it now in my mind. Ryle's attempt to analyse such claims purely in terms of behaviour was unconvincing because it seemed to deny what we all know, through introspection. Armstrong tries to develop a more convincing account, though still one that remains purely physicalist. Mental images are like perceptions. We will all agree on this although we may disagree over how like perceptions mental images are. Some have tried to exploit the point that perceptions seem more vivid and lively than mental images. But the problem here is that I might sometimes perceive in near darkness or in a fog where my perception is not vivid at all. Armstrong takes a different approach. His account of perception is that it consists in belief acquisition. The having of mental images can then be likened to "idle" perceptions. They resemble the acquiring of beliefs but they are not caused directly by the environment, as in the case of perception. Indeed, they are often caused just by an act of will. Because of this, they are "of all perceptual events, ... the most completely divorced from belief" (MTM: 301). Genuine perceptions and mental images are distinguished, therefore, by the latter being neither caused through stimulation of the senses, nor involving the inclination to belief (MTM: 303).

While this shows that there is no special problem of mental images, once one has a theory of perception, it might yet be wondered whether this is a credible theory of perception. In saying that perception is mere belief-acquisition, or the gaining of a disposition to believe, is Armstrong also denying what introspection tells us: that there are pictures in our minds when we see things? This need not be the case, however. Armstrong is not denying that there is a central, mental state involved in perception. Indeed, a correct perceptual process will involve the causing of such a state: a state that can go on to be a cause of behaviour. This mental state may well be one that we believe involves pictures in the mind (or sounds, smells, etc. in the mind). What is difficult to grasp, if anything, is the claim that this mental state is really – is identical with – some physical state. It is some state of our brains or central nervous system that seems to us, first-personally, to be a mental image. The claim means that the way we understand our own minds does not uncover all its aspects. But this is a conclusion Armstrong thinks correct, as we have already seen. And we have also seen in Chapter 7 that the argument in favour of a direct realist theory is stronger than one that posits mental images as real entities in the mind, as the representative theory of perception would have it. Through suchlike arguments, and careful analysis, Armstrong thinks that a physicalist account of consciousness is, after all, a realistic contender.

The other chief problem area for the mind is intentionality. Intentionality is often presented as a mysterious and problematic phenomenon. The possibility of a purely physical account of the mind appears to exacerbate the problem. With his causal theory of mind, however, Armstrong seeks to demystify intentionality and show it not to have any special magical qualities. Indeed the features of intentionality, correctly described, are perfectly compatible with physicalism. Physicalism might actually illuminate the problem.

It will be recalled that mental states are said to be directed towards intentional objects, where such an object might be a proposition in the case of belief, another person in the case of some emotions, or just ordinary physical objects in our environment in the case of perception. There seems to be a special power of the mind to "point out" beyond itself, or be "about" something else. Physical things do not seem to have this power, which suggests a possible criterion by which we might distinguish the mental and the physical (Brentano 1874).

Certainly there can be some pointing, in physical cases, as when an arrow drawn on a map may point to the city of Nottingham, but there is no sense in which the arrow is "about" Nottingham. Furthermore, intentionality permits a phenomenon known as "intentional inexistence", where a mental state can be about something that does not really exist. I may fear a burglar in my living room, for instance, when really there is nothing there except a cat knocking over a vase. My fear can be real enough in such a case, however, and it is fear of a burglar, even though there is no such burglar. In contrast, an arrow cannot point to something that is not there. If there really is a sharp distinction between the mental and physical in this respect, then that would make the prospects look bad for a physical theory of mind. Such a theory would have to make a claim that purely physical states were, after all, capable of intentionality.

In what Armstrong calls "the central chapter of the whole book" (MTM: 245), he tries to an extent to deflate this mysterious power of intentionality. His aim is to show that sense can be made, in a purely physical theory of mind, of states being directed to or about their intentional objects. But instead of saying that the state is about some other thing, the talk is of states apt for being caused by situations in a perceiver's environment or own body, and of states apt for discriminatory or selective behaviour towards such situations in the perceiver's environment or body (MTM: 269). Essentially, Armstrong is aiming to show that what is really needed is a correct causal theory of perception and will (intending, motives, and so on), which will then be able to account for everything that is more traditionally "explained" in terms of this special quality of mental intentionality.

The account becomes complicated, however, because, as Armstrong's analysis proceeds, it emerges that perception and intending can only be explained together. Perception should be understood in terms of the acquisition of belief and knowledge. But to have a belief is to have a disposition. To understand what disposition it is, we have to be able to say what behaviour would count as the manifestation of the belief. The behaviour that counts is only the purposive behaviour I have towards something. I have perceived that there is a cat in front of me when I am disposed to purposely stroke it if I want to comfort it. Stepping on the cat accidentally would not count as purposive behaviour so would not count as a manifestation of belief acquired through perception. To fill out the account of perception, therefore, we need to invoke purposes for a correct account of belief. But, then, how can we give an account of purposes that does not involve perception? If I have a purpose, I need to be able to perceive when it has been achieved and also when my behaviour needs to be modified or corrected so that I can achieve it (MTM: 251). Purpose and perception, it turns out, cannot be defined independently, "because they are two sides of one hugely complex process" that enables "goal-seeking behaviour" (MTM: 252).

Instead of the invocation of intentionality as some inexplicable, almost magical, power of the mind, therefore, what we need are naturalistic accounts of the various human phenomena that we label mental. If we go though accounts of perception, knowledge, belief and the will, we find that, with some work (see MTM: chs 7–11), naturalistic accounts are available. Understanding the mind in causal terms, as an interconnected series of causal processes, allows us to understand all the phenomena that Brentano and his followers referred to as intentional. The slightly surprising consequence of this is that, in at least one place, Armstrong subscribes to the view that there is physical intentionality (MTM: xvii–xviii). This is surprising because in another context he has resisted Molnar's (2003) physical intentionality account of dispositions. But Armstrong, in offering a materialist theory of the mind, is of course saying that where there is intentionality, it is a property of, or ability of, a physical being.

In many ways, a materialist theory of the mind is the greatest task facing Armstrong's naturalistic programme. But at the very least, he has shown that it is not absurd to say that the mind is identical with certain parts of the body. More than that, he may have shown that this is the most attractive explanation of the mind.

Chapter 9

Knowledge and belief

We saw in Chapter 8 what consciousness is and how a naturalist like Armstrong might account for it. Traditionally, philosophers like Descartes and Hume thought of our minds like theatres of consciousness. All the contents of our minds were visible and transparent to us. Hume had this view of beliefs, describing them as vivid ideas associated with a present impression (1739: I, pt III, sec. 7). An impression is always a conscious experience, so beliefs as such are always conscious occurrences. When I believe that today is Wednesday, for instance, it is a conscious event in my mind, having a beginning, duration and an end.

The inadequacies of this account have been known for some time, but we saw that Ryle offered the classic demolition. Our ascription of belief, and understanding of the way beliefs work, just does not fit the model of beliefs as conscious episodes. If I consider how many beliefs a person may have at present, I would expect that they run at least into the thousands and probably hundreds of thousands. I doubt very much that anyone could be consciously thinking of so many different things simultaneously. Indeed it is most common that a person entertains only one thought at a time but it would be a very strange theory of belief that declared each person to have at most one belief at a time. Very often people are asleep, unconscious, or have their minds focused on an experience. We may grant that they are thinking of no beliefs consciously at those times but do we want to say that they have no beliefs at all at those times? Again, belief ascription just does not behave that way.

Suppose you ask whether I believe that Tromsø is in the Arctic Circle or that zebras have black and white stripes. These are indeed two things that I believe. But then you ask me for how long I have had those beliefs. In the first case: for a few years, since I discovered Tromsø in my atlas. In the second case: for many years, since I first learnt about zebras at school and saw them on television. I have held these beliefs continuously for years but it is of course psychologically and phenomenologically vastly implausible that I have entertained those beliefs continuously in my consciousness for those years. It is also implausible to say that I held these beliefs only at the times I consciously entertained them. Did I believe zebras had black and white stripes for two minutes in 1969, then not again until I visited a zoo in 1973, and then not at all for another ten years? To say so would look like a clear confusion of belief with something else: some conscious experience that may be associated with my belief but is not constitutive of it.

This chapter deals mainly with Armstrong's epistemology as developed in *Belief, Truth and Knowledge*. This book was an attempt to provide a theory of belief that would avoid some of the absurdities of the Humean view, which have just been exposed. Such ideas first made their appearance in Part Two of *A Materialist Theory of the Mind*.

Natural beliefs

Ryle's alternative account was, as we have already seen, to say that beliefs (and various other mental phenomena) were not conscious states, indeed not states at all. They were dispositions: dispositions to be in various states. When I believe that today is Wednesday, I am disposed to do certain things, such as attend the weekly research seminar at the university, start making plans for the weekend and preparing the Wednesday night pasta. We have already seen the way in which Armstrong finds this view unsatisfactory. But this is not so much a problem with the account of the mind as dispositional. To a large extent Armstrong agrees with that. The disagreement is not over the issue of whether there are mental dispositions but over the nature of those dispositions. Armstrong criticizes Ryle's phenomenalist account on the grounds that he has no truthmaker for the disposition ascription. More precisely, Ryle understands a disposition ascription to be nothing more than affirming as true some such conditional as "if A, then B". Ryle has no account at all of why such conditionals are true and it looks as if he could have no account because he explicitly denies that dispositions are states (Ryle 1949: 43).

We have seen in earlier chapters that Armstrong's solution to this problem is to allow that dispositions are states. To have a disposition is to have a certain non-relational state, what he elsewhere calls a categorical basis, that makes it true that if A, then B, where A is the stimulus and background conditions and B is the manifestation. This categorical basis is to be discovered by empirical science and, in Armstrong's view, is to be identified with the disposition, even though it is only a contingent identification (BTK: 16). This claim is a controversial one.

Armstrong is thus in a position to account for beliefs as dispositions, but the account is not entirely straightforward. There are some *prima facie* differences between beliefs and other, non-mental dispositions (BTK: 16–21). Dispositions such as fragility and solubility need some stimulus in order to manifest. The fragile thing has to be knocked or struck to break. The soluble substance needs to be placed in liquid to dissolve. But beliefs at least appear to just manifest themselves without any stimulus. Second, ordinary dispositions have but a single kind of manifestation, such as solubility manifesting itself in dissolving and only in dissolving. But beliefs seem capable of manifesting in lots of different ways, as does my belief that it is Wednesday. A third significant difference is that beliefs appear to have a structure, with which we can find nothing in dispositions to correspond. The belief that the cat is on the mat is a different belief from the belief that the mat is on the cat. They have the same constituents but are different beliefs because of the ways those constituents are structured. It is not clear that there is anything in a non-mental disposition that corresponds to this kind of structuring that we find in belief. A dispositional account of belief is therefore left with work to do.

Let us begin by considering the manifestations of beliefs. A distinction can be drawn between the manifestations of a belief that are voluntary, or by one's own will, and those that are beyond our control. Suppose I learn that a certain lady finds me attractive. I may then blush in her presence. The blushing could be considered a manifestation of my belief but it is not done on purpose. In contrast, there are some manifestations that are also actions because they are performed intentionally. Armstrong calls these *expressions* of my beliefs (BTK: 24).

What will count as such an expression? If I assert "today is Wednesday" it seems to be a clear-cut case. Beliefs can be expressed linguistically. But must they always be expressed linguistically? There is a view, against which Armstrong argues, that one may hold a belief only if one is a language-user with the requisite concepts. Armstrong does not name his opponent but may have in mind a view many took from Wittgenstein, that the limits of my language are the limits of my world (Wittgenstein 1921: §5.6). Thus I would only be able to believe that today is Wednesday if I were able to understand the words that express that belief. Contrary to this view, however, Armstrong accepts that there can be non-linguistic belief and that the linguistic expression of belief is just one kind of expression that there may be. A dog that digs for a bone believes that it has buried it there (BTK: 25). Because a dog has no (sophisticated) language, Wittgenstein doubts that a dog could have a belief that his master will return the day after tomorrow (Wittgenstein 1953: 174). But Armstrong thinks there are plausible circumstances in which one could ascribe such a belief to a dog. Suppose one dog is used to his master leaving him for a day at a time. The next day this dog becomes agitated and expectant, waiting by the door and listening for footsteps on the path. Another dog is accustomed to being left for two days at a time. This dog does not wait by the door until two days have passed. So when the master leaves, it is fair, according to Armstrong, to ascribe the belief that his master will return the day after tomorrow. Armstrong admits that "the belief involved is quite simple. It is hardly comparable with a dog's believing the truth of Goldbach's conjecture [that every even number is the sum of two primes]". But, startlingly, "it may be that one could work up through a series of ever more complex cases culminating in the providing of behavioural but non-linguistic expression of beliefs in the truth of abstruse mathematical hypotheses" (BTK: 32). So a dog could indeed believe Goldbach's conjecture.

There is a basic theory of belief acquisition that drives Armstrong's view of expression. One view is that we acquire beliefs when we acquire and use language to communicate our thoughts. But if we recall Armstrong's account of perception from Chapter 7, it will be remembered that he thinks perception consists in belief acquisition, or acquisition of a disposition to believe. Animals and small children have some form of perception and thereby may acquire beliefs even if they are incapable of expressing them linguistically. There is no reason, therefore, why Armstrong should give a privileged status to the *linguistic* expression of belief.

Belief states as maps

What are the objects of belief: the things that are believed? A standard answer is that it is propositions that are believed. But Armstrong has yet to find a credible account of propositions (he will, however, have produced one by the time of his final book: see Chapter 10, p. 167). Certainly he does not see propositions as real things or objects (BTK: 46). Nevertheless, two different people may have belief states that have the same structure. It is belief structures that play the role propositions would play, therefore. The structure is not identical with what is believed but it does determine what is believed (BTK: 47).

To have a belief requires representation of the elements and representation of the relations that hold between the elements. Armstrong is happy to call both these representations *Ideas* (BTK: 51). Thus, to believe that the cat is on the mat I must have Ideas of the cat, the mat, and of the relation of *being on*. Such Ideas can map the world. Where the belief is true, they map the world correctly; where it is false, they map the world incorrectly (BTK: 54). Armstrong distinguishes Ideas from concepts, however. A concept of X is a capacity to have Ideas of the X sort (BTK: 52). I can have only one concept of X but I can have two different Ideas of X: for example, that X is round and that X is red. There are two different Ideas of X here, because there are two X-representing elements in numerically distinct belief states but there is only a single concept of X, which is the same in both instances (BTK: 51). Concepts themselves come down to selective or discriminatory capacities (BTK: 60). To have a concept of red is to be able to select red things, this capacity being caused by contact with red things.

To have a concept is to have a capacity for Ideas and to have an Idea is to have a capacity for beliefs. Nevertheless, one can entertain a belief structure without having the corresponding belief. So what is the difference between me considering that there are eight planets in the solar system and actually believing it? The difference comes down to whether we are prepared to act according to the belief structure or "map". Beliefs are like action-guiding maps (BTK: 4), which is a view that Armstrong takes from Ramsey (1929). When I merely entertain or think of a belief structure, it will not be a guide to my actions. Beliefs are thus thoughts *plus* this additional action-guiding role (BTK: 72).

An interesting anomaly for Armstrong's theory, however, is philosophy itself. Philosophical thoughts are abstract and cannot relate to action. How can I act *as if* trope theory is true? That seems absurd. Thus philosophical thoughts cannot be action-guiding. Rather than take this as a counterexample to his thesis, though, Armstrong rules that such abstract belief is only belief in a secondary sense (BTK: 66). The sense is at least secondary in that we make all the same kind of sincere linguistic expressions that we make of ordinary, non-abstract beliefs that can also be expressed non-linguisitically. Is this a persuasive way of avoiding the difficulty? Armstrong could, of course, have said that philosophical beliefs guide at least these vocal actions but a belief that guides *only* vocal actions may seem to misrepresent the theory he has developed and make belief and utterance look too close.

With Ideas of a cat, a mat and a relation of being on, it is relatively easy to see how a belief structure can be formed for the belief that the cat is on the mat. But not all beliefs can have such a simple structure. Armstrong progresses to consider the case of general beliefs, which pose a particular difficulty because they range over an infinite class of objects. How can an infinite class be represented in a map? We will come back to this in a short while but before that it will be useful to consider Armstrong's theory of knowledge.

Knowledge

An initial task in accounting for knowledge is to distinguish it from closely related phenomena such as belief and certainty. This would delineate the epistemological terrain. We can consider questions such as whether belief entails knowledge, whether knowledge entails belief, whether certainly entails knowledge, whether belief entails certainty, and so on.

There is a traditional definition of knowledge that Armstrong uses as his starting point. This is the classical tripartite definition that knowledge is justified true belief. There are in this three conditions to knowledge. To know that p, (i) p must be true, (ii) one must believe that p, and (iii) one must have good justification for believing p. The motivations for these three traditional requirements on knowledge are not hard to fathom so I will not dwell on them. The third condition is perhaps the one that needs most work to motivate. Suppose there was someone, call them the Irrational Believer, who asserted with complete conviction that the next toss of the coin would land heads. Let us assume that they act in good faith so they really do believe that the next toss will land heads. The coin is a fair one, with a head and a tail side and evenly distributed weight. It is tossed and it does indeed land heads. Did the Irrational Believer really know that it would be heads? Plausibly they did not. They believed it would land heads and it was true that it landed heads but, we think, they did not know it would be heads because they could not have had any adequate justification for their belief. The evidence pointed to a head and a tail in equal measure. We are likely, therefore, to dismiss our Irrational Believer's true belief as a lucky guess.

The tripartite definition of knowledge is attractive, therefore, but Armstrong is critical of it in a number of respects. Most significantly, he does not see that the first and third conditions are required, as they stand. The definition is not hopeless, however, and Armstrong is willing to defend the belief condition (ii), at least in its weak form. If a knows that p, a believes that p, though this is not to say that if a knows that p, a is certain that p. These claims can be expressed in the formulae $(Kap \rightarrow Bap)$ [if a knows that p, then a believes that p] and $\neg(Kap \rightarrow Cap)$ [it is not that case that if a knows that p, then a is certain that p] (BTK: 139). The belief condition has been challenged with such examples as someone knowing that their spouse is dead yet not quite believing it. But Armstrong already accepts the possibility of someone holding contradictory beliefs (BTK: 104) so he understands this as a case where Kap and Bap but also $Ba\neg p$. The case is remarkable because a believes that p and that not-p. But the case is possible because we do sometimes have contradictory beliefs that we do not bring together so do not see as contradictory.

Another case that mounts a challenge to the belief condition is the Unconfident Examinee. This is a person who is questioned on English history and produces some answers that they think are just guesses. They nevertheless get the right answers because they studied English history some time ago and forgot that they had done so. Armstrong is willing to accept that they know the answers (BTK: 146) but should we say that they do not believe them? Not according to Armstrong. Instead, this is a case where Kap with neither $KaKap$ nor $BaKap$. That is, you can know that p without knowing that you know that p and you might not even believe that you know that p. Armstrong rejects the so-called KK-principle (to know is to know that you know). Rejecting it allows that possibility of knowing that p without being certain of p.

On the evidence or justification condition (iii), which was motivated above by the case of the Irrational Believer, there is much that

155

we will need to say to make it at all plausible. We will have to say that the evidence must be conclusive and we will have to say that it is operative. I might, after all, believe p where p is true and also believe q, where q is a conclusive justification for p. But still I might not know that p as I might not "put two and two together" (BTK: 151). Miss Marple may have only the same beliefs as everyone else in the room concerning the guilty suspect. But only she is able to see that those beliefs prove the suspect's guilt conclusively. What is needed, then, is that the justification q be causally operative in *a*'s mind for q to be the justification of p for *a*.

There are even further difficulties that must be overcome for the traditional account, but one major problem is an alleged regress that emerges. For q to be a justification for *a*'s knowledge that p, q must itself be known. But then it seems that our analysis of what it is to know p will be incomplete. The analysis must employ the very same notion of knowledge – knowledge of the justification – that it is supposed to analyse. Unless I already know what knowledge is, this account will not therefore help me. And it is clear that this inadequacy of the analysis can produce a regress. Knowledge of p will be dependent on knowledge of q, which can be knowledge only if I have knowledge of r, which can be knowledge only if I have knowledge of s, and so on.

There are various responses that one could have to the apparent regress. One might use it, for instance, as the basis for scepticism: no knowledge is possible because it can never be fully justified. Descartes, in a renunciation of scepticism, sought to resolve the problem by identifying some non-inferential and self-evident knowledge. This rested on nothing else and could not be doubted, and upon it all other knowledge was purported to stand. Both these reactions are unsatisfactory for Armstrong. He rejects scepticism but looks for some firmer grounds on which to place our knowledge. Knowledge that is non-inferential would be a promising strategy but for this to be plausible we will need a credible account of such knowledge. Saying that it is "clear and distinct", as Descartes does, is inadequate. Armstrong tries to provide a firmer footing in the form of an externalist theory of non-inferential knowledge.

Externalism

Descartes's response to the problem is inadequate, among a number of other reasons, because it provides only an internal criterion of adequacy for knowledge. I am said to know something when I cannot doubt it. But not only does it seem possible to doubt everything; my own internal states do not seem a reliable guide to what I know. Instead, whether I know something ought plausibly be determined by the relations that hold between my belief states and the world. This is the idea that Armstrong develops.

Where might acceptable non-inferential knowledge be found? The likely source, as Armstrong has already argued in his work on perception, is in the simpler judgements of perception, such as that "there is a noise within earshot", "there is something red and round over there" and "there is something pressing on my body" (BTK: 163). These things can be known immediately, that is, non-inferentially, and can therefore end the regress of justification. They are unjustified, in the sense of being non-inferential, true beliefs, but count as immediate knowledge. We had best call them *simpler* perceptual judgements, instead of *simple*, as there may be no such thing as an absolutely simple perceptual atom.

What Armstrong has in mind now is a form of reliabilism, where "Knowledge is empirically reliable belief" (BTK: 159). Inferential beliefs may require further justification, or at least it seems so to begin with, but non-inferential beliefs will rest on nothing else. For them, there must be some other reason that they count as knowledge and according to a reliabilist view, it is that they are reliable. The simpler judgements of perception are empirically reliable, meaning that if I perceive a noise within earshot, there is indeed a noise within earshot. Non-inferential knowledge can then be likened to a thermometer and Armstrong sometimes calls this the *thermometer view* of non-inferential knowledge. If I have a reliable thermometer, then I know that if it gives a reading of T°, then the temperature is indeed T°. There is a true conditional that if the thermometer says T°, then it really is T°. What is the truthmaker for this conditional and why is the thermometer reliable? Here, Armstrong's account invokes laws of nature again. There is a *law-like* connection between the thermometer reading T° and the temperature really being T°. This will be so in virtue of the properties of the thermometer, of course. Let us call the relevant property or set of properties H. We have already seen (Chapter 3) that laws of nature are best understood as relations between universals. The law-like connection, in this case, would then be a relation holding between H and temperature T°. The connection between H and T° ensures that whenever the thermometer reads T°, it is T°.

We can now say something exactly analogous in the case of non-inferential knowledge. Of it, Armstrong says the following:

> What makes such a belief a case of knowledge? My suggestion is that there must be a *law-like connection* between the state of affairs Bap and the state of affairs that makes "p" true such that, given Bap, it must be the case that p. (BTK: 166)

In epigrammatic form, Armstrong also states the view as: "Knowledge is a state of mind which as a matter of law-like necessity ensures that p" (BTK: 189). If someone holds a non-inferential belief concerning their simpler perceptions, then Armstrong's view is that this can constitute knowledge. From their belief that p, it follows that p simply because there is a law-like relation connecting the belief that p and p itself or, rather, the state of affairs that is the truth-maker of the proposition "p" that is believed.

There are, of course, limits to this reliability and cases where an individual may have a simple perceptual belief that p, when p is not in fact the case. But this does not challenge the theory as such cases can be explained by the thermometer model. There are some bad or faulty thermometers. These may systematically give the wrong reading. But they do so because they fail to instantiate the relevant property H that all the reliable thermometers have. The law-like relation connecting H and temperature still holds. (We know from Armstrong's account of laws that the law connecting H with temperature will be a functional law, which really is a set of connections holding between H and specific temperatures such as T°.) The faulty thermometer does not have H so is not a counterexample. One might try to doubt the thermometer model on the ground that some person might have a simpler judgement of perception that p, although p is not the case. Perhaps this person has a form of synaesthesia and judges that "there is a noise within earshot" when really there is something red and round nearby that they misperceive. But this person is really like the faulty thermometer, failing to instantiate the property H that forms the reliable connection through being nomologically related correctly to the world. That there is synaesthesia does not show, therefore, that non-inferential judgements are unreliable in general, including those of non-synaesthetes.

The themometer model also shows how justified true belief that is not knowledge is possible: the so-called Gettier cases (after Gettier 1963). A faulty thermometer may, on occasion, give the correct reading, just as a stopped clock can tell the right time twice a day. My thermometer might be stuck on 20°, in which case it gives the right reading when the temperature is in fact 20°. This would be analogous to a justified true belief that fell short of knowledge. Similarly, I may ingest some bad gravy and begin to hallucinate a noise within earshot. It may be true that there is a noise within earshot and I believe there is such a noise with justification: I have a simpler perceptual experience. But I am like a faulty thermometer. I do not instantiate the H-property that makes my beliefs reliable. Instead I have some other property, H′, that is incompatible with H, that renders my non-inferential perceptual beliefs unreliable.

More on non-inferential knowledge

Some points can be drawn out of this account. First we can note that the connection between a belief state and the world is only *law-like*. It is not, strictly speaking, a law of nature itself. In *Belief, Truth and Knowledge*, Armstrong does not clarify why the relation is only law-like rather than fully lawful. It was, of course, another four years before he would present his worked-out account of laws of nature. Indeed, this gap in the account may have led Armstrong to concentrate next on the metaphysics of laws. But it is not hard to see why, in the light of the theory of laws that Armstrong did present, this connection could not be fully lawful. The connection cannot be a law because its instances cannot be causal. B*a*p does not cause p (strictly, the truthmaker of "p", which is henceforth taken as read) so there is no natural necessitation running from the belief to the thing believed. To be knowledge: "a belief must ensure (not, of course, causally ensure) its own truth" (BTK: 209). The reliabilist claim is simply that whenever B*a*p, then p. It would be absurd to claim that B*a*p standardly caused p. To grant that would be to grant a rather extreme form of idealism. There are special cases where it might happen, however, such as when a child's belief that they will get a certain toy for Christmas causes his kind parents to get him that toy for Christmas (BTK: 180–81). We simply cannot generalize from such a special case to all cases of belief, however. The instances of a law, as we saw in Chapter 3, are particular causal transactions. So if B*a*p does not typically cause p, then the general connection between B*a*p-types of states and p-type states, is not a law of nature. But what more can we then say about the law-like connection that the account invokes? Is there something in the world that explains this correlation?

Given the naturalistic view to which Armstrong subscribes, were there to be any causality involved, it would almost certainly go the other way. *a*'s belief that p will be caused by p being the case. Something in the world must cause our simpler perceptual judgement. This will undoubtedly be the case and we can, of course, fall back on Armstrong's theory of perception and sensation, as presented in Chapter 7. But even here we will have to complicate the story to an extent. We would certainly not want to say that if p then B*a*p. That would have us believing every truth; that is, it would make us omniscient. So Armstrong rules this out and, in so doing, draws attention to the limitations of the thermometer model. There is a symmetry in the operation of the thermometer. When it reads T°, it is indeed T°. But also, when it is T°, the thermometer reads T°. The case of knowledge does not support an analogue of the latter conditional. It may be the case that p without B*a*p.

We may, though, be able to explain why some states of affairs cause simpler perceptual judgements in us and some do not. I can hardly be directly perceptually affected by some quiet sound on the other side of the world, for instance. Some proximity might be a factor we begin with. But the connection between B*a*p and p is law-like, according to Armstrong, because it exhibits some of the features we often ascribe to laws. The connection can be empirically investigated and tested. We can experiment on the thermometer and find why it will be T° when it reads T°. Why it should always be p when B*a*p will be a far more complicated thing to investigate, test and explain. But it is possible in principle that we do so (BTK: 168). The connection between B*a*p and p supports counterfactuals such as that if p had not been the case, B*a*p would not have been the case. And while the connection that brings B*a*p into existence is not simply a causal one, it is nevertheless a natural and perfectly objective relation (BTK: 169). The key thing is, then, that this relation be a natural connection that ensures the reliability of B*a*p for non-inferential knowledge. This connection may not be simply the nomological relation, but that does not matter for this account.

This account of the law-like basis of reliabilism shows that the truth condition of the classic tripartite definition of knowledge is redundant. The traditional account defined knowledge as justified true belief. But examination of the notion of justification showed that a regress would be produced unless we could find beliefs that counted as knowledge without justification. The reliabilist account that Armstrong offers tells us that if a has some non-inferential belief, such as that c is J, then a has some property H and there is a law-like connection such that if anything instantiates H, and believes that anything is J, then that thing is J. This is a complicated idea so a more formal account may be preferable to some readers. Armstrong's semi-formalizations is as follows:

$(\exists H)$ [Ha & there is a law-like connection in nature such that (x) (y) {if Hx, then (if BxJy, then Jy)}] (BTK: 182)

Justified belief, or non-inferentially reliable belief, will be true in any case, and will count as knowledge in any case. Not only does the account offer a necessary condition of knowledge; it is also sufficient for knowledge as there does not seem to be anything else we would need to add to this to get knowledge (BTK: 184). On this reliabilist picture, therefore, one does not need to add a separate truth condition.

Inferential knowledge

Armstrong has ended a potential regress of justification by vindicating non-inferential knowledge, which can be known without further justification. But what should be said of inferential knowledge? Clearly some knowledge does depend on other knowledge. One belief may be based on others.

Armstrong had already laid the groundwork for a theory of inferential knowledge in his treatment of general belief, earlier in the same book. One belief can be disposed to create and sustain another and when it does so it is a reason for the second belief (BTK: 88). Reasons thus have a causal and dispositional nature. Such dispositions take the form of general principles, such as that $\forall x \ (Fx \rightarrow Gx)$ [all that is F is G]. According to Armstrong, general beliefs like this are just dispositions to infer from one thing to another. For example, I may believe that x's head is cut off. This generates and sustains my belief that x is dead. My belief that x's head is cut off will generate and sustain this belief for any value of x. The disposition to cause this further belief is thus constitutive of my general belief that *all decapitated are dead* (BTK: 89). Armstrong began with an idea of beliefs as maps. We should now restrict this, however, and say that only beliefs about particular states of affairs should be compared to maps. General beliefs cannot be so simply mapped because they concern open classes of a potentially infinite extent. But general beliefs can instead be understood as dispositions to extend the map or to create sustaining relations between one part of the map and another (BTK: 99), for instance, a disposition for the particular belief that *c* is decapitated to sustain the further particular belief that *c* is dead.

Inferential knowledge should then be understood on the following model. If one knows that p on the sole basis of evidence q, one must believe that p, know that q, and know q to be a conclusive reason for believing p. We now understand that the latter clause amounts to q causally sustaining the belief that p or, in other words, exemplifying a general principle from q to p. Effectively, this is a disposition to move from belief to belief (BTK: 199).

How, though, do we *know* that q is a conclusive reason for believing p? How can we know the general principle? If this knowledge is to rest always on further knowledge, then we encounter the regress of justification again. At some point, therefore, we will have to know of some general principle non-inferentially. How is that possible when all my experiences are of particular matters of fact, and the account of non-inferential knowledge presented thus far explains knowledge only of particular matters of fact?

To answer this, Armstrong extends his account of general belief to general knowledge. General beliefs were understood as dispositions to pass from belief to belief. A general belief is a belief-transmission belief. Non-inferential general knowledge is then understood as a disposition to pass from knowledge to knowledge, or as knowledge transmission (BTK: 202). The same externalist and reliabilist account can then be given of knowledge of general principles. To know a general principle, such as that $\forall x \, (Fx \to Gx)$, one must first believe it, which, as we have seen, is to have a disposition. And, second, if this disposition is manifested, then if one knows that Fx, then one knows that Gx. This is, therefore, merely a more complicated version of the account of particular knowledge, where to have a reliable belief that p is to know that p, and thus (pleonastically) for p to be true. Here one can be in a position to reliably believe a general principle that $\forall x \, (Fx \to Gx)$, and thus to know $\forall x \, (Fx \to Gx)$. Armstrong was vague about what non-inferential knowledge we had in the particular case and in the general case he is even more vague. That question is, after all, an empirical matter. But it may be plausible to suggest that the "relatively simple logical necessities and principles of scientific method" (BTK: 204) could be general principles known non-inferentially.

In a roundabout way, this line of reasoning suggests that the distinction with which we started, between inferential and non-inferential knowledge, breaks down under analysis. Inferential reasoning rests on general principles but unless we are to admit an infinite regress of justification, such general principles will at some point have to be known non-inferentially. Armstrong presents an account of how a general principle could be known non-inferentially and hazards a guess at which general principles are so known. To avoid the regress, therefore, inferential knowledge must rest ultimately on some non-inferential knowledge. This brings home a major weakness of the classical definition of knowledge as *justified* true belief. The justification of a true belief must always be some further knowledge. Similarly, inferential knowledge would always have to rest on some further knowledge. For any case of knowledge, therefore, it must at some point invoke knowledge that has no further justification, that is, non-inferential knowledge. That is why the key idea of Armstrong's theory is the externalist/reliabilist account of non-inferential knowledge. It may be unsatisfactory or seem obscure in some places, but if it is not right we need something that will do the same or a similar job if we are to have a theory of knowledge that has any plausibility at all.

Armstrong's account of knowledge contains many complications, clauses and caveats. I have attempted here to provide only an overview of his theory and for the sake of brevity I have had to pass over or ignore many of the complications. Consulting the original work will be worthwhile to the reader, not least because these issues are among the most important in epistemology. Armstrong offers an alternative to some engrained ways of thinking that have landed philosophers in difficulties over many centuries. A new perspective seems well worth considering, therefore, and it is one that fits with Armstrong's overarching naturalistic project. Belief must be disabused of its Cartesian explanation and knowledge must be freed from the shackles that scepticism would impose. A naturalistic, externalist and reliabilist account is far more promising than many of the other options.

Truth

Armstrong's theory of knowledge and belief is set in the context of a certain understanding of truth. I have purposefully avoided the subject until this point because truth, or the theory of truthmaking, has a chapter of its own. A brief statement of Armstrong's view as it stood in 1973 will, however, be of some use here. It certainly contains the seeds that would much later grow into the book *Truth and Truthmakers*.

Armstrong is inclined towards a version of the correspondence theory of truth (BTK: 113), where propositions or belief-state types correspond or fail to correspond with reality – beliefs that p will be true when p is true, which is to say when p corresponds with reality. But this correspondence is not simply a one-to-one correspondence. The relation between truth bearers and the world is not as simple as an unqualified statement of the correspondence theory might suggest. The relation of truth bearer to world might be one–one but it could also be one–many and many–one. This leads Armstrong to draw the surprising conclusion that the correspondence relation is not of the same sort in every case (BTK: 133). As we saw in his work on universals, a relation cannot vary its adicity. It must be identical in every instance; that is, it must always relate the same number of terms. If the relation of truth to world can be one–one, one–many or many–one, then we must conclude that there are many different correspondence relations involved.

It is worth noting in passing that Armstrong proposes here a solution to the problem of negative truth. Negative truths are true propositions that say something is not, for example that there is not a hippopotamus in the room or that this pen is not blue. This solution is in essence the same as he will later offer in a more fully worked-out version (see Chapter 10, p. 176). <There is not a hippopotamus in the room> (with the angled brackets marking off the truth-bearer) will be true in virtue of the room in question and its entire contents and properties. This seems to be an attempt to reach towards a general fact, which he will indeed later go on to postulate. He says here that this will avoid us having to posit negative facts (BTK: 132), although Armstrong does not at this stage realize or acknowledge that a general fact is a kind of negative fact.

Given the externalist and reliabilist account of knowledge developed in *Belief, Truth and Knowledge*, truth is the least important of those three related concepts so does not receive an extended treatment. Truth does not have a major role in our theory of knowledge. But we still must understand what truth is if we are to understand the claim that reliable belief is true. In Chapter 10, however, the subject of truth will be considered for its own sake.

Chapter 10
Truthmaking

What is it for a truth to be true? What makes it true? This is one of the oldest problems in philosophy and one to which Armstrong turned in *Truth and Truthmakers*. His concern was not with the epistemological question of how we know some particular statement or utterance to be true or false, but in what truth itself and falsehood itself actually consist. Armstrong's concern was therefore with the metaphysics of truth.

As Armstrong is a realist and naturalist, we are not surprised to find that he opts for something akin to the correspondence theory of truth: *"propositions correspond or fail to correspond to reality"* (T&T: 16). The correspondence theory has faced much criticism throughout its history: see for example Lewis (2001) but also M. David's (2004) reply. Critics of the theory have demanded that it be made more substantial. What are the two things that enter into correspondence, what is the correspondence relation, and how are these two different things able to correspond in the required way? (For more on the theory, see Engel 2002.) Truthmaker theory is an attempt to answer these questions and make the correspondence theory substantial. It is, however, a characteristically Australian take on the correspondence theory, which Armstrong credits to C. B. Martin's residence at the University of Adelaide.

The requirement for truthmakers has been encountered already in Chapters 5 and 8, on dispositions and the materialist theory of mind. Ryle's phenomenalist theory of dispositions was inadequate because there were no truthmakers for disposition ascriptions. Brain states could, however, be truthmakers for mental disposition ascriptions, taking us to Armstrong's central-state materialism. Although *Truth and Truthmakers* is Armstrong's most recent book, therefore, it is plausible to suggest that Armstrong was a truthmaker theorist for decades before its publication. As Armstrong says, Martin introduced him to the idea in the late 1950s (T&T: 1) and he invokes the principle in various places throughout his work: ToU: 157; WLN: 77; U: 88, for example.

How truthmaking works

The idea that truths are made true by something in the world has at least *prima facie* appeal. Whether it is finally acceptable will depend on whether that opening intuition can be developed into a robust and defensible philosophical theory. *Truth and Truthmakers* in intended to provide this and I now look at how Armstrong builds on the opening intuition.

A first question, if we are to take the intuition seriously, might be how truth can be *made*. For this, we need to understand the nature of the truth-bearers, the nature of the truthmakers and the nature of the truthmaking relation that may hold between them.

Armstrong understands the bearers of truth to be propositions: a truth is really a true proposition and a falsehood is really a false proposition (T&T 12). But what is a proposition? Russell (1903) and many others have thought that truth-bearers cannot simply be things like sentences, utterances or speech acts because it is possible to state the same thing in many different ways. What is true or false is understood to be the content of the sentence or statement, with the sentence or statement itself true or false derivatively in virtue of expressing or signifying that content. This could lead to a problem if propositions take on a life of their own. They could become eternal Platonic objects that exist whether or not they are expressed or thought about, and therefore whether or not any human beings exist at all. We have already seen, however, that Armstrong is in general against Platonic objects. Universals, and laws of nature *qua* universals, exist only in their instances. If he is to preserve his naturalism, therefore, one would have thought that propositions can exist only in their instances too. This is indeed the approach Armstrong takes: he aims for a naturalistic theory of propositions. In *A World of States of Affairs* he had argued (WSA: 10.3.1) that propositions were classes of synonymous sentences. But that theory is now rejected. Sentences are synonymous in virtue of their meaning. They do not have (the same) meaning merely in virtue of synonymy, for what could make sentences synonymous other than their meaning? In *Truth and Truthmakers*, therefore, Armstrong offers a new theory: propositions are the intentional objects of beliefs, thoughts and sentences. They are the *that* which beliefs, thoughts and sentences are *about*. A proposition is an abstraction of the content from beliefs, statements, speech acts and various other meaningful devices (T&T: 13). They are types, rather than tokens; that is, they are universals existing in their instances, like all other universals. We will see shortly that this generates a problem for Armstrong when it is coupled with his truthmaker necessitarianism, but we will leave the theory of propositions for now and move on to the question of what the truthmakers are.

Again we find a neat connectedness in Armstrong's philosophy. The truthmakers are the same facts or states of affairs that he had studied and advocated previously in *A World of States of Affairs*. They fit the bill perfectly. As Armstrong understands facts, it might be recalled, they are the units of existence in the world. They are not merely true propositions, as that would make them entirely unfit for the task of truthmaking, on pain of circularity. As we saw in Chapter 6, a state of affairs or Tractarian fact is a particular-having-a-property, correctly understood. It is thus a worldly existent, which is entirely appropriate for a theory of truth. Do we not, after all, still demand in any realist theory of truth that truth consists in the truth-bearer standing in an appropriate relation to something in the world? Truth has to be connected with reality (T&T: §2.7) and the search for truthmakers is the search for the appropriate parts of reality that make the truth-bearers true.

Why, then, does Armstrong think that it is specifically states of affairs that make propositions true, rather than some other entities such as individual objects? To see why, let us consider a proposition such as that the apple on my table is red. It is now standard in the truthmaking literature to pick out such a proposition inside angled brackets, "<" and ">". Let us simplify slightly and refer to this apple simply as "the apple", assuming there are no problems of reference to complicate the matter. Hence we are considering the truthmaker for <the apple is red>. Could the truthmaker for this proposition be simply the apple itself? In a sense, yes, but this would not be specific enough as a truthmaker. The object itself contains lots that is irrelevant to the truth of <the apple is red>. The apple contains four pips, perhaps, but these seem to make no contribution to the truth of <the apple is red>. Similarly, the apple has a certain weight and a certain circumference yet, again, these properties do not seem to be truthmakers for <the apple is red>. What we are looking for is what Armstrong calls a *minimal* truthmaker for a proposition. A minimal truthmaker is something in the world that makes a proposition true but from which nothing could be subtracted while that proposition remains true. It should be clear why minimal truthmakers are sought. Were we to treat the universe as a single object, it is obvious that it could stand as truthmaker for every truth. But if I wanted to find the truthmaker for <I am in Nottingham> or <Charlotte Church is famous> and was told it was the entire universe, I would have been given a vastly uninformative answer. As far as we know, nothing about the planet Neptune is of relevance to <Charlotte Church is famous> so it does not seem to deserve to be called a truthmaker for that truth. Neptune is extraneous to this truth. That which contains nothing extraneous to a particular truth <p>, yet is nevertheless sufficient for the truth of <p>, is the minimal truthmaker of <p>.

Returning now to our apple, what then would be the *minimal* truthmaker for <the apple is red>? It seems we have already decided that it is not just the apple, which would contain lots that is extraneous to this truth. Similarly, it is not just redness, the property, as that is instantiated in lots of things other than this apple. The truthmaker will then have to be the fact that this apple possesses redness. We should be able to see straight away that this is a state of affairs – the worldly fact of this apple-having-redness. It can be noted, however, that there are occasional exceptions where objects alone stand as truthmakers. This happens in the case of necessary truths, as will be described below, and plausibly also with statements such as <David Armstrong exists>.

The bearers of truth are propositions and the makers of truths are usually states of affairs. How do states of affairs make certain propositions true? According to Armstrong, they do so by necessitating the truth of those propositions. There is a truthmaking relation that can hold between states of affairs and certain propositions. Between most states of affairs and propositions this relation does not hold but between the apple-having-redness and <the apple is red> it does hold. The truthmaking relation is described as an "absolute necessitation" (T&T: 5). Armstrong offers a *reductio* argument for this view (T&T: 6, 7). If T is the suggested truthmaker for <p> but does not necessitate the truth of <p>, then T could exist without <p> being true. But this would suggest that something more than T is needed for <p> to be true and this other thing, call it T+U, would be a better candidate for the truthmaker of <p> than is T. This is also the case for any subsequent candidate for the truthmaker of <p> until we reach something where it is not possible for it to exist and <p> not be true. This is the same as saying, however, that this thing is the truthmaker for <p> and necessitates the truth of <p>. The thesis that truthmakers necessitate the truth of certain propositions is known as truthmaker necessitarianism and the claim is one of the distinctive features of Armstrong's theory.

That *any* relation holds between states or affairs and propositions is problematic but this is perhaps even more so the case with a relation of necessitation. As Armstrong accepts, the relation of necessitation is a cross-categorial one. One relatum is a concrete, worldly state of affairs; the other is abstract, as propositions are abstractions from actual beliefs, speech acts and so on. This is a necessitation, therefore, that runs across two categories. The standard cases of necessitation, with which philosophers are most familiar, have relata of the same category. We are familiar with necessitation as entailment but where entailment is a relation that holds between propositions. Hence, <John is in the room> entails or necessitates that <someone is in the room>. Here, both relata of the entailment relation are abstract but Armstrong explicitly rules that such entailment will not suffice for truthmaking (T&T: 5, 6). We are interested not just in truths that are entailed by other truths but, at the fundamental level, by truths that are necessitated by the things that exist in the concrete world. Logico-linguistic entailment is not, therefore, what we are looking for. The other model we have of necessity – causal necessity – is also inappropriate for truthmaking. By making truth, we do not mean a causal making (T&T: 5). The causal relation, for those philosophers who think it something real, something like natural necessity, holds only between concrete objects, whether these are understood as events, facts, properties or substances. For the type of truthmaking relation Armstrong seeks, one relatum is concrete – the state of affairs – the other is a proposition, therefore abstract, so the relation must be cross-categorial.

Although the available models of necessitation – entailment and causation – are inappropriate for truthmaking, we cannot say that Armstrong's cross-categorial necessitation is a non-starter. But if some posit of philosophy is of its own kind, *sui generis*, then that often makes it an object of suspicion. Armstrong has responded to this issue by arguing that there clearly are some cross-categorial relations (2005: 275). Indeed, any realist theory of truth seems committed to truth consisting in an appropriate relation holding between non-linguistic reality and linguistic reality. It is then a separate matter whether this cross-categorial relation is one of necessitation, for which Armstrong has his *reductio* argument. If there are separate reasons for finding truthmaker necessitation to be plausible and for finding cross-categorial relations plausible, then why not find cross-categorial necessitation plausible?

What happens when Armstrong's theory of propositions is coupled with his truthmaker necessitarianism? The existence of a particular state of affairs will necessitate the truth of a certain proposition. Presumably, however, there are some states of affairs that we do not know about and have not yet even conceived. This tells us, what we ought already to realize, there are can be truths that we do not know. How, though, can Armstrong allow this if a proposition is an abstraction from actual beliefs and utterances? If no one has ever uttered or thought about a proposition, it seems that it does not exist. And if a proposition does not exist, how can it be true? Armstrong's problem here is his familiar instantiation requirement. Were Armstrong to hold a Platonist view of propositions he would not have this problem. We could hardly expect Armstrong to give up his immanent realism at this stage, but he must find some way of reconciling the view with his truthmaker necessitarianism.

Armstrong's way out of the difficulty is to modify his theory of propositions slightly (T&T: 15–16). To begin with, he had said that propositions were the intentional objects of beliefs, statements, thoughts, and so on. But the world of states of affairs cannot necessitate that some particular belief is actually thought. Armstrong needs an account of the existence of propositions that will suffice whether or not they are actually expressed. His move is to say that unexpressed propositions are *merely possible* objects of belief, speech, and so on. All propositions will be possible objects of belief but the unexpressed ones will be merely possible. Again, this is not a comfortable position for Armstrong. What we have is the mere *possibility* of the instantiation of such a proposition and what we really need, therefore, is an account of the truthmakers for modal truths, which will show how it can be true that such a proposition is (merely) possible. An account of modal truths is offered later in *Truth and Truthmakers*.

Further claims in Armstrong's theory

So far we have considered only the basic mechanism of truthmaking, as described in Armstrong's version. We should now be able to understand how a state of affairs may necessitate the truth of a proposition through cross-categorial necessitation (and it is the *truth* of a proposition that is necessitated, not the proposition itself, as Armstrong has made clear, 2005: 275). There is much more to be said, however, for all we have here is a model of how truth can be made by a worldly fact. But we may wonder, straight away, whether this model can apply to every case of truth, in all its diverse instances. What about negative truths, modal truths, truths in mathematics, and general truths? Can there be worldly truthmakers for all these types of truth? Armstrong's view is that there can be and, indeed, every truth has a truthmaker in virtue of which it is true. This is a position widely referred to as *truthmaker maximalism* and subscription to the view is the second main distinctive feature of Armstrong's version of truthmaker theory.

Truthmaker maximalism is a very bold position to take. Armstrong used to say (in talks) that he was "going for the jackpot". It is bold because just one case of truth for which there is no truthmaker would render it false. How are we really to know that there is no such case of truth? Armstrong would have to produce a credible theory of truthmakers for any awkward case we throw at him.

Armstrong offers no direct argument for maximalism although he does offer weaker considerations in its favour. He thinks he has a quasi-inductive argument for it. If we see the success of the theory in dealing with a host of difficult cases, we may well become optimistic that the theory will be able to deal with any further case (T&T: 7). While there is no direct argument for maximalism, therefore, the work as a whole may be considered an argument. In addition, however, there are a number of other suggestions that make maximalism seem plausible.

First, Armstrong supports what he calls the entailment principle. If T is a truthmaker for <p>, and <p> entails <q>, then T is also a truthmaker for <q> (T&T: 10). Given that Armstrong is searching for relevant truthmakers, however, the entailment in the entailment principle cannot be classical. In classical entailment, any contingent truth entails any necessary truth. We cannot say, however, that <John Howard is Prime Minister> is a *relevant* truthmaker for <Jersey is not both an island and not an island>. The entailment principle must, therefore, concern some notion such as relevant entailment. The way Armstrong expresses this is to say that it is an entailment relation that holds only between purely contingent truths. A truth is purely contingent when it has only contingent truths as components so that it is contingent through and through (T&T: 11). A conjunction that has a necessary truth as a conjunct is not purely contingent in this sense, though it would be contingent in the normal sense.

The entailment principle reveals a very important thesis of Armstrong's truthmaker maximalism. The truthmaking relation is not necessarily, indeed is seldom, a one-to-one relation. Where the entailment principle comes into play, a single truthmaker can make many truths true. For instance, T can make <p> true and all that <p> relevantly entails. Not every truth, therefore, requires a unique truthmaker that makes it true and nothing else. We can see how this aids the case for maximalism when we consider the regress of truth. If <p> is true, then it is true that <p> is true. In other words, when <p> is true, <<p> is true> is true, and <<<p> is true> is true> is true, and so on forever. We see from the regress of truth that there are an infinite number of truths. Were there to be a unique truthmaker for every truth, there would have to be an infinite number of facts. The world would have to be infinitely large. But we cannot say for certain that the world is infinitely large. The regress of truth is only a problematic regress, however, if we assume the relation between truths and truthmakers is one-to-one. The entailment principle shows us, however, that if T is the truthmaker for <p>, then it is also the truthmaker for <<<p> is true> is true> because <<p> is true> entails <<<p> is true> is true>.

This seems a perfectly acceptable result because there are, after all, independent reasons why a single truthmaker can make many truths true and why a single truth can have many truthmakers. Suppose David Armstrong were to be in the room with me now. His presence in the room would make <David Armstrong is in the room> true but also that <an Australian is in the room>, <a man is in the room>, <someone is in the room>, and so on, are true. A single fact, David Armstrong being in the room, can therefore be a truthmaker for many truths. But it is easy to see that it goes the other way too. <A man is in the room> is made true by David Armstrong being in the room but it is also made true by me being in the room. Here we have two distinct facts both of which are sufficient for, or necessitate, the truth of <a man is in the room>. We can have, therefore, relations between truths and truthmakers that are many–one and one–many, as well as one–one (if a truth happens to have a unique minimal truthmaker). Because there is no demand for a one–one relation in every case, the plausibility of truthmaker maximalism is greatly improved.

Negative and general truths

Most of Armstrong's general theory of truthmaking has now been explained. As he said, however, the argument for maximalism is in the work as a whole. To accept maximalism, we would have to be convinced that there are truthmakers for all truths, including those for which it has so far been difficult to find truthmakers. Armstrong moves on, therefore, to consider some of these difficult cases of truth in detail. He starts with the related subjects of negative and general truths.

The so-called negative truths are the apparent truths such as <there is no hippopotamus in this room>, <there are no unicorns>, <David Armstrong is absent> and <my pockets are empty>. It is very difficult to offer a firm criterion that distinguishes negative truths from the ordinary, positive truths. Stated in a general way, however, the problem concerns how we can truthfully say that something is not the case. As the above examples show, this is not done simply by using the word *not* because I can use words such as *absent* or *empty* to signify much the same thing.

The problem of saying what is not is an ancient one and can be found in Plato's *Theaetetus*, but we can see that the problem is particularly pressing for truthmaker maximalists. Many pro-positions state that something is not the case. If they do so truly then the truthmaker maximalist has to find something that is the case and can be a truthmaker for a statement that something is not the case. What, then, among all the things that exist, can make <there is not a hippopotamus in this room> true (Russell's example, 1918: 189)? The proposition is about something that is *not* but to be true it must have a truthmaker, which is some-thing that *is*. The late George Molnar, sometime associate of Armstrong, stated the problem of negative truth succinctly. There are four theses, each of which seems attractive. They are (Molnar 2000: 84–5):

(i)   The world is everything that exists
(ii) Everything that exists is positive
(iii) Some negative claims about the world are true
(iv) Every true claim about the world is made true by something that exists

Taken together, (i)–(iv) entail that there are positive truthmakers for negative truths. Truthmaker theorists, it now seems, have a duty to either name the positive truthmakers for negative truths or, if they cannot, reject (at least) one of theses (i)–(iv). The problem of finding truthmakers for general truths amounts to much the same. The truthmaker for <all men are mortal> must include at some stage that there are no more men than the mortal ones. That there are no more men seems to be a negative truth for which, again, we require a positive truthmaker. Hence, Armstrong identifies two kinds of negative truth. There are *absences*, such as when I say some thing is not (a unicorn) or some property is absent from a thing (I am not tall) and there are *limits*, when I say that these things are all there are.

Philosophers have not had much success in finding positive existents that can be truthmakers for negative truths. There is one initially attractive line of thought, but it is not regarded as being ultimately successful. Russell attributes this strategy to Demos (1917). This room contains a number of positive existents, such as tables and chairs, a man and a sofa. Being a sofa is incompatible with being a hippopotamus, as is being a man or a table or a chair. Let us then take the sum of everything that is in the room. Given that these things are all incompatible with being a hippopotamus, then perhaps, as a sum, they can be the positive truthmaker for the negative truth that <there is not a hippopotamus in this room>. There is, however, what seems to be a fatal problem with this line of thought. It relies essentially on a notion of incompatibility. The solution "works" by accounting for the truth of <not-p> in terms of some other positive truth <q> where <p> is incompatible with <q>. That p is incompatible with q, however, seems to mean that it is not (perhaps cannot be) both p and q together. For instance, nothing can be both a table and a hippopotamus. This seems quite clearly to be invoking another negative truth: *not* both p and q. And what is the positive truthmaker for this negative truth? We do not know. In short, this so-called incompatibility solution merely displaces the problem. Initially it offers an apparent positive truthmaker for a negative truth but it turns out to require a further negative truth to work and at no point do we genuinely get a positive truthmaker for a negative truth.

At this point, assuming we cannot salvage the incompatibility solution, we can either search for some other positive truthmakers for negative truths or we can instead reject one of the four motivating theses. This is what Armstrong chooses to do in developing his totality solution. To understand Armstrong's solution, however, it will help if we consider Russell's solution, upon which Armstrong is aiming to improve.

Russell's move is basically to reject Molnar's thesis (ii). Russell argues, perhaps astonishingly, that there are negative facts. Like Armstrong, Russell has an ontology of facts, rather than of things. Some of them can be negative facts that are fit to be truthmakers for negative truths. Hence, when <there is not a hippopotamus in this room> is true, there is a truthmaker for this truth that is a negative fact. A negative fact is a fact that something is not the case, such as that the apple is not red or that there are no unicorns. It is an admittedly negative existent. Philosophers are immediately repulsed and puzzled by such things, as Russell conceded (Russell 1919: 287) but he saw no better solution.

Let us just consider a little further what is so ontologically repugnant about negative facts. This issue is seldom taken seriously so I am venturing into the unknown at this point. We have seen that a fact can be understood as a particular having a property. How would such a fact be negative? There seem to be at least two ways. First, a particular could have a negative property. So when it is true that <my pen is not blue>, my pen may have a negative property of being not-blue. We have already seen what Armstrong thinks of negative properties in Chapter 2 (p. 33). Another way is for the particular to be a negative, so that it may be true that <there is not a hippopotamus in this room> when the room contains a non-hippopotamus, this negative existent bearing the property of being in the room. (Of course, the truthmaker might also be understood as the room having the property of non-hippopotamus-containment, which is a negative property of the kind previously mentioned.) Neither negative properties nor negative particulars are the sorts of things we usually would want in a naturalistic ontology. I may be providing the wrong analysis of a negative fact here but, even if I am, its advocates already concede its nature as a negative kind of existent.

Now let us move to Armstrong's solution. The truthmaker for a negative truth is a complex consisting of a number of positive, first-order facts plus a higher-order fact about those facts. According to Armstrong, <there is not a hippopotamus in this room> is true for the following reason. Let us imagine that we could gather before our minds every simple, positive fact about the room: that there is a sofa in it; that there is a chair, that the walls are white, and so on. Unlike the number of truths about the room, the number of facts about the room will be finite. Let us underestimate grotesquely and assume that there are 1,000 such facts. That there is a hippopotamus in this room is not among the 1,000 facts about the room. This, alone, would still not necessitate that <there is not a hippopotamus in the room>, for reasons we have already encountered when truthmakers for general truths were considered. To get the necessitation, we would need to add to our list a 1,001st fact, which is the higher-order fact (a fact about the other facts) that facts 1 to 1,000 are all the first-order facts there are about the room. If there being a hippo in the room is not among our 1,000 facts, and we add to those the higher-order fact that these are all the facts about the room, then we do get the necessitation of <there is not a hippopotamus in this room>.

There is a conspicuous difficulty with this solution, however, namely that this higher-order fact is itself a negative fact. It is a totality fact that "totals" the first-order facts. We have already encountered these. But the totality fact means that these are all the facts: there are no more facts than these (T&T: 58). Armstrong admits that this is a negative fact. It is a limiting fact, of the same kind that we need for general truths. In a way, therefore, Armstrong's solution is the same as Russell's: they both reject Molnar's (ii), that everything is positive, so they then do not need (solely) positive truthmakers for negative truths.

Nevertheless, Armstrong can claim plausibly that his account is an advance over Russell's, albeit only an advance in economy. Russell, it seems, was prepared to countenance many negative facts. As well <there is not a hippopotamus in this room> being true, let us assume also the truth of <there is not a red hippopotamus in this room>, <there is not a Scotsman in this room> and <George Bush is not in this room>. Russell would require four different negative facts to stand as truthmakers for these four different negative truths. We can see, however, that Armstrong's single negative, totality fact will be enough to make all negative truths about the room true. There are undoubtedly many negative truths about the room, perhaps infinitely many, and if we need invoke only a single negative fact to account for them, then that is certainly more ontologically economical than invoking countless many.

Furthermore, Armstrong argues, such totality facts are needed anyway in order to make general truths true (see Chapter 6, p. 106), so "let them really earn their keep!" (T&T: 58). Indeed, the problem of negative truth has been reduced, through the totality facts, to the problem of limits. It may be recalled that Armstrong began with two kinds of negative truths: absences and limits. The absence case, like the hippopotamus being absent from the room, now has a negative truthmaker that is a limit – a totality fact that "totals" the first-order facts about the room. Absences do not, therefore, have to be admitted into our most austere ontology but, we will be somewhat startled to discover, limits do. Limits are ontological realities.

Is there any alternative solution to the problem of negative truth? Armstrong claims that while this is not a palatable solution, it is better than all the other options: it is "the least evil" (T&T: 82). It does, nevertheless, clash with the naturalistic view that existence is univocal. The admission of some negative existents seems to threaten Armstrong's most fundamental commitment, in which case the naturalistic programme may falter at the final hurdle.

I have already mentioned that we may continue the search for the positive truthmakers of negative truths but with the passage of time, and the great minds that have been exercised on the search, there are few current grounds for optimism in this direction. Molnar seems to be suggesting that this is the only way forward because it seems to him out of the question that any of (i) to (iv) should be rejected.

We have seen how (ii) can be rejected, but what about (i), (iii) and (iv)? As far as I know, no one has ever seriously maintained that (i) should be rejected, that the world is everything that exists. This is sometimes referred to as the Tractarian thesis. Thesis (iv) has indeed been rejected and other truthmaker theorists, such as Peter Simons (2005), now see this is the least costly option. Thesis (iv) is the maximalist thesis – to reject it is to reject truthmaker maximalism – but many truthmaker theorists are prepared to do this. Negative truths, and perhaps some other classes of truth, may be true primitively or true by default. When we say that something is not the case, why should we need anything in the world corresponding to it or making it true? Armstrong's opponent may also point out that his maximalism is so far only weakly motivated: Armstrong could offer only a quasi-inductive argument in its favour. Maximalism was, therefore, motivated by the success of truthmaker theory in accounting for problems like that of negative truth. But Armstrong's solution to the problem of negative truth now seems motivated by a desire to preserve maximalism. Why else would one prefer the ontologically daring rejection of thesis (ii) to the ontologically conservative rejection of thesis (iv)? There is a kind of circularity, therefore, in Armstrong's strategy.

Nevertheless, it would have to be admitted that the rejection of (iv) creates its own problems. If a truthmaker theorist rejects (iv), then they are admitting that a proposition can be true without having a truthmaker. And if there can be truth without truthmakers, then what is the motivation for any kind of truthmaker theory at all? On the other hand, were the truthmaker theorist to say that there are special reasons why we do not need truthmakers in just this case, of negative truth, then they at least owe us a principled account of why some sorts of truth need truthmakers and others, such as these, do not.

The final option is one that I do not think has been taken seriously until fairly recently. This would be to reject Molnar's (iii), that some negative claims about the world are true. One would assume that few have considered this because it just seems so obvious that there are negative truths. If one were to be a convinced truthmaker maximalist, however, one would think a proposition true if and only if it has a truthmaker. Many truthmaker theorists now seem to concede that there are no truthmakers for negative truths. Perhaps the obvious conclusion should be that these propositions are just not true. If they lack truthmakers, should these propositions instead be thought of as falsehoods (Mumford 2007a)? A putative negative truth could, on this solution, be understood instead as a disguised falsehood. For example, the apparent truth of <there is not a hippopotamus in this room> has, let us assume, no truthmaker. It is not, therefore, true. Instead, however, we can say that it is false that <there is a hippopotamus in this room>. Being a falsehood, this proposition requires no truthmaker. We do not have to find any positive existent that makes it so. Rather, it is false because there is no truthmaker making it true. There are many potential objections to such a view though it may be possible to answer enough of them that such a line carries at least some hope.

There is much more that can be said about this whole issue, which is perhaps now the most hotly contested area of truthmaker theory. But now I will consider Armstrong's approach to other problem areas of the theory.

Modality, numbers and time

Modal claims present a problem. How are they made true by the facts of our world? How can a truth about what is merely possible be made true only by what is actually the case? Similarly, how can truths about what is necessary be made true by just the facts there happen to be in our world? These two issues have to be addressed separately.

The mere possibilities, it will be recalled, are those which are possible without being necessary or actual. Mere possibilities appear to be capable of truth and only if one thinks there are no contingent falsehoods is one likely to claim otherwise. How then can we provide a naturalistic account of truths of possibility? Armstrong offers the following proposal (T&T: 84). First, let us assume that T cross-categorially necessitates <p>, that is, makes <p> true. Assume also that <p> is contingent. If <p> is contingent then it is a necessary truth that it is contingent. If that is so, then <p> necessitates <it is possible that not-p>. T is therefore, by the entailment principle, the truthmaker for <it is possible that not-p>. We have found, therefore, an actual state of affairs that is also a truthmaker for a mere possibility.

The case where it is not-p, but <possibly-p> is true, is slightly more complicated. The truthmaker for not-p, as we saw above, is a complex of first-order facts plus a totality fact. These are all contingent, so could be otherwise. If they are contingent then they are necessarily so. Therefore, they necessitate <possibly-p>. So where there is no fact that there is a hippopotamus in the room, among the first-order facts about this room, and there is a totality fact that these are all the first-order facts, the totality fact could have been otherwise. This means that there could have been more facts about the room, such as that it contains a hippopotamus.

We now move to truthmakers of necessary truths. Here Armstrong feels he needs a separate account to that of possibility. To understand the truthmakers for necessary truths, he offers two main claims. First, he says, the truthmakers are the objects alone, rather than states of affairs involving those objects. The necessary truths of mathematics, for instance, are made true by mathematical objects, such as numbers. The truthmakers for <7 + 5 = 12> are the numbers 7, 5 and 12. The proposition <7 + 5 = 12> asserts a relation between those numbers and all that is needed for the relation to hold is the numbers themselves. They bear internal relations to one another. As we have already seen, it is sufficient for an internal relation to hold just if the relata exist. To be 12 is, among other things, to be equal to 7 + 5. Second, Armstrong opts for a *possibilist* account of such objects and the truths in which they partake. This means that necessary truths are hypothetical in nature (T&T: 100). When we are asserting such a truth, we are asserting a conditional such as "(necessarily) if there are seven things and five further things, then the sum of all these things is twelve". Possibilism is especially attractive in the case of truths about large numbers, where there may not be that number of things in the whole universe.

One concern there might be about Armstrong's account of possibility and necessity is that it does not appear to be a unified account. A reason one might want a unified account is the purely logical consideration that the two modal operators that express possibility and necessity are interdefinable (given the non-modal operator of negation). If we have an account of possibility, then we also have an account of necessity because necessarily-p can be defined as not-possibly-not-p. Armstrong accounts for truths of possibility in terms of actual states of affairs and then truths of necessity in terms of relations between hypothetical objects. With a proposition such as <not possibly not-p>, which of these two accounts should we invoke? Is it a truth about necessity or a truth about possibility?

Armstrong moves on to consider mathematics and set theory in more detail (T&T: ch. 9). What, if anything, is the truthmaker for the claim that the number 4 exists? As would be expected, Armstrong rejects the Platonic view that the number four is an eternal existent or Form. He also rejects the extensionalist view of Russell, which has it that the number 4 is the class of all four-membered classes. Armstrong prefers the intensionalist response to such a view: it is because these classes have four members that they form a class of classes; they do not have four members because they belong to this class of classes. That a particular class has four members is an intrinsic matter, quite apart from what goes on in other classes.

Armstrong's naturalistic theory requires, following Forrest and Armstrong (1987), only the notion of a mereological whole. The mereological whole, comprised of four men, is the truthmaker for there being four men. There is a relation holding between the property *being a man* and the whole that the four men constitute. The mereological whole "fours" the property of being a man, as Armstrong says (T&T: 114). The property serves the function of determining the unit of which, in this case, there are four. Classes serve the same function. What, then, is the number 4 itself? On this account it is a universal – a dyadic universal or *four*-relation – instantiated by a mereological whole and some unit-determining property. Effectively, this means that the four men themselves instantiate the number four. In the case of very large numbers, they have only possible instantiations.

Truth and Truthmakers ends with a discussion of time, in which Armstrong argues for omnitemporalism or four-dimensionalism, which we already encountered in his work on universals. It is accepted, certainly by Armstrong, that there are truths about the past. He also accepts that there are truths about the future, though admits this to be slightly more controversial. What are the truthmakers for these truths? An omnitemporal view provides them at a stroke. Past, present and future are equally real, as are the states of affairs within them.

Consider the proposition <Caesar existed>. The presentist thinks that only the present is real. What do they have, in all existence, that could make such a proposition true? It cannot be Caesar himself, whom the presentist thinks is non-existent. Nor can the presentist say <<Caesar exists> was once true> because this itself would have to be a truth and, again, it seems to have no truthmaker in the present. The omnitemporalist will admit Caesar to be a real existent, even though he is in the past relative to our experience. Past existents can be truthmakers for truths about the past and future existents can be truthmakers for truths about the future. It is, again, most satisfying to see that truthmaker considerations support an earlier commitment in Armstrong's metaphysics.

This completes Armstrong's survey of difficult cases of truth. Truthmaker theory works for them, he contends, and we should be encouraged enough to think it will work for any future difficult case. Hence we should be maximalists. Whether Armstrong really has considered enough cases is a decision I leave to readers.

The programme completed?

Armstrong said (in conversation), just before the publication of *Truth and Truthmakers*, that it would be his final book. This was not because he expected an imminent demise but because he had said everything he had wanted to say. Unlike some philosophers, cut down before their work is complete, Armstrong has lived a long enough life to see his programme of naturalistic metaphysics completed and presented to the world. Despite a few minor changes of view along the way, Armstrong's books present a beautifully integrated and systematic view of the world, with numerous interconnections between the topics of properties, laws, causation, facts, truth, powers and minds.

Armstrong is pleased he does not have followers. There are no Armstrongians. If this is thought to be because there is not an Armstrongian philosophy, that would be a mistake. The books from *Perception and The Physical World* through to *Truth and Truthmakers* present a unified and coherent account of the world. It does offer a philosophy: a naturalistic, immanentist one. Perhaps, instead, there are no Armstrongians because his interest has not been in attracting followers but in the philosophy itself. Those who have been taught or informed by Armstrong's work are happily not likely to become disciples. Rather, they are likely to want to investigate these or other philosophical issues further. Armstrong has offered a model of clear enquiry, where a position is exposed nakedly to our understanding. The effect has been to enthuse readers, make them see that philosophy need not be confusing or esoteric. That there are no Armstrongians is indeed a tribute to the man and his work.

In Chapter 11, however, I shall consider one additional aspect of *Truth and Truthmakers*, about which I have remained deliberately silent until this point. Armstrong puts forward a new view of instantiation, inspired by the work of Don Baxter. Despite previously offering us a singular vision of the world, this new direction in his thinking threatens to overturn much of what he has argued hitherto.

Chapter 11

Necessity

In Chapters 1 to 10 we have seen Armstrong's naturalist programme develop. It forms a remarkably integrated and exceptionally consistent body of work covering the entire operations of the natural world, with some detailed attention paid to the operation of minds within that world. We might think of this body of work as the official Armstrong philosophy. It is at least the view that he has spent the majority of his career developing and extending with thorough and detailed argument. One distinguishing feature of the entire programme is the all-pervading presence of contingency. Things could have been different. Everything could have been otherwise. Even the fundamental elements of the world are contingent existents. Any necessity, such as it is, is usually classed as analytic necessity, grounded in the meaning of words rather than the nature of things, or concerns merely the internal relations of objects such as numbers.

Let us take stock and recapitulate this contingentist position. We can start with the particulars and universals. Every particular thing is a contingent existent. No particular exists of necessity. Only God, Platonic Forms and transcendent numbers were ever seriously proposed as necessary existents, but Armstrong's naturalism already rules these out. But while the idea of necessarily existing particulars has never had great intuitive appeal, many have thought that universals are necessary existents. Redness, for instance, was thought to be an eternal existent because it cannot be created or destroyed. It was not thought to be dependent on the existence of red things. But Armstrong argued, to the satisfaction of many, that the attraction of this view does not bear detailed scrutiny. Universals are best thought of as immanent rather than transcendent phenomena and therefore, *qua* second-order particulars, also contingent existents.

That does not exhaust the basic components of the world. The world is a world of states of affairs and these are something additional to the particulars and universals that make them up. The particular *a* can exist and the universal F exist without there being a state of affairs that *a* is F. Even where *a* being F is a state of affairs, its existence is not necessitated by its constituents. States of affairs are, therefore, also contingent beings.

We then move on to some of the higher-level features of our world. There are laws of nature, existing as relations of natural necessitation between universals. But as relations, laws are themselves universals: higher-order universals. And like all other universals, they are also contingent existents. Even if there is a law that N(F,G), F and G do not themselves ensure the existence of the law N(F,G). That has to be some further universal in addition to F and G. Once the law exists, it necessitates that anything which is F is also G. But this is a contingent, natural necessitation. It is not as strong as logical necessity.

Laws, like all universals, exist only in their instances. But the instances of nomological relations are to be found in particular causal sequences. As it is contingent what laws exist, it is therefore contingent what causal relations there are. Laws and causes could have been different. But we can take this even further. The dispositions of things are not fundamental parts of reality and do not show that properties necessitate other properties or have essential features. All properties are categorical. Dispositions come about simply when something has a property that is, with some stimulus, nomologically related to something else (Armstrong 2005a). What a property is disposed to do, depending on the applicable laws of nature, is thus also contingent. This features large in Armstrong's theory of mind because many mental phenomena are dispositional in nature. Which properties or states are responsible for such dispositions is a contingent matter as it will depend on what the laws of nature are. If one is to identify mental states with the physical states that cause mental behaviour, it will have to be, therefore, a contingent identification only. Other physical states could have been the causal bases of mental dispositions, had the world been different.

The last major subject where we find contingency is in the topic of modality itself. Armstrong sees that the world allows free, unrestricted recombination of all the existents that are wholly distinct.

All and only the recombinations of these existents are possible. His combinatorial theory of modality was limited to a theory of possibility. Little was said of necessity. A distinction between necessary and contingent truths was nevertheless maintained (for example, WSA: 183). But necessary truths were to be found in the restricted domains of logic and mathematics and, along with traditional empiricists, Armstrong saw them typically as analytic truths. Some truths of mathematics required a slightly more complicated account. Some such truths may be about particulars, such as numbers, but truths about them will be truths about their internal relations, such as 7 + 5 being internally related to 12. Internal relations are no additions of being over and above the existence of the numbers themselves. Because of this, we can have necessary truths without adding *de re* necessity to the world. The Armstrong who developed the core programme of metaphysics was thus not a believer of necessity *in re*, as a real, additional feature of the world.

For a long time, that was Armstrong's official view. But *Truth and Truthmakers* saw a radical shift of view and admission of a major new kind of necessity in the world. The rest of this chapter is concerned with that new view and the implications it would have for the contingentist view just summarized.

Instantiation as partial identity

Armstrong's change of mind came about through a reconsideration of the issue of instantiation prompted by a reading of Baxter (2001). It may be recalled that instantiation cannot be regarded as a relation, on pain of Bradley's regress. Relations are themselves universals, which would have to be instantiated by their relata, so no progress would be made. We wonder how it can be that Fa; for instance, an apple being red (which is by no means a fundamental state of affairs). If we think that the apple, a, bears a relation of instantiation to redness, F, we face exactly the same question again: how can it be that I(a,F), where I is a relation of instantiation? Instantiation would have to be instantiated and the regress is under way. Hence one of Lewis's chief criticisms of Armstrong's view is that the instantiation invoked in his theory of universals cannot be analysed (Lewis 1983: 23). Yet Armstrong had criticized forms of nominalism and transcendent realism for failing to fully analyse their key notions, such as falling under a predicate, being a member of a class, resembling, participating in, and so on. All these views were accused of producing regresses (Chapter 2, pp. 21–2) but the charge is that the same would be true of instantiation.

A particular and a universal, united in a state of affairs, cannot therefore stand in a *relation* of instantiation. But we need an account of how a state of affairs is composed: "We have somehow got to get particulars and their properties together" (T&T: 48). Instead, Armstrong spoke of the "fundamental tie" between *a* and F (U: 94, for example). He argues that there is no regress involved in instantiation understood as the fundamental tie (U: 111–12). No extra state of affairs is required over and above *a* instantiating F – being fundamentally tied to F – because that same state of affairs is also the truthmaker for any further instantiation claim (such as that *a*'s instantiating F *instantiates* instantiation). But this is hardly completely satisfactory, consisting as it does in the pretty loose metaphor of a "tie". He also offered "nexus" (U: 108), which is little more illuminating. It is no surprise, then, to see that Armstrong revisited this issue, clearly unimpressed with his own earlier dismissal of the problem, where he had said "I do no think that the problem of characterizing the nature of the tie should detain us" (U: 108).

One may be able to pursue the line of the tie or nexus further, and spend time characterizing it in detail, but after reconsideration Armstrong opts for a brand new theory instead:

> I have had a change of heart about the instantiation of universals. In previous work I conceived of the instantiation as a matter of contingent connection of particulars and universals. New work by Donald Baxter . . . has made me think that the link is necessary. . . . I have been convinced by him that what is involved in a particular instantiating a property-universal is a *partial identity* of the particular and universal involved. It is not a mere mereological overlap, as when two streets intersect, but it is a partial identity. This in turn has led me to hold that instantiation is not contingent but necessary.   (T&T: 46–7)

Let us first get clear on how this new account of instantiation is to be understood before we go on to consider its implications and viability. We shall see that while Armstrong accepts that the basics are taken from Baxter, he makes of it something quite different from the original author.

For Baxter, a universal is a strict identity running through many particulars and, likewise, a particular can be thought of as a strict identity running through many universals. Where we have a particular instantiating a universal, Armstrong says we have "an intersection of the two sorts of oneness, a point of partial identity" (2004: 141). This is not simply a mereological relation. As we have seen, Armstrong's states of affairs were supposed to have a non-mereological mode of composition. However, the attraction of the partial identity view is that no additional mode of composition is required: "Because the suggested link between the two is partial identity, any need for a fundamental tie, a copula, or what have you, seems to be eliminated" (*ibid.*: 142). Clearly this is a big attraction for Armstrong. The problems that he had in explaining the nature of the fundamental tie or nexus vanishes. There is no tie or nexus whose nature is to be explained.

Armstrong has likened the new view to the early account of instantiation found in Plato's *Parmenides*. Socrates was asked how particulars stand to the Forms. His answer was that they *participated* in the Forms. While Armstrong cannot see that this could be the case if the Forms are transcendent universals, where we are instead immanent realists this might be the best way to understand instantiation. Particulars can be said to participate in the universal in the sense that they are partially identical with the universal. The *first* theory of instantiation might have been the right one after all.

A difficulty this leaves us with, however, is how to distinguish universals and particulars. Both are now depicted as Ones running through Manys. Previously, universals alone had this distinguishing feature. Now the same is being said of particulars. But there remain key differences, Armstrong alleges. In the first place, a universal has a fixed number of terms. It is either monadic, dyadic, triadic, and so on, and never varies from what it is. Particulars can instantiate any number of universals, in alleged contrast (2004: 147). And, second, universals are repeatable with no logical limit on them getting instantiated at any time and place (*ibid.*). We will return to these "differences" in a short while.

The necessity of instantiation

The new view of instantiation has major implications for Armstrong's philosophy. I will go on to argue that instantiation is not for him just some local problem that permits a local solution. In changing his mind on instantiation, Armstrong has to change his mind on virtually everything. The key point to this change is that instantiation as partial identity means that instantiation is necessary. As Armstrong remarks, "Particulars and universals are, on this theory, an inseparable package deal because they each help to constitute the other" (2004: 143). This produces a major consequence of the theory. Contingency has to be jettisoned. Referring to instantiation as intersection, instead of partial identity, he asks:

> Is it not a central idea in classical logical atomism – in the *Tractatus* in particular – that any state of affairs (fact) might not have existed, *yet everything else remain exactly the same?* The trouble is, though, that in the intersection theory neither the row that is the universal, nor the column that is the particular, would *be* exactly the same. Is the theory forced to say that, given the actual universals and the actual particulars, each intersection, each state of affairs, is then necessary? . . . We are indeed forced to say this. (2004: 144)

Let us reconsider the red apple again, as an example state of affairs though not a fundamental one. The apple and redness are partially identical or intersect. This means that redness is constituted (at least in part) by the particulars it runs through. The apple is constituted (at least in part) by the universals it runs through (or run through it). Were the apple not red, then it would not be the particular that it is. Similarly, were the apple not red, then redness would not be the universal that it is. The upshot is that if redness exists, this very redness of our world, and if this apple exists, this very one, then it is necessary that this apple is red. This universal and this particular might not have existed, perhaps, but given that they do, it is necessary that they intersect. Being instantiated in this apple is part of what makes redness what it is. And being red is part of what makes this particular apple the apple that it is.

The new view that Armstrong offers, he once criticized in strong terms. He was criticizing a certain view of trope theory for having the sort of consequences his theory now has.

> A heavy price is paid . . . The price is the huge amount of necessity *in re* that this . . . has to postulate. Every property and (it would seem) every relation that exists must be instantiated where it is actually instantiated . . . the arrangement of the world is fixed. (WSA: 117)

With instantiation as partial identity, the arrangement of the world does indeed look fixed. Just how fixed it would be is the next matter to which we turn.

Consequences for Armstrong's programme

Let us consider once more the grid-like representation of the world from Chapter 2. We could consider this to be a complete description of the world at a time or, more in keeping with Armstrong's four-dimensionalism, we could consider it as a complete account of the whole world at all times. For the latter, certain states of affairs would have to be, in some way, indexed to certain times.

We can see that a is F; for example, our apple is red. a being F was originally understood as a state of affairs, something additional to the existence of a and of F. It is, of course, no longer clear that this is an additional entity because its existence has a kind of necessity, albeit with a conditional character. If a and F exist, then the state of affairs, a being F, also exists. Let us put that aside, for the moment, as the point to be considered here is how little is left of contingency

	A	B	C	D	E	F	G	...
a	✓		✓		✓	✓		
b		✓				✓		
c	✓						✓	
d				✓	✓			
e		✓		✓		✓	✓	
f	✓						✓	
g			✓	✓		✓		
...								

Figure 11.1 Grid for instantiation of properties

189

once we accept the partial identity view. Suppose that *a* is indeed F and we tried to imagine a world just like ours but in which *a* is not F. We shall try to subtract this state of affairs from our world. We might begin by thinking that we can imagine such a world. This certainly seems to respect our pre-theoretic modal intuitions. After all, it is just a world like ours but in which this apple is not red. We see quickly, however, that by eliminating just this one state of affairs from our world, we would almost certainly eliminate the whole of the world.

If it were no longer the case that *a* is F, then *a* would no longer be *a* and F would no longer be F. *a* and F would have ceased to exist. One still might not take this to be too high a price to pay, if one thinks that the partial identity view is appealing, but we can see that it does not end there. We are not just talking about a world lacking one individual and one universal. F is also instantiated, in our grid, by *b*, *e* and *g*. If F no longer exists, then the state of affairs *b* being F can no longer exist. And because instantiation is partial identity, this means that *b* no longer exists. By the same argument, *e* and *g* no longer exist. That only leaves us with the individuals *c*, *d* and *f*. They will not survive long, however. We have also said that *a* no longer exists. But *a* also instantiated A, C and E, as well as F. Because instantiation is partial identity, and *a* no longer exists, that means that A, C and E no longer exist. That leaves us only with universals B, D and G. But these will not survive long either. One of our few remaining individuals, *c*, instantiated universal C, which no longer exists. So *c* no longer exists. *c* instantiated G, however, so G no longer exists. And if G does not exist, then nor does *f*, and so on. We can now see that every particular and every universal would cease to exist just because the state of affairs, *a* being F, ceased to exist. Take away the one small fact – that this apple is red – and most likely the whole universe ceases to exist. This is because all particulars and universals are interrelated in some way, as we have just seen. To take away one state of affairs is to take away every particular that instantiates the same universal and every universal that is instantiated in that particular. And then we have to take away every particular that instantiates any of those universals that have been taken away and any universal that is instantiated by any of those particulars. We set in motion a domino effect at the end of which nothing is likely to be left standing.

We have seen the importance of naturalism in Armstrong's philosophy. There is but a single world of spacetime. Everything is therefore spatiotemporally related to everything else. But only if there are unrelated "island-universes" could anything survive once we try to remove but one state of affairs. And such an escape route is surely not open to Armstrong unless he throws off the naturalism that is his chief commitment. This has led one critic to liken Armstrong's new philosophy to Leibnizian rationalism and describe the new position as "disastrous" (Simons 2005: 259): "everything in the world necessarily coexists with everything else" (*ibid.*: 260). A world would then come as a complete package, consisting of every single state of affairs, or not at all. The only other possible worlds would be completely alien worlds, containing none of our particulars and none of our universals, in clear violation of Armstrong's commitment to naturalism.

Armstrong has, after reflection, tried to prevent this domino effect:

> I now think that the situation does not spread to the properties. "Partial identity", I now think, is a somewhat misleading phrase. Particulars enfold their universals – and that is a sort of partial identity – but universals do not enfold their particulars. In the envisaged "deleting", the universal continues to exist identically in other particulars, unless, indeed, *a* is the only particular to instantiate that universal. (2005: 274)

But this response looks *ad hoc* and an unconvincing retreat to a halfway position that will satisfy no one. Partial identity seemed like a way of treating particulars and universals equally. Partial identity looks symmetrical. There seems little reasoned justification for now saying that universals are exempt from the constraints of partial identity. All we have is this notion of "enfolding", which is supposed to apply to particulars and universals asymmetrically. But it is not clear what this is, nor how it exempts universals from the domino effect. The position looks a mish-mash: half-Leibnizian and half-empiricist.

Some further implications of the new position should by now be all too apparent. But here are some of the main points. First, it is clear that Armstrong no longer has a theory of possibility. The blanks on the combinatorial grid are no longer possibilities at all (2004: 148). One might think that this is all well and good. We have seen that various things that seem intuitively possible no longer are on the new view of instantiation (notwithstanding the fact that we saw in Chapter 10, p. 179 how to provide truthmakers for modal truths). But the combinatorial theory of possibility, as outlined in Chapter 4, had at least something going for it. Everything, or almost everything, is in the new theory either actual or necessary. Should we not have a modal theory that allows *mere* possibilities: things that are neither necessary nor actual? Are we really willing to give up our modal intuitions, and a modal theory, just on the basis of a theory of instantiation?

Laws of nature would also now be necessary (2004: 153 and 2006: 246). Laws are higher-order universals that will run through the second-order particulars – the first-order universals – that they relate. These, in turn, are instantiated in particular causal sequences. All these will become necessary in a very strong sense. The universal F would not be the universal it is unless it partakes in the law N(F,G). If F exists, so does the law, and also all the particular causal transactions that are the instantiations of the law. Again, take any of these away and the whole universe ceases to exist. And if we do away with this contingency then it becomes obvious that the dispositional properties, which are endowed by a categorical property together with a law of nature, are also a matter of necessity. Given a certain categorical property, it would then be necessary what dispositions would follow. This has clear implications for Armstrong's philosophy of mind. Which categorical properties formed the causal bases of mental dispositions would now be a matter of necessity. The notion of contingent identity, that Armstrong fought at length to defend, would also be sacrificed.

It is clear that adoption of the new theory of instantiation would be a serious business. But are there any advantages to it, other than it being a putative solution to the general question of instantiation? On the plus side, general facts need no longer be posited to account for general truths. Each instantiation of F is necessary and no other instantiation is possible. The truthmaker for the universal statement that every F is a G can now just be all the Fs (2004: 148). We will not need an additional fact that these are all the Fs because there could be no more Fs than the actual Fs. It should also be conceded that at least some contingency does remain. The universals are themselves contingent existents in a sense. Assuming that *a* is F, then had *a* not been F, F would not exist. But there could be some other property very like F that exists. Suppose that F* is just like F except that it is not instantiated by *a*. This allows some contingency still in the world, though F* is not identical with F. But it is just like F except for the fact that it is not instantiated by apple *a*. The alleged domino effect might then be just a scare story. Take away the Fa state of affairs and it is not as if the world would cease to exist. All the particulars and all the universals would merely be different particulars and universals, $a*$ to $n*$ and A* to N*. We would not even notice the difference because $a*$ is so like a and A* is so like A. What we have, therefore, is "a necessary connection between contingent entities, the particular and the universal" (2006: 243).

The case for the new theory may be understated but, if we come to the balance sheet, it looks like we have, in the credit column, a solution to Bradley's regress, no need for general facts, and now a surrogate for the world's contingency. But on the debit column, we have the considerable minus that most of our ordinary modal intuitions will have to be rejected as almost everything comes out, strictly speaking, as necessary.

Even parts of the new theory itself look endangered by this all-consuming necessity. On p. 187 we described how Armstrong tried to maintain a difference between universals and particulars even though both were now Ones running through Manys. But the necessity of instantiation seems even to undermine this claim. Universals were said to have fixed adicities: they always had to be instantiated by the same number of particulars. Armstrong had called this his Principle of Instantial Invariance (ToU: 94). But, taken as a four-dimensional whole, necessity would entail that each particular instantiated (or was partially identical with) a fixed number of universals. It could not have instantiated one fewer, or one more, universal and remained the particular that it is. Instantial Invariance seems, therefore, to apply also to particulars. That criterion of difference is left hard to uphold and so is the second, for similar reasons. Universals could be instantiated at any number of places and times, it was argued, while, standardly, particulars are seen as restricted. But has Armstrong not now imposed a modal limit on a universal's instantiations? It may well exist in various places and times but could it be at any more places and times than it actually is and still be the universal it is? We must recall that Armstrong has now effectively rejected his combinatorial theory of possibility. He no longer has any ground, therefore, for invoking the possibility that a universal have a further, additional instantiation to the one it has, nor that a particular could instantiate one further universal over and above the ones that it does. The difference between particulars and universals now looks to be a very uncertain matter.

David Armstrong

Afterword

There has been a twist in the tale of Armstrong's philosophical career. So often the proponent of Humean distinctness and unrestricted combinatorial freedom, he now presents us with a radical alternative in which almost everything is connected and necessary. We are faced with a choice where we cannot accept both the contingentist programme, outlined in Chapters 1–10 below, and the necessitarian view that has just been introduced. We may, of course, choose to accept neither. The contingentist view has much going for it. Armstrong demonstrated how it could generate a systematic and integrated view of the world. That it is able to do so surely counts in favour of its truth. The alternative, though it has been branded Leibnizian, may yet be developed in an equally systematic way. The necessity involved, throughout the intersection view, is also something from which philosophers no longer shy away (see Bird 2007 and Mumford 2004). It is by no means clear-cut, therefore, which of these directions, if either, we should take. In particular, I would urge that the new view of the later Armstrong be considered seriously, for it is by no means as far-fetched as it could seem at first sight.

Bibliography

Books by Armstrong

1960. *Berkeley's Theory of Vision: A Critical Examination of Bishop Berkeley's Essay Towards a New Theory of Vision*. Melbourne: Melbourne University Press.

1961. *Perception and the Physical World*. London: Routledge & Kegan Paul.

1962. *Bodily Sensations*. London: Routledge & Kegan Paul.

1968. *A Materialist Theory of The Mind*. Revised edition (London: Routledge, 1993).

1973. *Belief, Truth and Knowledge*. Cambridge: Cambridge University Press.

1978. *Nominalism and Realism* (*Universals and Scientific Realism*, Volume 1). Cambridge: Cambridge University Press.

1978. *A Theory of Universals* (*Universals and Scientific Realism*, Volume 2). Cambridge: Cambridge University Press.

1981. *The Nature of Mind and Other Essays*. Brighton: Harvester Press.

1983. *What is a Law of Nature?* Cambridge: Cambridge University Press.

1984. *Consciousness and Causality* (with Norman Malcolm). Oxford: Blackwell.

1989. *Universals: An Opinionated Introduction*. Boulder, CO: Westview Press.

1989. *A Combinatorial Theory of Possibility*. Cambridge: Cambridge University Press.

1996. *Dispositions: A Debate* (with C. B. Martin and U. T. Place), T. Crane (ed.). London: Routledge.

1997. *A World of States of Affairs*. Cambridge: Cambridge University Press.

1999. *The Mind–Body Problem: An Opinionated Introduction*. Boulder, CO: Westview Press.

2004. *Truth and Truthmakers*. Cambridge: Cambridge University Press.

Other works by Armstrong

1958. "Educating Sydney?". *Observer* 19/4/58: 152.

1968. "The Headless Woman Illusion and the Defence of Materialism". *Analysis* **29**: 48–9.

1969. "Dispositions are Causes". *Analysis* **30**: 23–6.

David Armstrong

1980. "Against 'Ostrich' Nominalism: A Reply to Michael Devitt". *Pacific Philo-sophical Quarterly* **61**: 440–9.

1982. "A Search for Values". *Quadrant* **26** (6): 65–70.

1984. "Self Profile". In *David Armstrong*, R. Bogdan (ed.). Dordrecht: Reidel, 3–51.

1987. (with P. Forrest) "The Nature of Number". *Philosophical Papers* **16**: 165–86.

1988. "Can a Naturalist Believe in Universals?". In *Science in Reflection*, U. Ullmann-Margalit (ed.). Dordrecht: Kluwer, 103–15.

1989. "C. B. Martin, Counterfactuals, Causality and Conditionals". In *Cause, Mind, and Reality: Essays Honouring C. B. Martin*, J. Heil (ed.). Dordrecht: Kluwer, 7–15.

1991. (with A. Heathcote) "Causes and Laws". *Noûs* **25**: 63–73.

1992. "Properties". In *Properties*, D. H. Mellor and A. Oliver (eds). Oxford: Oxford University Press, 1997: 160–72.

2003. "Review of Rodriguez-Pereyra's *Resemblance Nominalism*". *Australasian Journal of Philosophy* **81**: 285–6.

2004. "How Do Particulars Stand to Universals?". In *Oxford Studies in Metaphysics* 1, D. Zimmerman (ed.). Oxford: Oxford University Press: 139–54.

2005. "Reply to Simons and Mumford". *Australasian Journal of Philosophy* **83**: 271–6.

2005a. "Four Disputes About Properties". *Synthese* **144**: 309–20.

2005b. "Review of Mumford, *Laws in Nature*". *Australasian Journal of Philosophy* **83**: 607–10.

2006. "Particulars Have Their Properties of Necessity". In *Universals, Concepts and Qualities: New Essays on the Meaning of Predicates*, P. F Strawson and A. Chakrabarti (eds). Aldershot: Ashgate, 237–47.

Works by other authors

Adams, R. 1974. "Theories of Actuality". *Noûs* **8**: 211–31.

Anderson, J. 1962. *Studies in Empirical Philosophy*. Sydney: Angus and Robertson.

Anscombe, G. E. M. [1971] 1981. "Causality and Determinism". In *Metaphysics and the Philosophy of Mind*, Oxford: Blackwell, 133–47.

Ayer, A. J. 1954. *Philosophical Essays*. London: Macmillan.

Baxter, D. 2001. "Instantiation as Partial Identity". *Australasian Journal of Philosophy* **79**: 449–64.

Bird, A. 2005. "The Ultimate Argument Against Armstrong's Contingent Necessitation View of Laws". *Analysis* **65**: 147–55.

Bird, A. 2007. *Nature's Metaphysics: Dispositions, Laws and Properties*. Oxford: Oxford University Press.

Black, R. 2000. "Against Quidditism". *Australasian Journal of Philosophy* **78**: 87–104.

Brentano, F. [1874] 1973. *Psychology From an Empirical Standpoint*, L. L. McAlister (ed.). Atlantic Highlands, NJ: Humanities Press.

Campbell, K. 1990. *Abstract Particulars*. Oxford: Blackwell.

Crane, T. (ed.). 1996. *Dispositions: A Debate*. London: Routledge.

David, M. 2004. "Don't Forget About the Correspondence Theory of Truth". *Australasian Journal of Philosophy* **82**: 42–7.

Davidson, D. 1963. "Actions, Reasons and Causes". *Journal of Philosophy* **60**: 685–700.

Demos, R. 1917. "A Discussion of Certain Types of Negative Proposition". *Mind* **26**: 188–96.

Devitt, M. 1980. "'Ostrich Nominalism' or 'Mirage Realism'". *Pacific Philosophical Quarterly* **61**: 433–9.

Dretske, F. 1977. "Laws of Nature". *Philosophy of Science* **44**: 248–68.

Ellis, B. 2001. *Scientific Essentialism*. Cambridge: Cambridge University Press.

Ellis, B. 2002. *The Philosophy of Nature*. Chesham: Acumen.

Ellis, B. 2006. "Looking for Laws". *Metascience* **15**: 437–41.

Engel, P. 2002. *Truth*. Chesham: Acumen.

Franklin, J. 2003. *Corrupting the Youth: A History of Philosophy in Australia*. Sydney: Macleay Press.

Gettier, E. L. 1963. "Is Justified True Belief Knowledge?". *Analysis* **23**: 121–3.

Goodman, N. [1955] 1983. *Fact, Fiction, and Forecast*, 4th edn. Cambridge, MA: Harvard University Press.

Goodman, N. 1966. *The Structure of Appearance*, 2nd edn. Indianapolis, IN: Bobbs-Merrill.

Handfield, T. 2005. "Armstrong and the Modal Inversion of Dispositions". *Philosophical Quarterly* **55**: 452–61.

Heil, J. 1998. *Philosophy of Mind: A Contemporary Introduction*. London: Routledge.

Heil, J. 2003. *From an Ontological Point of View*. Oxford: Oxford University Press.

Hempel, C. G. and Oppenheim, P. 1948. "The Logic of Explanation". In *Readings in the Philosophy of Science*, H. Feigl and M. Brodbeck (eds). New York: Appleton Century Crofts, 319–52.

Holton, R. 1999. "Dispositions all the Way Round" *Analysis* **59**: 9–14.

Hume, D. [1739] 1888. *A Treatise of Human Nature*, L. A. Selby-Bigge (ed.). Oxford: Clarendon Press.

Hume, D. [1748] 1975. *Enquiry Concerning Human Understanding*, in *Enquiries Concerning Human Understanding and Concerning the Principles of Morals*, L. A. Selby-Bigge (ed.), 3rd edn rev. P. H. Nidditch. Oxford: Clarendon Press.

Jackson, F. 1977. "Statements about Universals". *Mind* **86**: 427–9.

Kripke, S. 1980. *Naming and Necessity*. Cambridge, MA: Harvard University Press.

Lewis, D. 1966. "An Argument for the Identity Theory". *Journal of Philosophy* **63**: 17–25.

Lewis, D. 1973. *Counterfactuals*. Oxford: Blackwell.

Lewis, D. [1983] 1999. "New Work for a Theory of Universals". In *Papers in Metaphysics and Epistemology*, Cambridge: Cambridge University Press, 8–55.

Lewis, D. 1986. *On the Plurality of Worlds*. Oxford: Blackwell.

Lewis, D. 1986a. *Philosophical Papers* II. Oxford: Oxford University Press.

Lewis, D. [1994] 1999. "Reduction of Mind". In *Papers in Metaphysics and Epistemology*, Cambridge: Cambridge University Press, 291–324.

Lewis, D. 2001. "Forget About the 'Correspondence Theory of Truth'". *Analysis* **61**: 275–80.

Lewis, D. Forthcoming. "Ramseyan Humility". In *Naturalism and Analysis*, D. Braddon-Mitchell and R. Nola (eds). Cambridge, MA: MIT Press.

David Armstrong

Mackie, J. L. 1962. "The Philosophy of John Anderson". *Australasian Journal of Philosophy* **40**: 265–82.

Martin, C. B. 1984. "Anti-Realism and the World's Undoing". *Pacific Philosophical Quarterly* **65**: 3–20.

Martin, C. B. 1997. "On The Need for Properties: the Road to Pythagoreanism and Back". *Synthese* **112**: 193–231.

Maurin, A.-S. 2002. *If Tropes*. Dordrecht: Kluwer.

Melia, J. 2003. *Modality*. Chesham: Acumen

Mellor, D. H. 1974. "In Defense of Dispositions". *Philosophical Review* **83**: 157–81.

Mellor, D. H. 1991. *Matters of Metaphysics*. Cambridge: Cambridge University Press.

Mellor, D. H. 2000. "The Semantics and Ontology of Dispositions". *Mind* **109**: 757–80.

Michotte, A. 1963. *The Perception of Causality*. London: Methuen.

Mill, J. S. 1843. *A System of Logic*. London: Parker.

Molnar, G. 1969. "Kneale's Argument Revisited". *Philosophical Review* **78**: 79–89.

Molnar, G. 2000. "Truthmakers for Negative Truths". *Australasian Journal of Philosophy* **78**: 72–86.

Molnar, G. 2003. *Powers, a Study in Metaphysics*, S. Mumford (ed.). Oxford: Oxford University Press.

Moore, G. E. [1925] 1993. "A Defence of Common Sense". In *Selected Writings*, T. Baldwin (ed.). London: Routledge, 106–33.

Mumford, S. 1998. *Dispositions*. Oxford: Oxford University Press.

Mumford, S. 2004. *Laws in Nature*. London: Routledge.

Mumford, S. 2005. "Kinds, Essences, Powers". *Ratio* **18**: 420–36.

Mumford, S. 2007. "Powers, Dispositions, Properties". In *Revitalizing Causality: Realism About Causality in Philosophy and Social Science*, R. Groff (ed.). London: Routledge.

Mumford, S. 2007a. "Negative Truth and Falsehood". *Proceedings of the Aristotelian Society*, **107**: 45–71.

Musgrave, A. 1981. "Wittgensteinian Instrumentalism". *Theoria* **46**: 65–105.

Nagel, T. 1974. "What Is It Like to Be a Bat?". *Philosophical Review* **83**: 435–50.

Place, U. T. 1956. "Is Consciousness a Brain Process?". *British Journal of Psychology* **47**: 44–50.

Plantinga, A. 1974. *The Nature of Necessity*. Oxford: Oxford University Press.

Plato, *Theaetetus*. In *The Collected Dialogues*, E. Hamilton and H. Cairns (eds). Princeton, NJ: Princeton University Press.

Plato, *The Republic*. In *The Collected Dialogues*, E. Hamilton and H. Cairns (eds). Princeton, NJ: Princeton University Press.

Plato, *The Sophist*. In *The Collected Dialogues*, E. Hamilton and H. Cairns (eds). Princeton, NJ: Princeton University Press.

Plato, *Parmenides*. In *The Collected Dialogues*, E. Hamilton and H. Cairns (eds). Princeton, NJ: Princeton University Press.

Popper, K. R. 1959. *The Logic of Scientific Discovery*. London: Hutchinson.

Price, H. H. 1953. *Thinking and Experience*. London: Hutchinson.

Quine, W. V. O. [1948] 1953. "On What There Is", in *From a Logical Point of View*, Cambridge, MA: Harvard University Press, 1–19.

Quinton, A. 1957. "Properties and Classes". *Proceedings of the Aristotelian Society* **48**: 33–58.

Ramsey, F. 1928. "Universals of Law and of Fact". In *Philosophical Papers*, D. H. Mellor (ed.). Cambridge: Cambridge University Press, 140–4.

Ramsey, F. 1929. "General Propositions and Causality". In *Philosophical Papers*, D. H. Mellor (ed.). Cambridge: Cambridge University Press, 145–6.

Rodriguez-Pereyra, G. 2002. *Resemblance Nominalism*. Oxford: Oxford University Press.

Ruby, J. [1986] 1995. "The Origin of Scientific 'Law'". In *Laws of Nature: Essays on the Philosophical, Scientific and Historical Dimensions*, F. Weinert (ed.). Berlin: de Gruyter, 289–315.

Russell, B. 1903. *The Principles of Mathematics*. London: Allen & Unwin.

Russell, B. 1912. *The Problems of Philosophy*. Oxford: Oxford University Press.

Russell, B. [1918] 1986. "The Philosophy of Logical Atomism". In *The Collected Papers of Bertrand Russell* 8, J. G. Slater (ed.). London: Allen & Unwin, 160–244.

Russell, B. [1919] 1956. "On Propositions: What They Are and How They Mean". In *Logic and Knowledge*. London: Allen & Unwin, 1956: 283–320.

Russell, B. 1940. *An Inquiry into Meaning and Truth*. London: Allen & Unwin.

Russell, B. 1948. *Human Knowledge: Its Scope and Limits*. London: Allen & Unwin.

Ryle, G. 1949. *The Concept of Mind*. London: Hutchinson.

Searle, J. 1991. *Minds, Brains and Science*. London: Penguin.

Shoemaker, S. [1980] 2003. "Causality and Properties". In *Identity, Cause and Mind*, expanded edn, Oxford: Oxford University Press, 206–33.

Shoemaker, S. [1998] 2003. "Causal and Metaphysical Necessity". In *Identity, Cause and Mind*, expanded edn. Oxford: Oxford University Press, 407–26.

Simons, P. 2005. "Negatives, Numbers, and Necessity: Some Worries About Armstrong's Version of Truthmaking". *Australasian Journal of Philosophy* **83**: 253–61.

Skyrms 1981. "Tractarian Nominalism". *Philosophical Studies* **40**: 199–206.

Smart, J. J. C. 1959. "Sensations and Brain Processes". *Philosophical Review* **68**: 141–56.

Smart, J. J. C. 1963. *Philosophy and Scientific Realism*. London: Routledge & Kegan Paul.

Squires, R. 1968. "Are Dispositions Causes?". *Analysis* **29**: 45–7.

Strawson, P. F. 1959. *Individuals*. London: Methuen.

Swinburne, R. 1983. "Reply to Shoemaker". In *Aspects of Inductive Logic*, L. J. Cohen and M. Hesse (eds). Oxford: Oxford University Press, 313–20.

Swoyer, C. 1982. "The Nature of Natural Laws". *Australasian Journal of Philosophy* **60**: 203–23.

Tooley, M. 1977. "The Nature of Laws". *Canadian Journal of Philosophy* **74**: 667–98.

Van Cleve, J. 1985. "Three Versions of the Bundle Theory". *Philosophical Studies* **47**: 95–107.

Warnock, G. 1953. *Berkeley*. London: Pelican.

Williams, D. C. 1953. "The Elements of Being, I". *Review of Metaphysics* **7**: 3–18.

Wittgenstein, L. 1921. *Tractatus Logico-Philosophicus*, trans. 1961. London: Routledge & Kegan Paul.

Wittgenstein, L. 1953. *Philosophical Investigations*. Oxford: Blackwell.

Index

David Armstrong